OVERTURE AND BEGINNERS

A Musical Autobiography

by

EUGENE GOOSSENS

METHUEN & CO., LTD. LONDON

36 *Essex Street, Strand, W.C.*2

First published September 27th, 1951
Reprinted 1951

TO MY FATHER

I.2
CATALOGUE NO. 5350/U

PRINTED IN GREAT BRITAIN

FOREWORD

THIS first instalment of chronological happenings pretends to neither great literary or self-revelatory interest. In it I have attempted a record of the modest, though not exactly passive, roles played by the Goossens family throughout a period of some fourscore years of musical activity in both England and America.

If, in the process of factual recital, I succeed in evoking for the reader scenes or memories of people, places and performances which made those years the musically exciting ones they were, I shall count the main object of this volume achieved.

Autobiographical as my narrative is, it has been difficult to avoid at times an excessive use of the personal pronoun, except in the 'overture' of the opening chapters. Certain press notices essential to the narrative I have reluctantly included in spite of their often too laudatory character. And just as when the opera call-boy summons the singers on stage with his 'Overture and beginners, please', so my 'beginners' duly appear at their appointed times.

Acknowledgements are due to my dear father and my friend, J. Gregson of Liverpool, for their help in furnishing certain indispensable data.

I wish also to thank the following for permission to reproduce copyright material: J. Curwen & Sons, Ltd., *The Musical News*; Victor Gollancz, Ltd., *My Life of Music*, by Sir Henry Wood; The Oxford University Press, *Cyclopedic Survey of Chamber Music*, by W. W Cobbet; the Executors of H. G. Wells and the Editor of *The Times* for the letter by H. G. Wells; Mrs. Dorothy Cheston Bennett for the quotations from Arnold Bennett's letters; and the Editors of the *Daily Express, Daily Mail, Daily Telegraph and Morning Post, Evening News, Evening Standard, Observer, The Times*, and *Yorkshire Post*.

EUGENE GOOSSENS

STATE CONSERVATORIUM OF MUSIC
SYDNEY, N.S.W.
1950

ILLUSTRATIONS

Plates

The Author   *Frontispiece*

My Father: Eugene Goossens II   *Facing page* 6
   (*Photo: H. J. Whitlock & Sons Ltd., Birmingham*)

My Great-Grandfather   12

My Great-Grandmother   12

My Grandfather: Eugene Goossens I   20

Queen Victoria's Silken Programme for a Command
   Performance in London at which my Grandfather
   conducted *H.M.S. Pinafore* (1878)   24

My Maternal Grandfather, Aynsley Cook   40
   (*Photo: Chancellor, Dublin*)

My Father in 1888   56
   (*Photo: Chancellor, Dublin*)

The Author, 1898   72
   (*Photo: Brown, Barnes & Bell, Liverpool*)

Adolphe, Leon, Mother, Sidonie, Eugene and Marie;
   Liscard (1902)   90

Adolphe, Marie, Eugene, Leon and Sidonie;
   Liverpool (1904)   90

My Mother, Annie Cook (1914)   102

Adolphe Goossens   136
   (*Photo: Naudin Ltd.*)

Leon Goossens   136

Marie Goossens   152
   (*Photo: Lenare Ltd.*)

Sidonie Goossens   152

Sir Thomas Beecham   200

Achille Rivarde   *Facing page* 200
  (*By courtesy of Miss Freda Mackenzie*)

William Murdoch, Albert Sammons, Cedric Sharpe,
  and the Author (1916)   216

Sir Dan Godfrey and the Author at Bournemouth
  Festival (about 1920)   216

Eugene Goossens III conducting the Los Angeles
  Orchestra at the Hollywood Bowl (1931)   264
  (*Photo: Keystone Press Agency Ltd.*)

The Author and Sir Henry Wood at Appletree Farm
  House, Chorley Wood, Bucks (1932)   280

In the Text

Programme of Command Performance at Balmoral
  of *The Daughter of the Regiment* (1892)   *Page* 9

Autograph Letter of Massenet, regarding the conditions under which my father could enter his
  composition class at the Paris Conservatoire (1890) 14-16

Invitation to Harry Payne's Benefit (1857)   19

Two autograph letters from Edward Elgar to my
  Grandfather concerning a performance by the
  Goossens choir of Elgar's *Te Deum* and *Benedictus*
  (1902)   30-35

Programme of Orchestral Concert at Queen's Hall
  (1921)   160

CHAPTER I

IF you ever visit Bruges, and are architecturally inclined
—there seems little point in going there if you are not—
one of the first things you will probably want to do is to see
the Church of Notre Dame. Making your way along Rue
Notre Dame, you will notice at the corner of the Rue du
Vieux Bourg a yellow house with shuttered windows,
typically Flemish gables, and a statue of the Virgin in a
niche in the angle of the walls. My great-grandfather put the
statue there, for this was his birth-place, and, like all good
Flemings, he was a devout Catholic. The tall spire of the
old church has cast its shadow over the house for nearly a
hundred and fifty years since the day the name of Jean-
Baptiste Maria Goossens first appeared in the Record of
Births of Notre Dame. That was on 20 May 1793.

Great-grandfather Goossens began as a jeweller's ap-
prentice, and ended as a master silversmith. (So, by a strange
coincidence, did my mother's grandfather.) The old house
in the Rue du Vieux Bourg served as his home and workshop; later, when he married, a modiste's atelier was added
to it. My great-grandmother was a *couturière*, and had a
large class of student-apprentices, who doubtless added
many a lively note to the quiet street.

Great-grandfather, judged by his portrait, was stolidly
Flemish, like a Van Eyck painting. Great-grandmother,
Brugeoise in appearance and temperament, shouldered her
domestic responsibilities as dutifully as her professional
ones. She had three children: my Great-uncle Adolphe
(1841), my Grandfather Eugene (1845)—known hence-
forward in these pages as Eugene I—and my Great-aunt
Julia. The two boys showed a precocious talent for music,
else this chronicle might never have been written. Aunt
Julia was—well, just Aunt Julia.

I

When the children were quite young, it happened that M. Mechelaere, Choirmaster of Notre Dame, decided to change his lodging, and, being a friend of my great-grandfather, he was invited to live with the Goossens family. Mynheer Mechelaere discovered that Jean-Baptiste's two sons possessed beautiful voices. He arranged to place the lads in his choir, and very soon, it is said, the excellence of their singing became the talk of the town. Mynheer Mechelaere said they were 'born musicians'.

Of the two boys, Eugene was musically the more gifted, so at nine began the inevitable violin lessons at the Bruges Conservatoire. (Nowadays, it's the clarinet or trumpet, which are easier and quicker to learn.) After only two years' study he won the medal of the Société Renaissance, awarded by the school on the occasion of the twenty-fifth Anniversary of Leopold I. In those days, medals were perhaps easier to come by than they are to-day, but obviously the institution had found a promising talent. The Conservatoire Royale at Brussels was the next logical step, and there both boys were sent, Eugene to continue his violin studies with Meerts and Beumer, and Adolphe to study piano and singing with other worthy masters. What violin student hasn't at some time or another encountered those Meerts exercises!

The Brussels Conservatoire was at that time second only in repute to the Conservatoire of Paris and the Berlin Hochschule. Fétis, the celebrated musicologist and teacher of composition, was its much admired Director, and the certificate of excellence he presented Grandfather in 1870 strikes me as a much more picturesque document than the printed or typewritten scrolls presented by present-day music schools. At nineteen, Eugene had already won the Premier Prix of the Conservatoire for violin playing,[1] besides distinguishing himself in solfège, harmony, counterpoint, and composition. A virtuoso should also be an expert theorist. At Brussels, it was all or nothing: the musical

[1] Cincinnatians should know that he graduated in company with Hugo Heermann (father of Emil, former concert-master of the Cincinnati Symphony Orchestra), who was also in Meerts's class and who also won the Premier Prix for violin.

2

sugar-coating which nowadays so frequently passes for an education in music was not, and still is not, tolerated there.

Great-uncle Adolphe, who had previously graduated from the Conservatoire with rather less *éclat* than the more brilliant Eugene, was to devote almost his entire lifetime to choirs and choral training. His only existing portrait shows him wearing decorations bestowed by half the crowned heads of Europe during the course of the tours he made with his many choruses. Chief of these groups was the choir of 'Les Artisans Réunis' of Brussels, a reputedly superb body of voices of which Uncle Adolphe was rightly proud. Later, he succeeded Beuwens as conductor of 'L'Orphéon'—generally considered Belgium's finest choir. Gone, alas, are those sonorous male-voice choruses whose vocal feasts in the dramatic *a capella* pieces of the nineteenth century Flemish school were the pride and joy of every Belgian. True, England has its fine mixed choirs, such as the Leeds and Three Choir Festival groups, and America has its Schola Cantorum and Cincinnati May Festival Choir. But these fine organizations can hardly be compared to the Belgian choirs I have mentioned, since they specialize in a different and more conventional type of singing. Perhaps in happier days to come some enterprising spirit will let us hear those exciting, albeit dated, works of Gevaert, Ries and Blockx, designed specially for the dramatic emphasis of vigorous yet subtly shaded male-voice choruses.

Grandfather Eugene, on graduating from the Conservatoire, lost no time in renouncing his state of single blessedness. Célanie van Dieghem, a pretty young dancer, known later in London as Madame Sidonie, was the lady of his choice. With her, he toured France and Belgium, appearing sometimes as solo violinist, but more frequently in the humbler role of theatre musician, when better and more profitable engagements were not forthcoming. On one of these tours, in 1867, my father—Eugene II—was born in Bordeaux,[1] and shortly after this event the young parents

[1] His French birth did not, however, affect his Belgian nationality, and to this day, in spite of years of English residence, he remains a staunch Fleming.

3

returned to their father's house in Bruges, which became their headquarters. A few years later, mourned by neighbours and friends, my great-grandfather, Jean-Baptiste Maria Goossens, went to his rest; the funeral bell of Notre Dame tolled the passing of an honest burgher, and there was sadness at the yellow house in the Rue du Vieux Bourg.

By the time my father was six years old, his parents had decided on a drastic step. The unremunerative nature of touring in Belgium and the limited opportunities for an ambitious musician in a small Flemish city were forcing Grandfather to look further afield for new professional outlets. Failing to find these in his native country, he decided to venture across the Channel and prospect the great unknown territory of musical London, in the belief, like Mr. Micawber, that something was bound to turn up. It was a difficult decision to come by, for in those days the stranger from another country could count with much less certainty than to-day on finding elsewhere the employment he sought. The field was at that time small and restricted, and opportunities few. But a successful solo appearance at St. James's Hall or the Portman Rooms might bring fame and fortune, failing which there were possible orchestral vacancies available. And there was conducting. Yes, there was always conducting. . . .

CHAPTER II

WITH heavy hearts, and leaving their small son at the College of St. Louis in Bruges, Eugene I and his wife departed in the winter of '73 for London. They arrived with slender resources, and a still slenderer knowledge of English, to try their fortune in a strange land. For some time, Grandfather eked out a bare existence playing the violin at Cremorne Gardens, the gay night-spot of London—a far cry from the St. James's Hall of his dreams. Later he joined the orchestra at Covent Garden Opera House, where his longing to conduct opera became an obsession. His aspirations as concert-soloist had long since disappointingly evaporated, and he sought a post as conductor of one of the travelling companies of light opera and musical comedy then in vogue.

The chance came when one day the impresario, Kate Santley, suddenly found herself without a conductor for one of her London seasons of operetta, and despairingly invoked the aid and advice of the Covent Garden management. They referred her to an importunate Belgian violinist in the orchestra who seemed more interested in conducting opera than in playing the violin. And so it was that Grandfather found himself engaged for the princely salary of £20 a week to conduct *Olivette*, *La Périchole*, *La Marjolaine*, and *Orphée aux Enfers*. How this miracle came to pass, and by what feat of salesmanship he succeeded in convincing the management of his ability to carry out the task are not known to-day. But if Miss Santley seemed unduly venturesome in her choice of a young unknown, let it be said that the London critics heartily endorsed it, and without exception praised the work of the boyish foreigner who, it was rumoured, had never held a baton in his hand before, much less ever been associated with first-class

5

operetta. But he knew the works, and seemingly that's what counted.

One engagement led to another, and eventually an organization called the Comedy Opera Company Ltd. engaged Eugene I as its conductor at the Opéra Comique in the Strand. The manager of this group was Rupert D'Oyley Carte, Senr., founder of the D'Oyley Carte Opera Company of Gilbert and Sullivan fame. Reproduced facing page 24 is a programme of a gala performance of *H.M.S. Pinafore* which took place in May 1878 in the presence of Her Majesty Queen Victoria. The names of George Grossmith, Junr., and Richard Temple will have a familiar ring to old London theatregoers. My grandfather conducted the performance. Sullivan, who wasn't by any means easy to please in the matter of his interpreters, must have thought much of the Belgian conductor to confide such an important event to his direction. By so doing, he incidentally disposed of the idea that only an Englishman can handle the racy idiom of Gilbert and Sullivan.

Grandmother Sidonie, after a few years of touring, appeared as leading dancer in the productions of Offenbach's *La Belle Hélène* and *Geneviève de Brabant* at the London Alhambra in 1882. In the late 'eighties, after my grandfather joined the Carl Rosa Company, she devised and produced many of the ballets for the newer operas staged by the company.[1] She was the toast of the 'balletomanes' of the day, for her fame certainly rivalled that of Adeline Genée, her successor of thirty years later. Her early death put an end to a brilliant career, and the memory of Mme. Sidonie lives on to-day in England in her harpist namesake, my younger sister.[2]

At the age of sixteen, my father was sent to the Brussels Conservatoire. After quiet preliminary years at the College of St. Louis in Bruges, and rather tame violin lessons from the local *maestro*, this must have been something of an adventure. At Brussels he found himself in the class of Gevaert for composition, and Cornélis for violin. Gevaert

[1] See Appendix A, p. 306.   [2] Also in my harpist daughter in Australia.

MY FATHER
EUGENE GOOSSENS II

had succeeded Fétis as Director of the Conservatoire, and is still remembered as the author of much worthy music and a treatise on orchestration. As a teacher of composition he was, like his predecessor, a strict disciplinarian, and none such as he is to be found anywhere to-day. Composition lessons then were not the casual affairs they often are now. It is extremely doubtful, indeed, whether the average pupil of the 1950s would submit to the iron discipline of those old-time classes, much less subscribe to the technical requirements demanded for admittance to them. Most modern student-composition is a witness to this. Sloppy, ill-kempt and disorderly I find much of it. Small wonder one is hard put to it to find effective-sounding novelties by graduate students. The fault lies usually with the teacher, often more concerned with the manner than the matter of his pupil's work. Conspicuous exceptions were the late Sir Charles Stanford and Rubin Goldmark, while in more recent years the astonishing Nadia Boulanger continues her series of musical 'transformation acts' with the young and pliable.

Father's five years in Brussels began—in 1883—at the same time as my grandfather (still in London) was invited by Carl Rosa to join his opera company as second conductor. For ten years, as the august Grove's *Dictionary of Music and Musicians* records, the latter 'distinguished himself by his admirable work with that troupe when at the height of its artistic fame and prosperity'. As the term 'opera in English' and the name Carl Rosa are synonymous, and as the Rosa Company was for long bound up with the fortunes of the Goossens family, it seems appropriate to tell something of its founder. Carl Rosa, a German violinist and remarkable combination of musician and business-man, married the well-known soprano, Madame Parepa, whereupon he gave up his virtuoso career and became interested in opera in English. He established his first company in 1872 and opened with a season at the Prince's Theatre, Manchester, in the same year. Liverpool later became the company's headquarters, and the old Amphitheatre, afterwards the Royal Court Theatre, was its permanent home for many

7

years. The Company's seasons in Liverpool ran from ten to twelve weeks, as compared with a maximum of four to five weeks in the other big provincial cities. Rosa's first London season took place in 1875, with *The Marriage of Figaro* (in English, be it observed) given on the opening night. Here is the cast:[1]

Count Almaviva	. .	Campo Bello
Figaro .	. . .	Charles Santley
Dr. Bartolo	. . .	Aynsley Cook [my maternal grandfather]
Basilio .	. . .	Charles Lyall
Countess Rosina	. .	Torriani
Cherubino	. . .	Josephine York
Susanna .	. . .	Rose Hersee

Two years later Rosa turned his group into a limited company, and eventually, as a result of a command performance given before Her Majesty Queen Victoria at Balmoral,[2] the word 'Royal' was added to the title. Among the factors which contributed to Rosa's success as an operatic impresario were his sagacity in picking out embryonic musical stars, very often from among the chorus; his choice of operas, combining the new with the old, the classical with the popular; and, finally, the issuing of books of subscription tickets for all parts of the theatre. There was always a tremendous demand for these tickets. Some enterprising people, indeed, used to buy up the books and dispose of them at a profit, a practice not unknown in our own day. Rosa was an idealist, and always insisted on a high standard of performance. At first he invariably conducted the operas himself, but when he was later joined by my grandfather he began to take more interest in the business, and less in the musical side of his venture.

Outside England, the name of the Carl Rosa Company is

[1] My late friend, Herman Klein, writes concerning this performance (at which he was present): 'Santley's masterly interpretation of Figaro was the gem of a performance universally acclaimed as the best that had ever been given in the vernacular. What is more, I have never heard it better in any language.' Charles Santley had at that time just turned forty, and was unquestionably the greatest English baritone of his day.

[2] See Appendix A.

8

BALMORAL CASTLE.

Carl Rosa Opera Company,

BY COMMAND OF

HER MAJESTY THE QUEEN.

Tuesday, November 8th, 1892.

Her Majesty's Servants will perform Donizetti's Comic Opera in Three Acts, entitled the

"DAUGHTER OF THE REGIMENT."

TONIE (a young Tyrolean peasant)	...	MR. E. C. HEDMONDT.
SERGEANT SULPICE (of the 20th)	...	MR. AYNSLEY COOK.
BRUNO (Steward of the Countess)	...	MR. L. PRINGLE.
CORPORAL MAX (of the 20th) ...	...	MR. CHARLES CAMPBELL.
DELVE (a peasant)	...	MR. P. SOMERS.
COUNTESS OF BERKENFELDT ...	...	MISS MADGE STAVART.
BABETTE	...	MISS KATE DREW.
MDLLE. BEAUPRE	...	MISS WILLIAMS.
MADAME DUVAL	...	MISS NEUWIRTH.

AND

MARIE (the Daughter of the Regiment)	MDLLE. ZELIE DE LUSSAN.

Conductor ... ... MR. E. GOOSSENS.

Manager ... MR. T. H. FRIEND.

B

little known. Yet when we stop to consider its pioneer work on behalf of opera in English, and the fact that the grand old company still survives, true to its traditions, after an existence of over seventy years, it would seem not out of place to consider some of its more spectacular but now almost forgotten achievements. That list of some thirty-three operas and singers to be found in Appendix A at the end of this book is in itself an imposing—indeed, a remarkable—record of real artistic enterprise. The names of both operas and artists set down there will arouse a great nostalgia in the minds of those older readers familiar with them. Especially is this so in the case of dates and other particulars connected with some of those historic 'first productions' of opera in English. And if there was ever a greater quartet of English singers than Zélie de Lussan, Kirkby Lunn, Ben Davies, and Lemprière Pringle, I have yet to learn of it.

CHAPTER III

WHEN Carl Rosa died in 1889 Eugene I succeeded to the principal conductorship of the company. A strict disciplinarian, Grandfather often set himself unattainable artistic standards, yet while he was feared as an irascible martinet, his artistic integrity made him respected, though not always loved, by those who worked with him. At that time the conductor could rehearse his players as long and arduously as he chose. Grandfather did not scruple to take the utmost advantage of this. He would often keep the orchestra working up to a couple of hours before the curtain rose on the evening performance. This sort of thing hardly endeared him to the players, most of whom called him tyrannical and unfeeling. He refused to tolerate any temperamental exhibitions from the singers, and there are stories about him concerning scenes said to have taken place at rehearsals. While some are apocryphal, the following is typical: A Russian bass, whose Mephistopheles was considered his masterpiece, had been engaged by Rosa. He did not show up at the rehearsals of *Faust*, and sang his part at the performance so badly that my grandfather called him for a special rehearsal. The renowned *basso* objected to being so frequently pulled up that he lost his temper, and said that he had sung the role of Mephistopheles in all the great capitals of the world, under the batons of many great conductors, 'whose boots *you*, Mr. Goossens, are not fit to brush!' He added: 'I know the part upside down.' Grandfather replied, 'That's quite evident. But we don't play it that way in this company!'

During the ten years Grandfather spent with Carl Rosa, he conducted about forty operas,[1] many of which were first

[1] See Appendix A for list of the operas produced and conducted by my grandfather, together with a list of many first productions and names of principal singers.

productions in English. Among these were the first English performance of *Tannhäuser*, in Liverpool in 1892, and in the same year a command performance[1] of *The Daughter of the Regiment* before Queen Victoria at Balmoral, with my maternal grandfather, Aynsley Cook, singing his famous role of Sergeant Sulpice.[2] In connection with this command performance, the following seems worth the telling. Eugene I discovered that the orchestra had to play in a window recess at the side of the State Rooms in the castle, in order that the players would not have to turn their backs to, nor sit in front of, Her Most Gracious Majesty. At rehearsal, he could not conceal his annoyance at the unfortunate arrangement, and it needed only a spark to cause an explosion. The spark was duly applied. In the course of the rehearsal there appeared upon the scene a noisy, inebriated theatre manager who proceeded to bustle about and make himself generally obnoxious. Grandfather turned on him angrily, and asked who he was. The manager replied, 'What's that to you; I'm McPherson from Aberdeen.' 'Mr. McPherson,' said Grandfather, 'kindly go to the devil, and mind your own business!' McPherson made a tipsy lunge at Grandfather, but a watchful attendant seized the Scotchman by the arm and reminded him that the State Apartments were no fit spot for a set-to with the conductor. Just at this moment Her Majesty in person appeared on a tour of inspection, and, quickly sizing up the situation while Mr. McPherson was being gently but firmly escorted from the room, said very nonchalantly to Grandfather, 'I trust, Mr. Goossens, that everything is now to your liking!' It is recorded that Mr. Goossens beamed with gratitude at Her Majesty's solicitude, but more particularly at the discomfiture of the objectionable McPherson.

Father returned to England from the Brussels Conservatory shortly after Carl Rosa's death. His father immediately made him leader of the second violins, and gave him

[1] See Appendix A, p. 311, for a contemporary report of this event.

[2] See p. 9.

MY GREAT-GRANDFATHER

MY GREAT-GRANDMOTHER

The Marriage of Figaro to conduct as a test of his fitness for the role of assistant conductor. This was a stroke of luck for the youngster, even though his newly acquired beard did make him look older than his years! He was then twenty-two, as I was when I conducted my first opera in London. He doubtless revelled as much as I did in the first taste of newly acquired authority. My grandfather, however, was not so enthusiastic, and decided after a few weeks' observation that Eugene, Junr., needed more theoretical study. He decided to send him back to school for a further period of study, and asked Marie Roze—the French soprano of the company—to persuade Massenet to accept Father as a pupil in his class at the Paris Conservatoire.[1] For some unknown reason, this plan did not mature, so Eugene II was sent to the Royal Academy of Music in London, then situated in Tenterden Street, off Hanover Square. Frederick Corder was Director, and father began a two-year studentship under Davenport for harmony, counterpoint, and composition. The resumption of student life after a brief taste of the colourful life of the Opera Company must have proved a bitter pill to swallow. So depressed did he become, and so strenuously did he attempt to drown his sorrows in work, that, having got halfway through the composition of a *De Profundis*, he became seriously ill and was compelled to abandon all further thoughts of composition. After a

---

[1] *Translation of Massenet's letter reproduced on pp. 14–16:*

Paris, 19 May 1890.

DEAR MADAM,—Thanks firstly for your always nice letter.

Here is the information. There is no examination in order to become a pupil in my class, but it is necessary to spend at least a year in my class as listener. One can compete in the second year as a student (fugue exam. at the Conservatoire), but a foreigner cannot enter for the Prix de Rome given by the Institut de France. If Mr. Eugene Goossens comes to live in Paris, he will be received in my class as listener, and then, according to his progress, as pupil (with the obligation of competing in fugue in the second year). I promise you and assure his father that I shall be absolutely devoted to this young man.

All my best wishes to Colonel Mapleson [head of Covent Garden], and to you my faithful and affectionate admiration.

J. MASSENET.

13

Paris - 19 mars /90

Chère Madame,

merci d'abord pour votre lettre
si aimable toujours pour moi -

Voici les renseignements:

pour entrer Élève dans ma classe
il n'y a pas d'examens -
mais il faut avoir passé dans
une classe au moins une année

AUTOGRAPH LETTER FROM MASSENET TO MARIE ROZE

comme auditeur —

— on peut concourir la 2de année
comme élève (concours de fugue au
Conservatoire) — mais comme étranger
on ne peut prendre part au
concours du 5e prix de Rome
décerné par l'Institut de France —

— Si Mlle Lugia Goossens vient
habiter Paris il sera reçu
à ma classe comme auditeur —
puis, selon ses rapides progrès,

comme élève (avec l'obligation de
concourir à la fugue la 2de année).

— Je vous promets, et je l'assure
à son père, que je serai absolument
dévoué à ce jeune homme —

— Tous mes meilleurs souvenirs
au colonel Mapleson et à vous
ma fidèle et affectueuse
admiration.

J. Massenet

long convalescence, he returned to the opera company. There he became engaged to the young contralto, Annie Cook, whom he married in 1892.

Mother was the daughter of Aynsley Cook, the eldest son of Thomas Cook, a London silversmith who had his establishment on Cornhill, at the beginning of the nineteenth century. Thomas Cook claimed descent from Captain Cook, the explorer, which probably accounts for my own propensity for 'living in a suitcase'. I will dispense with my maternal forbears in short order; family data makes tiresome reading. Many of them were prominent in the theatrical world, and their activities and connections may therefore be of interest to the reader interested in that remote period.

Grandfather Aynsley was born in London in 1835. He married Harriet, the daughter of W. H. Payne, a well-known theatrical producer of the time. There were six children of this marriage: Tom, Annie, Willie, Fred, Jim, and Katie. To-day Annie, my mother, no longer survives her brothers and sisters. She passed away in 1946 when in her eighty-fifth year; though, like my father, she had bravely endured her six years in wartime London. When in 1939 we begged her to leave for a safer refuge in anticipation of the Blitz, she replied: 'With the garden full of vegetables? I would never forgive myself.' So she and Father stayed on, confident in the protection of North Finchley's barrage balloons and anti-aircraft guns. I think of her as the type of all the heroic mothers of her generation.

In their youth my uncles Tom and Jim sang in the choir of the Chapel Royal, Windsor, and it is said that Queen Victoria often referred to the singing of the young Master Thomas Cook as the most beautiful thing she had ever heard in the Chapel. In later life the two brothers became well-known theatrical managers, and for some time Tom was associated managerially with the celebrated Mr. and Mrs. W. H. Kendal on their provincial tours. I remember going to 'Madge' Kendal's tea parties at her home in Portland Place just before the First World War. The most famous

Lady Teazle of her day had a caustic tongue. 'Yes, I remember your uncle,' she said once. 'Too good-looking for a manager. My husband couldn't stand him. I liked him. Have a muffin.' For several years Tom managed the Empire Theatre in Liverpool, where one saw the best vaudeville show in England. As a boy I was frequently taken backstage to meet some of the headliners—Dan Leno, George Robey, and Marie Lloyd (whose particular brand of humour I was too young to appreciate). I first saw the unknown Charlie Chaplin there in a sketch called *The Bricklayers*. He was for ever disappearing under a mountain of bricks. Once, I remember, Chung Ling Soo, a 'Chinese' magician, did a trick specially for my benefit—and I was cruelly disillusioned when told afterwards he was a Yorkshireman.

My great-aunt, Alice Aynsley Cook, grandfather's youngest sister, was well known with the D'Oyley Carte Company on its provincial tours. She took the soubrette roles in most of the productions, and was also a member of the old Gaiety Theatre Company, which included Nellie Farren, Kate Vaughan, and Connie Gilchrist. She was my liveliest relative, and at eighty still had a devastating sense of humour, as racy as in her palmy Gaiety days. In a fantastic bonnet and long silver curls, she would come to tea at our house in West Kensington, and convulse us all with a line of comic patter in the best Victorian tradition. Even in the finest weather she always carried a short cape and a parasol, which made her resemble the comic pantomime dame of tradition. My brothers and I adored her, and called her 'Sporty Aunt Al'.

The old Gaiety featured mainly performances of light and burlesque opera (not 'burlesque' in the American sense of the word!) and the composer of one of these Gaiety productions, a piece called *Faust Up-to-date*, was Meyer Lutz, the Gaiety's conductor, who married Elizabeth Cook, my great-aunt. This gentleman was also organist of the Catholic Cathedral at Southwark, and composed much sacred music of the maudlin kind then in vogue. Another great-uncle by marriage was Harry Payne, one of the best-known

MANCHESTER,
in the County of
LANCASTER,
TO WIT.

𝕿𝖎𝖈𝖙𝖔𝖗𝖎𝖆, 𝕼𝖚𝖊𝖊𝖓 𝖔𝖋 𝖙𝖍𝖊 𝖀𝖓𝖎𝖙𝖊𝖉 𝕶𝖎𝖓𝖌𝖉𝖔𝖒 𝖔𝖋 𝕲𝖗𝖊𝖆𝖙 𝕭𝖗𝖎𝖙𝖆𝖎𝖓, 𝕴𝖗𝖊𝖑𝖆𝖓𝖉, & 𝕾𝖈𝖔𝖙𝖑𝖆𝖓𝖉, 𝕯𝖊𝖋𝖊𝖓𝖉𝖊𝖗 𝖔𝖋 𝖙𝖍𝖊 𝕱𝖆𝖎𝖙𝖍.

WE command you after the serving of this Writ, to put in appearance *personally*, between the Hours of SEVEN and TEN at Night, at the **THEATRE ROYAL**, on **MONDAY, FEBRUARY 23rd, 1857,** or show some just cause why you think not of coming to **OUR BENEFIT,** so that we may be able to pay our Wine Bill, Tailor's Bill, and 999 other Bills ; when our well-beloved Subjects, we think, will be delighted with the Amusement intended for that Evening, if not, they shall be brought to the Bar of the House of Commons and be deprived of their dignities and privileges.———(*SIGNED,*) *by permission,*—**W. H. PAYNE,**

SEVEIHTYTTROFEHTFOFEIHCCARASSAH.

HY. PAYNE.—SELGNAPSDNASEHCTAPFOECNIRPNIUQELRAH.

clowns of the 'seventies, and famous for his antics in the 'Harlequinade' of the pantomime at Drury Lane Theatre, based on the old Commedia Dell' Arte. In his clown's dress, and armed with the familiar string of sausages and red-hot poker, he was the idol of the children who thronged the famous theatre Christmas after Christmas, to see *Aladdin*, *Sinbad*, *Jack and the Beanstalk*, and all those old perennial favourites of English pantomime lovers. His most famous exploit consisted in crawling on all fours round the edge of the dress circle, distributing buns to his hysterical young audience. Loving both clowns *and* buns, I lament never having witnessed this feat. . . .

MY GRANDFATHER
EUGENE GOOSSENS I

CHAPTER IV

GRANDFATHER COOK inherited little or no musical talent from his parents, but Edward Hopkins, organist of the Temple Church, thought him a good enough singer at the age of ten to give him the solo soprano position at his church. From thenceforward his career was so varied and colourful that I cannot refrain from noting some of its highlights. When he was eleven, he sang solos at the opening of St. George's Catholic Cathedral, Southwark (Pusey's 'Gothic Revival' church), and also at concerts directed by Mendelssohn and Spohr, neither of whom, according to Aynsley, conducted as well as they composed! A year later he became 'Chamber-Singer' to the Marquis of Anglesea, one of the heroes of Waterloo and a great amateur musician. (Imagine, if you please, an English general with a private *Kapelle*!) At fourteen, he was sent to the Conservatory of Wurzburg, and in a few years' time developed a fine bass voice, which led to his adopting an operatic career. His early professional engagements were in small Bavarian towns under conductor-composers, such as Franz Lachner and Meyer, and after five years in Germany he made his English début in the 'fifties with an organization styled the National English Opera. There he created Devilshoof in Balfe's *Bohemian Girl*, his most famous role, and shortly afterwards left England with his young wife Harriet for a transcontinental opera tour of America under the auspices of the newly formed Estcott Opera Company.

On 28 June 1860 my mother was born in Boston, Massachusetts. The Civil War broke out that year, and as a result of this melancholy event, the Cook family was compelled to take the first available ship back to England. The vessel on which they returned made her last regular sailing before the blockade.

On his return, Aynsley sang the role of Oroveso in *Norma*, with Grisi as the heroine, at the old Theatre Royal, Liverpool. Sir Augustus Harris, famed London impresario, engaged him to create the part of General Boom in Offenbach's *Grande Duchesse*, in which he became famous for the great staying power he displayed in a role which required tremendous swagger and bombast. Later, Hollingshead booked him at the Gaiety Theatre, London (in conjunction with Santley), to sing operas in English, proving that the 'Opera in English' movement was already in vogue in the 'sixties. Aynsley's best-known roles were in *Zampa*, *Fra Diavolo*, and *Peter the Shipwright*, a stodgy but not unattractive work by Lortzing. Carl Rosa offered him the principal bass parts in his newly formed company, with which group he again went off to America and sang during two long remunerative tours.

An old Liverpool opera-goer recalls in a letter to me a memorable performance of *Zampa* by the Rosa Company in about 1879: 'What a performance that was! Mr. (afterwards Sir) Charles Santley was Zampa, Mlle. Corriani was the Bride, Leslie Crotty (he was later also to found an opera company) the Manservant, Mr. Aynsley Cook Zampa's Lieutenant, Mr. Ludwig the First Robber, and Mrs. Aynsley Cook the Marble Image of Alice de Manfredi. Oh, that Marble Image!! It was absolutely thrilling, and no one in the vast audience was more stirred when the Image "raised a denunciatory hand" than was the writer.' (How I'd have enjoyed seeing my grandmother enacting a 'marble image'!)

Grandpa Cook remained with the Rosa Company till his death, which took place the year after my birth. He was a great character, generous, unselfish, and witty. Queen Victoria thought much of him, and when the Company's Command Performance was given at Balmoral Castle, Her Majesty sent for Aynsley to inquire whether she was right in thinking that she saw him in *Satanella* at Covent Garden in 1853. Aynsley Cook confirmed the royal recognition and received in return a royal scarf-pin. Later, when the

Queen attended a Carl Rosa performance of *Fra Diavolo*, she sent for *both* my grandfathers (Eugene and Aynsley). The interview affords a good example of their different personalities. Speaking first to Eugene in a most complimentary manner, she asked him his nationality. Instead of taking this opportunity of winning the good graces of Her Majesty by an ingratiating speech, Eugene merely replied, 'Belge, Madame.' Aynsley, on the other hand, before being presented, wanted to 'tidy up a bit', but was forced to appear in costume. With his usual charm, he explained to the Queen, 'I have to apologize, Your Majesty, for appearing before you in this guise.' To which Her Majesty replied, 'No, no, Mr. Cook. There is no ground for apology. Believe me, you are delightful in *any* guise!'

His last appearance was in Auber's *Fra Diavolo* in January 1894, and a month later his colleagues of the opera company sang Mozart's *Requiem* in St. Peter's Catholic Church, Liverpool, at his funeral. When the wreath from Zélie de Lussan (greatest of all English Carmens and Daughters of the Regiment) bearing the inscription, 'Farewell, Sergeant Sulpice', was placed in tribute at the grave, old opera-lovers who recalled his many fine performances of this role read the words and unashamedly wept.

Mother was fifteen when she was admitted to the chorus at Covent Garden—then called the Italian Opera—though as a little girl of five she had already made her début on the opera stage in *The Bohemian Girl*.[1] She was the child abducted by Devilshoof—played by her father. One night, in the escape scene, he tripped on the high bridge across which he was fleeing, and nearly fell to the stage with my mother in his arms. Fortunately, the side of the bridge averted a tragedy.

---

[1] It is interesting to recall Herman Klein's account of witnessing a performance of *The Bohemian Girl* at Norwich in his youth, probably in the 'seventies. In his book, *The Golden Age of Opera*, he writes: 'Could the finest operatic ballet ever yield a more exciting climax than the breathless dance of Devilshoof as executed by Aynsley in *The Bohemian Girl* . . . twisting, twirling, gyrating around the stage a dozen times or more, until everyone grew giddy save the leaping gipsy himself? Ah! Those were moments!'

In those days the choristers at the Italian Opera apparently experienced no difficulty in singing in foreign languages. Thanks to the parrot-like method of choral rehearsal then in vogue, they were able to memorize the music without particularly bothering to understand what they were singing about. So thorough was this training that even up to quite recently my mother could still recall the phonetic sounds associated with well-known choruses from both the standard French and Italian operas. (Judging by certain foreign-language performances in some of our opera houses to-day, the same mechanical condition still exists.) After a few years of this routine work, mother joined the Carl Rosa Opera Company as a principal. There, at any rate, she could sing in her own language.

At this time (about 1890) no fewer than four of my forbears were members of the same opera company: Eugene I, conducting the orchestra; Eugene II (my father) playing principal second violin; Grandfather Cook singing leading bass roles; and his daughter Annie (my mother) singing the smaller contralto parts. I doubt very much if such a unique record has ever been established anywhere else by any other family of musicians. It is said that clashes of temperament were by no means infrequent between my two grandsires. The bearded martinet in the pit must have had his hands full dealing with the boisterous *basso buffo* on stage, particularly in roles which called for a certain licence in interpretation and musical style.

In contrast to this, the romantic attachment which developed between the young contralto and the handsome violinist in the orchestra must have provided a valuable compensatory factor in current Cook-Goossens relationships.

An experience which befell my parents in 1892—the year of their marriage—was typical of those days. A certain venturesome Italian impresario, one Signor Largo, attempted to produce the new Tchaikovsky opera, *Eugene Onegin*, at the Olympic Theatre in the Strand. Deserting Carl Rosa for the time being, my mother and father were

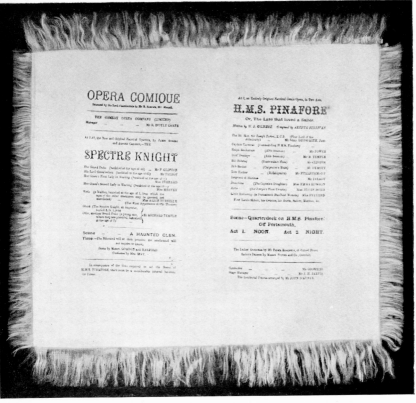

QUEEN VICTORIA'S SILKEN PROGRAMME FOR A COMMAND
PERFORMANCE IN LONDON ON 25 MAY 1878, AT WHICH MY
GRANDFATHER, EUGENE GOOSSENS I, CONDUCTED *H.M.S. PINAFORE*

engaged by the Signor for the production, but after three performances it proved a failure; Signor Largo bolted with the receipts, and the company went without any salary. This sort of thing, however, was not peculiar to those bygone days. My own experience in America with a defaulting management in the middle 'twenties proves that unscrupulous operatic impresarios still flourish in this day and age.

CHAPTER V

THE following year, 1893, was an eventful one for the Goossens family. Grandfather Eugene, tired of opera companies and their ways, resigned from the Carl Rosa Company and settled down to voice-teaching in Liverpool. Father left his post in the orchestra to become conductor of the Burns-Crotty Opera Company—an organization into which two singers, Georgina Burns and Leslie Crotty, threw their fortunes, with no very lasting results. Finally, the writer of this chronicle, Eugene III, was born in a theatrical boarding house in the suburb of Camden Town, London, on the morning of 26 May. It is said that early that day, there being a lively south-east breeze blowing at the time, the chimes of Bow Church were faintly heard in Camden Town. This fact automatically established me as a Cockney, and the date of my birth as a Geminian—a concatenation of circumstances which lends all the more strength to my fatal proclivity never to do to-day what can possibly be put off till to-morrow.

The boarding house in which I was born is situated in one of the most depressing sections of London. I suppose the railways have something to do with this, but it is chiefly the stucco-faced buildings of the locality—mostly rows of dwelling houses, small shops, 'rooms' and commercial hotels—which contrive to lend a forlorn and dingy note to all this part of North London. In 1903, the house adjoining my birthplace was the setting for the notorious Crippen murder, an event which set the final seal on a desolate neighbourhood. Yet the sulphurous atmosphere of trains which permeates Camden Town and the air of shabby gentility it still manages to retain are things for which I must always confess a strange fondness.

I should rightly here have been able to set down something

of my first vague impressions of infancy. To my intense relief—and I'm sure the reader's as well—I find myself unable to recall any single thing about it. The Burns-Crotty Company had promptly disintegrated by the end of the year, compelling my father to take a place as violinist at Covent Garden until the arrival of his next touring engagement. This occurred when he became, a few months later, conductor of the Arthur Rousbey Opera Company, another fairly short-lived organization. It seems that I successfully weathered these first fluctuating years of *va et vient*, surviving even such experiences as sleeping in chests-of-drawers and on horse-hair sofas when accommodation on tour proved difficult to secure. Outside of a penchant for immediately depositing all breakables on the pavement, my conduct in a perambulator was apparently beyond praise, and the only misgivings I ever caused were at my christening, when I was described by the priest as taciturn and aloof.

Rumour has it that I was immensely popular with the members of the Rousbey Company, presumably on the principle that 'all the world loves a baby', especially if it's the conductor's baby. Certainly I must have often taken my father's mind off the problems a travelling musical director had to contend with in those days in the matter of adequate personnel and rehearsal. The orchestral resources available to the Rousbey Company and its conductor were slender. Orchestra pits were of limited size in provincial theatres, and as this skeleton orchestra was usually reinforced by 'local' players the crush must have been disheartening. The 'locals' were chosen ahead of time by the advance representative of the company, an individual who, while probably an excellent business-man, was rarely much of a hand at picking potential orchestral material. The job of rehearsing the comparatively unskilled 'locals' in those days in each city visited by the company can well be imagined. For over twenty years father always undertook this task himself. Every morning, irrespective of whether he was in a big or small town, he would rehearse apprehensive little groups of players (never more than seven or eight in number) in the stuffy 'bar' of the theatre, in order that they should be tolerably familiar with the opera to be played that night. The execrable sounds produced at some of these rehearsals were unbelievable, yet at the performance, with the help of the regular players, the 'locals' usually managed to give a fair account of themselves. Father relates that in one small town, after a spell of bad business, the company's finances were so slender that he was reduced to conducting a performance of *Cavalleria* with five players—harmonium, cornet, horn, and two violins. The following day even the cornet and horn players deserted, and he had to conduct *Tannhäuser* with two violins and a harmonium. This performance prompted the manager's wife to remark that she had never heard the woodwind 'so well in tune!' In spite of those vicissitudes, the Rousbey venture survived for three or four years. During that time the Goossens family had increased by two members. Marie, my elder sister,[1] was born in London in 1894 and Adolphe (killed in the First World War) in 1896. With these new arrivals, family touring finally became impracticable, and so in the following year my father decided to establish domestic headquarters in Liverpool, where grandfather Goossens had previously installed himself in a roomy old house on Mount Pleasant, facing what is now the half-completed Catholic Cathedral. (Formerly the Brownlow Hill workhouse stood there—a gloomy augury, I always thought.)

At the close of 1893, Grandfather Eugene resolved to give four symphony concerts at the Philharmonic Hall in Liverpool, in the hope that the orchestra he gathered together for these concerts might become a permanent institution in that city. To this end, he organized a group of seventy players, at the same time inviting the public to subscribe to the new series. The first concert took place on 1 November, and was attended by a fairly large, very demonstrative audience. Judging by the local papers, it was an unqualified artistic success. With Lamprière Pringle, a well-known baritone, as his assisting artist, Grandfather's

[1] Now harpist of the London Symphony Orchestra.

first offering consisted of an all-Wagner programme.[1] The second concert, consisting of a mixed programme, took place before a smaller audience two weeks later. Alas for the fickleness of the public! The expenses of these two concerts had already far exceeded the takings, and, prudent man that he was (unlike his grandson on a later and similar occasion), Eugene I decided that it was wiser to cancel the final two concerts. To those, therefore, who had subscribed to all four concerts, the following letter was sent, headed 'Goossens Orchestral Concerts': 'Mr. Eugene Goossens begs to return your subscription for two concerts and to thank you very sincerely for your kind patronage; also to express his regret that the inadequacy of support accorded by the general public—resulting in a serious financial loss—necessitates his discontinuing the series.' Many subscribers wrote by return, asking him to retain the full amount of the subscription, but he refused to do so. (The indifference of the 'smart' Liverpool audiences towards these concerts was —and still is—typical of the conservative apathy of English provincial audiences.)

No sooner had the series been abandoned than, nothing daunted, Grandfather started organizing a male voice choir, to be devoted principally to the performance of music of the Belgian School. The Goossens Male Voice Choir was duly formed at a meeting held at the end of 1894, presided over by a Mr. Wynne, then Editor of the *Liverpool Mercury*. Grandfather explained at the meeting that his idea was to form a male voice choir similar to the fine Belgian choruses of the time. The organization was to be on co-operative lines, and there was a small entrance fee of half a crown, in addition to a weekly contribution of a few pence. The profits of the concerts were to be invested, and eventually divided among members of the chorus. The works to be performed would be in the nature of vocal symphonies. The names of about fifty members were enrolled at this meeting, many others being subsequently added. In due course the chorus appeared at a concert in Picton Hall, concerning which the

[1] See Appendix A, p. 311.

March 20: 1903

Dear Mr Goossens:

Many thanks for your
letter: I have such ex-
cellent accounts of your
Men's chorus that I feel
sure you chord really
with very great success:
I wish all good things.

[signature]

I am very glad you
contemplate

contemplate a performance,

the work is the property
of Messrs Novello & Co
& no doubt they would
assist your society — I
have sent on your
letter to them.

In the event your
performance taking
place I would suggest
that no cuts
be made on account
of the words. the Canticle

PERFORMANCE BY GOOSSENS' CHOIR OF ELGAR'S *TE DEUM AND BENEDICTUS* (1902)

should not be mutilated
but is to well known
to point out the failings.

I hope you will see
your way to give it
over.

Believe me

Yours very truly

Edward Elgar

E Groves, Esq.

March 26 1902.

Stephr. Goosens:

I have written
Messrs. Novello about
the Te Deum & Benediction,
& they will make
things necessary for
you regarding a
performance. Will
you kindly write
to them telling them
you

your requirements to all
particulars. Please
mention that I let
Mr. & Mrs. Novello
have written to me
or your application
will go into the ordinary
hire department.

I shall be very pleased
to hear that you
have arranged
the Concert with
your every success
in

[handwritten letter closing]

in your new society

Believe me

Yours very truly

Edward Elgar

local *Mercury* wrote: 'However high preliminary anticipations may have reigned, it is certain that last evening's performance must have transcended them.' Grandfather had chosen two works by the Belgian composer Limmander, *The Tomb of the Janissaries* and *The Smugglers*. The local Press went into raptures over these performances, and the Goossens Choir, by reason of its success, was soon able to move its concerts to the much larger Philharmonic Hall. Conspicuous in the repertory of the choir were such dramatic and virtuoso works as *The Survivors of Tydal*, by Hager, and the *Hymn of Life*, by Riga, composed originally for the competition of the Chants D'Ensemble at Cologne. The Goossens Choir continued as a vigorous organization up to its last appearance in 1906, when my grandfather's untimely death put an end to its activities.

CHAPTER VI

YOUNG as I was when we migrated to Liverpool and began occupying the gloomy, spacious house on Mount Pleasant (how a recluse like my grandfather could ever have reconciled himself to this invasion still remains a mystery), I can still conjure up memories of those early days. I remember particularly the rehearsals of the Goossens Choir, always held in the long first-floor drawing-room. Twice a week the gusty sounds from those evening meetings reached me in my attic bedroom and, far from lulling me to sleep, kept me wide awake. I was stimulated and sometimes a little frightened by what I heard, especially when Grandfather raised his voice over the tumult. Fortunately the houses on either side of ours were vacant, else we might have had to contend with some rather irate neighbours. Fifty or sixty tenors and basses crowded into a drawing-room can produce a gale of sound. I vaguely remember the people who came to the house during the daytime for singing lessons and auditions. I never saw these persons who came to sing scales and arpeggios, but I hated the sounds they made, and, for the most part, hate them still to-day.

My very earliest memory of Mount Pleasant, and indeed of my whole childhood, is of my father telling me in a quite matter-of-fact voice—probably assumed for the occasion—that I had suddenly acquired another small brother. This, to me, somewhat mystifying piece of news heralded Leon Goossens' arrival into the world, a source of much eventual gratification for all lovers of the grand manner of oboe-playing. Apart from his being probably the noisiest and worst-tempered baby I've ever heard, and a serious competitor of the Goossens Choir in its loudest moments, his arrival must have complicated the whole question of

36

Lebensraum for Eugene II and his steadily growing family. It certainly precipitated it, for a few months later my father decided to move his family from the city to the countryside. This not only left Grandfather and his choir in undisputed possession of the house on the hill, but proved highly beneficial to the health and happiness of his grandchildren.

So one day we bade farewell to depressing Mount Pleasant and, moving across the Mersey to the Cheshire side of the river, settled in what was then the small, quiet residential community of Liscard, on the Wirral Peninsula. Instead of the drab aspect of the Brownlow Hill Workhouse, which faced our house in Liverpool, we now revelled in the open fields and pure sea air of Wallasey and New Brighton. Ten years afterwards, Liscard was unrecognizable, so heavily did the blight of 'real estate' descend upon it. But how beautiful it all was when first we went to live there! The firm white sands were but a few minutes' walk away, and over to the west there was the distant purple line of the Welsh mountains, mysterious and wondrously remote. There were the lonely sands of Dee, formed by the estuary of the river, and inland stretched the gentle, windswept countryside towards Bidston Hill, with its old mill a landmark for miles around. Northward the choppy waters of the Irish Sea foamed over the 'Bar', across which, even at high tide, it took a skilful pilot to bring a big ship safely into the Mersey. And along the beach was New Brighton, at the very mouth of the Mersey, where half the shipping of the world used to pass by. You could stand near Perch Rock Lighthouse on Saturdays, and watch the big steamers and the tramps and the sailing ships leaving for all parts of the seven seas; and returning from them, too. How many recall those grand old liners whose names have long passed into legend? The big Cunarders and White Star ships, American and Dominion liners. Fine steamers like the *Oceanic, Campania, Lucania, Teutonic, Majestic, Umbria, Etruria, Virginian, Saxonia, Ivernia*; all of them, even then, carrying sail for an emergency. You could take a ferry from New Brighton pier and ride down the Mersey, keeping company with a big liner all the way to Liverpool until she finally tied up at the landing-stage. And whether you approached the 'stage' on a ferry-boat from New Brighton, Egremont, Liscard, Birkenhead, or Eastham, Liverpool was an exciting city to come to. They hadn't put up the splendid Mersey Docks and Harbour Board Building, nor the Liver Building at the pier-head in those days, but the big shipping offices of Water Street and the warehouses of Back Goree and the old Custom House and the tower of St. Nicholas Church and a jumble of quaint buildings formed the picturesque façade to a fine city. Uptown, there was the majestic St. George's Hall—containing then the largest pipe-organ in the world—and the severely classic and acoustically perfect Philharmonic Hall (later destroyed by fire), not to mention rows of aristocratic-looking Georgian homes; and, alas, wastes of dreary slums! Miles of granite-faced docks stretched in an unbroken line north and south of the landing-stage; in the south docks there were always forests of sailing ships, and in the north docks an endless array of big steamers. To-day, as I write, the Mersey still flows to the sea past its bomb-scarred mother city, but most of the big steamers, at least the *very* big ones, have gone. . . .

Father meanwhile, having severed his connection with the Rousbey Company owing to its financial instability, sought elsewhere an outlet for his activities. It wasn't until August 1898 that he became conductor of the Moody-Manners Opera Company, a group which, founded by the singers Charles Manners and Fanny Moody, eventually enjoyed a long and prosperous existence in friendly rivalry to the Carl Rosa Company. That two organizations specializing in the performance of opera in English could manage to command a big enough public while operating simultaneously over the same terrain is proof that the English provincial cities were, in those days, definitely fertile operatic soil. What a pity they didn't remain so! Manchester, Liverpool, Birmingham, Leeds, Sheffield, Newcastle, Bristol, Cardiff, not forgetting Glasgow, Edinburgh, Aberdeen, and (across the Irish Sea) Dublin, Cork, and Belfast, were some of the larger centres of operatic activity of those days. Smaller cities, such as Derby, York, Portsmouth, and others, also proved staunch citadels of the 'opera in English' movement for many years to follow. Not till the hectic 'twenties did the decline begin to set in, and with it a period of strain and stress for the few surviving opera companies, most outstanding of which was that survivor of Beecham days, the British National Opera Company. As these words are written, the future seems too problematical to predict flourishing days for any touring company.

In 1899 father was offered, and accepted, the principal conductorship of the Carl Rosa Company, and there began, as in the case of my grandfather, a long association with it which only the War of 1914–18 terminated. My sister Sidonie,[1] youngest member of the family, was born this year in Liscard, which meant that my mother now had a family of five on her hands. Father was on tour for eight months of the year, and had it not been for the fact that a small preparatory school nearby (proprietor and sole teacher, Sarah Perris) catered to the educational needs of the neighbourhood, Mother might have found herself faced with far too much all-day and all-night domestic responsibility. The school took some of this from her shoulders, and cared for Marie and myself each morning. But her task was an onerous one. That she accomplished it all is a tribute to her devotion and unselfishness, though, like many other women before and since, the relinquishing of a career seemed to her a small price to pay for the joy of bringing up a family!

Meantime, at the end of 1897 (the year of Leon's birth), Father Turner, Benedictine priest and composer of much excellent sacred music, died at St. Anne's Benedictine Church in the Liverpool suburb of Edgehill. He was organist and choirmaster of the church, and my grandfather, one of his parishioners, immediately volunteered to fill the post until a new organist could be found. His offer was accepted, and he remained at St. Anne's, not for a few weeks,

[1] Harpist of the B.B.C. Symphony Orchestra.

39

but for close on nine years. So much did he love his new work, and such a gap did it fill in his life of retirement, that the temptation to stay proved irresistible. He completely reorganized the choir, and brought to it a discipline previously unheard of at St. Anne's. In later years, when the three Goossens boys were inducted into it, that discipline was to be brought very close to home. . . .

MY MATERNAL GRANDFATHER
AYNSLEY COOK

CHAPTER VII

NEW BRIGHTON—referred to in the foregoing note on Liverpool—boasted in my youth two features which made it almost world-famous. One was the notorious 'Ham-and-Egg' Parade, a string of dowdy side-shows, cafés, and boarding houses familiar to everyone who took the ferry ride across the Mersey. There were also merry-go-rounds and shooting galleries and other paraphernalia of Coney Island. In later days my brothers and I patronized them whenever we had pennies to spend, but more often than not we had to be content with merely sightseeing. There were horses, too, which galloped you along the hard sands for 'tuppence' and knew exactly when to turn back, even when *you* didn't. I loved the sound of the galloping hooves on the beach against a background of steam-organs, boat-whistles, and the pounding of the waves on the shore.

The other feature was the New Brighton Tower, which stood at the mouth of the river, and was second only in height to the Eiffel Tower in Paris. (Blackpool boasts a similar one; they seem indigenous to Lancashire.) Its base was a lofty red-brick, circular building which contained an enormous ballroom, frequently used for orchestral concerts. Here the Liverpool Orchestral Society gave regular Sunday concerts, conducted by Mr. (later Sir) Granville Bantock, and here Father took me to listen to my first concert when I was six. Beyond recalling the sudden *fortissimo* chord in the *Oberon Overture* (at which I let out a dismal wail of fear and surprise, and as a result was immediately led from the hall to recover), I remember very little of this event. Subsequent concerts I do remember, particularly a recital given by the Czech violinist, Kubelik. Father and I had seats on the stage for this occasion, so that I was able to gaze wide-eyed at the young, frock-coated violinist who performed with ease feats on the violin which some swore hadn't been heard since the days of Paganini. (Thirty-five years later I conducted Kubelik's last concert in America with the Cincinnati Orchestra, a rather pathetic event by contrast.) The Tower,[1] with its frightening ascent by elevator to the summit—and what a view that was—its fair grounds, menagerie, tight-rope exhibitions by Blondin, and splendid concerts, gave me my first real musical and adventurous thrills.

All this was at the turn of the century, and though my memory of events *circa* 1900 isn't too clear, I do know that every time news of a British victory came from South Africa, I pinned a button (showing Generals Roberts and Baden-Powell) to my lapel, and hoisted the Union Jack on the flagpole at the end of the garden. My attitude towards violin lessons was less enthusiastic. Father had started to teach me when I was five years old, but, being away much of the time, he had turned over this part of my education to James Matthews[2] from Birkenhead. 'Jimmy' came once a week to give me lessons, and though I liked him, I hated having to practise. The daily routine of scales and exercises seemed aimless and depressing, though when Father returned home in the summer from his eight months of yearly touring, he managed to reconcile me to its inevitability by supervising practice hours with a firm but kindly hand. At such times no outside distractions were permitted to interfere with their solemn ritual. Cricket, picnics, and all such frivolities took second place where violin and piano were concerned. (The piano had now entered the picture; an upright Bechstein with a heavy touch.) Musically speaking, I was happiest when listening to Father preparing new operas at the piano. Not only did he memorize each bar of the

---

[1] The actual tower itself (612 feet high) was pulled down at the end of 1918, and I agree with the old seafaring men who say that with it there disappeared Liverpool's most famous landmark. Fortunately, the lighthouse and the nearby picturesque fort still remain.

[2] J. E. Matthews, formerly first desk member of the first violin sections of the Liverpool Philharmonic, and until recently conductor of the Southport Orchestral Society.

music, but as he went along marked in pencil in the score every nuance and inflection of the vocal line—a formidable task. No wonder singers used to say, 'Once you've coached a role with E.G., you don't forget it till you die.' When the Rosa Company gave its seasons at the Shakespeare Theatre in Liverpool, I used to accompany Father across the Mersey to his daily rehearsals. Sometimes I'd sit just behind him in the front row of the 'stalls', peering over the orchestra rail or watching the singers on the stage. I loved everything about those rehearsals, from the details of musical preparation to the mysteries of 'back-cloths', 'ambers', and 'props'. During them, I lived in a conflicting world of romanticism and reality. Even the sight of Lohengrin in a fedora and overcoat or Amneris in tippet and muff didn't disillusion me. The emotional impact of some of the operas sometimes proved a little too much for my sensitive imagination, but I always managed to keep an ear open for what was happening in the orchestra. At a time therefore when both operatic and symphonic tradition counted for more than they do to-day, I learnt much that was to prove invaluable in later years. Those were days of deliberate 'tempi' which did leisurely justice to the music rather than, as now, draw critical yawns from those who claim that speed is the secret of 'brilliant' interpretation. (Listen to the way they scamper through the preludes to *Carmen* and Act III *Lohengrin,* the first duet in *Tannhäuser,* the *Kermesse* and Soldiers' Chorus in *Faust* in most modern opera-houses for proof of this.)

But in opera, it is the singing which, after all, really counts. Of course if the 'old-timers'' accounts are to be believed, the calibre of to-day's singers hardly measures up with those of late Victorian days. ('It ain't necessarily so', as Gershwin's hero once said.) Then, it would seem, in addition to possessing a fine voice, diligence and apprenticeship were the requisites for success. Standards of artistry were high, and what now is looked upon by the average student as hard work would have been laughed at by some of the worthies of the 'eighties and 'nineties. Listen to Grandfather Cook talking to an interviewer of the *Liverpool*

43

Review in 1889. The interviewer is asking him his opinion of singing as a profession. Grandfather replies, 'Nowadays, when people can't do anything else, they see if they have a voice. You'd be astonished if you knew how many people *imagine* they can sing, and to-day they have opportunities they never had before. Years ago, it was considered a great privilege to be allowed the chance of trying one's voice before an impresario, but now, through the indulgence of Mr. Rosa, we have people coming to our company every day to have their voices tried by Mr. Goossens, and as a rule these aspirants are not fit even for the chorus, much less a leading part.' 'Early training has a great deal to do with it, I suppose,' says the interviewer. 'Yes,' replies Aynsley, 'Many people who have fine natural voices are ruined through bad training. Anyone who has a voice should place himself under a good singing-master, not under a piano-teacher (as is so often the case); in fact, I think every man and woman who goes on the lyric stage should have commenced life as a chorister. It teaches him deportment and how to appear before the public.' [Can you see the face of a singing-teacher of to-day if he were told that it was necessary to enter the chorus in order to make a successful début as an operatic artist?] 'Let me remind you, too, that the voice alone does not make a fine singer. A fine singer must have the ear, the brain, the soul of an artist. Indeed, the singer is always learning something, and in this respect he must serve a long apprenticeship.' The interviewer asks him about diet. 'The singer must keep his brain clear. If his brain is out of order, it throws his stomach out of gear, and that upsets his voice. On the day of a performance a singer should dine at three in the afternoon [*sic*], take simply a cup of tea about six. He should never use stimulants during singing. After his business is over, then let him take what he likes, but not during the day.' Asked about his repertoire, Aynsley replies: 'Well, I think I may venture to say that I am not exactly behindhand in that matter, for my repertoire consists of *ninety-two operas*.' (My italics.) 'In many of these, I take more than one part, so the parts I perform are about as many again.' The interviewer is puzzled as to how he remembers so many roles. 'Oh, well,' he replies, 'it's a special kind of memory, I suppose. Every man to his trade, you know. The other day, for instance, I sang in *Maritana* and *Faust*, and had not looked at the scores since first studying the parts nearly twenty years ago, but I managed to do them perfectly well. It comes back to you when you are once note-perfect.' Asked about his hobbies, he replies: 'Riding and driving; but I am too heavy for riding and can't afford to drive. Still, I have a hobby in my music, which more than serves my purpose, and my ambition is to die in harness—which I hope will not happen until I'm a centenarian.' He nearly realized the first, but not the second.

I am quite ready to admit that there is a tendency among those who write enthusiastically of bygone days to disparage the accomplishments of the living artist by comparison with those of his predecessors. Instancing the legendary figures of the past is sometimes a convenient method of belittling contemporary achievement. Yet can it truthfully be said that the critical judgement of the public regarding singing is higher, or even as high, as that of an age which knew neither the radio soprano nor the crooner? Are the standards of the past applied as critically—when they *are* applied—to a newcomer in the field of singing as they formerly were? Is the professional field for singers in America and Europe[1] wide enough to warrant the flood of mediocrities which now overwhelms it, so that our few really great singers emerge by sheer force of artistry head and shoulders above the lesser fry? The answer is an emphatic 'No'. There is nowadays a complacency in the vocal branch of the musical profession which takes many forms: lack of industry, resentment of criticism, and a strange indifference to perfection. I mean by this the tendency to take the short cut which eliminates tedious, but nevertheless essential, study of detail without which an artist is not fully equipped. Our economic conditions may be in part responsible, yet it is true that while

[1] And Australia, for that matter.

45

many of the great singers of the past suffered actual priva-
tion during their prolonged, intensive period of final study
before launching out into a career, young graduate students
and budding professionals nowadays must needs either make
an immediate London or New York concert début or land up
prematurely in a radio studio with a remunerative contract.
What chance for an apprenticeship is there in either case?

An old-time Carl Rosa tenor named Valentine Smith once
founded a company of his own. He made a point of advertising 'Valentine Smith's top C from the chest' in allusion
to his singing of an aria from *Trovatore*. Imagine such candour
to-day, much less a top C!

CHAPTER VIII

WHEN I was eight years old I was sent as a boarder to St. Francis Xavier's School in Bruges. There was a certain thrill about the prospect of leaving England for the Continent, especially as I was going to the city of my fathers. So with about a hundred other English boys, I left Victoria Station, London, on a murky September day in 1901, accompanied to the station by my tearful mother to wave me farewell. Sitting in a corner of a London, Chatham, and Dover Railway compartment and munching a Spier's and Pond's bath bun, a great loneliness of spirit descended on me. By the time we reached Dover, I had definitely decided that leaving home for a ten-month exile was not quite the joyous release it had been pictured. But a rough Channel crossing on the Dover-Ostend steamer soon changed my mood, and when I arrived in Bruges that evening I had entered another world. Its spires, old houses, canals and the music of its belfry cast a spell which obliterated my nostalgia for England. And, like Longfellow's traveller, I lay that evening—

> Listening with a wild delight
> To the chimes that through the night,
> Rang their changes from the Belfry
> Of that quaint old Flemish city. . . .

Life at St. Francis Xavier's was strenuous, and not unexciting. Every morning the chapel bell awakened us at five and, irrespective of creed, the whole school attended Mass at 5.30. Breakfast was at six, and school began an hour later for all excepting a handful of the musical élite, myself included. These unfortunates were taught their different instruments in a series of glass-houses, icily cold in winter and appallingly hot in summer. Each room in the

47

row was separated from the adjoining one by a glass partition, so that an individual at either end of the row enjoyed an uninterrupted view of professors and students working away in some twelve rooms. This prospect, plus the bedlam of sound produced by the mass banging and scraping of the inmates, always struck me as quite ridiculous. In winter-time the professors sat in thick overcoats, munching sausage and drinking hot coffee, while their miserable pupils—with great fortitude, it seemed to me—stumbled through badly prepared pieces and tried to forget the bitter cold.

Three afternoons a week we walked to the playing-fields outside the city, where we learned the mysteries of cricket and football, neither of which I ever really enjoyed. Here one acquired what is known as the 'team spirit', plus a taste for Belgian apples, pears, and cherries which I have never lost. The countryside around Bruges is typically Flemish. From the playing-fields of the school the towers of the city rise from the plain in the distance, looking just as they did when Van Eyck portrayed them five centuries ago. In the winter the view is indescribably beautiful, and when we skated on the lake of Minnewater close by, it was as though a painting by Breughel had come to life. Sometimes when the wind blew that way, the sound of the chimes could be heard drifting over the landscape. Not even the green meadows of England gave one a sense of such peace and tranquillity as did that lovely scene.

Belgians, French, and English made up the five hundred boys of the school. Consequently, I soon spoke fluent French (with a Belgian accent) and rather execrable Flemish. Between the Flemings and the English there existed always an hostility difficult to explain. It flared up badly on one occasion during the Russo-Japanese War, the Flemings and French siding with the Russians and the English with the Japs. Hard to believe, there was at that time an Anglo-Japanese naval alliance. One day we fought it out in the playground, and, armed with slings made of thick paper wads weighted with lead and tied to long pieces of string, we tried to crack each other's skulls, to the tune of numerous casualties. The whole school was 'confined to quarters' for three days as a result of the mêlée. The Xaverian brothers were, on the whole, a kindly and efficient body of men, and, compared with the far stricter Jesuit college in nearby rue St. Louis, life at St. Francis' was a pleasant affair. Musically I made very little headway during the first two years at Bruges, for if scholastic standards there were none too high, musical ones were almost non-existent; so Father decided that for my third year at Bruges I should enrol as a student at the local 'Muziek-Conservatorium.' By then I was considered old enough to make the trips from the school to the Conservatorium without supervision. Twice a week I went there for violin, piano, and harmony lessons, likewise large doses of *solfège*. The head of the Conservatorium, Carol Mestdagh, was florid and mediaeval, and might have stepped out of *The Mastersingers*. My violin professor was Léon Queekers of Brussels, a tall, emaciated man with a thick mop of hair which, seen under a black felt hat three sizes too small for him, caused him to be regarded by the students as an object of derision. But his violin technique was stupendous: he could play the twenty-four caprices of Paganini without missing a note. He had little opinion of my gifts, and at times let go a torrent of Flemish profanity which even I could hardly fail to understand. So when I left the Conservatorium in 1904 after a year's study, I was awarded honours—but no medal—at the final examination. I remember stumbling through the Twenty-third Concerto of Viotto badly enough; so badly indeed that a plaster bust of Schumann tottered to the floor during the finale and was destroyed. This the students looked upon as a very bad omen.

The newly-acquired freedom which permitted me to journey twice weekly to the Conservatorium made me much envied by the other boys at St. Francis, for we were never allowed into town except in groups in the inevitable crocodile formation. The temptation to prolong my excursions to the Conservatorium proved irresistible, so I gradually devised crafty excuses for staying away from school, each time longer than the last. Eventually I contrived to add almost a full hour to my leave of absence—a pleasant hour spent exploring the odd corners of the city and losing myself in its maze of streets. There were also the pastry-cook shops, into whose tills much of my scanty pocket-money disappeared. Sometimes there was a *kermesse* in the Grand Place, with its merry-go-rounds, swings, and shooting-galleries, where I squandered a whole month's pocket-money at one time. Once I forgetfully left my violin in the tent of the bearded lady, and had to pay another five centimes to retrieve it. The most embarrassing incident of these jaunts happened once when, having decided to see the city from a rowboat on the canals, I was rowed clean under a group of Xaverian brothers who happened to be crossing the bridge at the Quai Vert. I spotted them before they saw me, and was able to collapse into the bottom of the boat, (much to the astonishment of the boatman), without being identified and apprehended.

On one of these expeditions I decided to climb the belfry —something which I had longed for two years to accomplish. Leaving my violin with the custodian at the foot of the tower, I paid a franc and started the long climb of four hundred steps to the summit. Dusk was falling, the narrow stone circular stairway was eerily dark, and after long minutes of groping upwards, I wished heartily that I'd never begun the adventure. I had almost reached the top when suddenly the carillon started playing. In the dark, the sound was awe-inspiring; I hadn't reckoned on the power of the bells at close quarters. A few stairs higher, and from behind the great revolving barrel which operates the chimes suddenly appeared the little bearded cobbler who acted as watchman of the tower. He looked sinister, rather like Mime the dwarf in *Siegfried*. He was holding a pair of pliers, and his leather apron and wild appearance made him resemble a torturer of the Middle Ages. He mumbled at me in Flemish, but, to my surprise, turned out to be a kindly man. The throbbing of the clock pendulum was by far the most dramatic thing about the place; this was truly Longfellow's 'heart of iron'. (Or did it recall one of Edgar Allen Poe's most frightening tales?) A few more steps to the bell-chamber itself, and through open Gothic arches the fading daylight illumined the vast plain of Flanders unfolding itself in the haze all the way to the sea-coast. Beneath me, the city, with its crinkly red roofs and smoke rising slowly in the evening air, seemed an evocation of past centuries, and the belfry on which I stood a part of it.

Reassured at emerging again into the open after the gloom of the tower stairway, I counted the forty-eight bells of the carillon, the largest the size of Big Ben and the smallest the size of a muffin-bell. For over two hundred years wind and rain have mellowed them and given them an unearthly, melancholy beauty. Their music falls on the ears as the most majestic buffeting of sound imaginable when you stand among them. But when you listen to them from down below in the Grande Place during a recital by the town *carilloneur* you can never forget their haunting beauty. The old master, Jef Denyn, used to perform prodigious feats of virtuosity on the wooden keyboard in the belfry; so do his successors, who to-day carry on his traditions. The difference between the actual sound of the mechanical chimes with their stilted old-world charm and that of the performer's human touch on the keyboard must be heard to be believed. The cascades of music falling from the towers of Bruges, Antwerp, Mechlin, and Ghent are as much a part of the Belgian scene and the Belgian people as the Sunday-morning pealing of bells over the shires of England is a vital part of English rural life. And when the bells of Flanders were silenced by an inhuman fate,[1] their silence was a mute protest against the sufferings of the people they watched over. Then in later days they rang out joyously, and their music proclaimed again the triumph of free men and the doom of tyrants.

[1] Since these lines were written, the full sum of German iniquity has been revealed. Many priceless bells of different Flemish carillons were removed from the towers during the war and melted down for their metal.

I said farewell to Bruges on a rainy day in June,[1] and as the train pulled out and I caught a final glimpse of grey towers, red roofs, and canals, I vowed to return often to the old city. I have done so many times. Was it grim coincidence, too, that, driving to the station that day, a procession passed by with three generations of kings in its midst; Leopold, Albert, and *his* son, Leopold, who recently abdicated. They rode together in one landau through a flag-bedecked and garlanded city—a tragic trio. The chimes were playing 'La Brabançonne'. . . .

[1] 1904.

CHAPTER IX

BACK to Merseyside and home, to discover that we no longer occupied the house in Liscard. Father, deciding that his growing family had to live closer to the centre of things, had forsaken the Cheshire side of the Mersey for the dingier but more convenient Abercromby Square section of Liverpool, close to the Mount Pleasant home of former years. Our new abode in Chatham Street was only a short walk from the Philharmonic Hall, then the handsomest and most acoustically perfect concert hall in England. There the Hallé Orchestra under Richter gave its concerts, making frequent trips from nearby Manchester to do so. I lost no time in getting parental permission to attend them, and always found a seat by the organ, on the topmost tier of the orchestra and immediately behind the percussion section, which I appropriated for all the concerts. Up there, it was easy to follow the conductor's indications and get a close-up of the players in action, invaluable experience for a boy my age. Once the cymbal player in my vicinity miscounted his bars in the finale of the *New World Symphony*, and the 'Doctor' transfixed him with a stare which endured to the end of the movement, and which, I heard later, resulted in the player's dismissal from the ranks. It is related that the next time the orchestra rehearsed this movement the 'Old Man' stopped the musicians two bars before the unforgettable spot and, in a reminiscent mutter, inquired ominously, 'Iss he still alive?'

A martinet Richter most certainly was, but the men loved him, and the Hallé Orchestra under him was without doubt one of the finest in Europe. There is a tendency among my older colleagues to disparage his conducting powers in the light of flashier and more recent stick technique. The Doctor, for all his years, was a musician of pretty catholic tastes; nowadays we are overprone to think of him

53

only as a Wagnerian conductor. Opinions may differ regarding his merits as an interpreter. I was too young at the time to form an estimate. But I *do* remember his stirring versions of the then new Strauss tone-poems and much other fairly provocative music. It is quite possible that his rigid beat missed some of the subtler nuances in these works realized by the more fluid indications of modern conductors. But it certainly suited *The Mastersingers* and works of that category well enough. And the tempi behind the beat were good, too!

Richter's stick technique was simplicity itself. He used a short, thick piece of cane with a padded grip, and indulged in few superfluous gestures. The elaborate arabesques of contemporary conducting were totally unknown—and superfluous—to him. The beat was a square one, vehement, simple, and best suited to classic and romantic styles. Especially in long sustained rhythmic patterns did he preserve a marvellous continuity of style. At least, I thought so. His manner was the antithesis of the Nikisch school, and little the worse for that, except that French impressionism utterly escaped him.

There was plenty of other music at the hall on Myrtle Street. First of all the concerts of the august Liverpool Philharmonic Society itself, announced on yellow posters bearing the legend, 'A few choice seats still available for ladies and gentlemen'. (The endless line of private carriages on Tuesday nights had to be seen to be believed.) The concerts of the old Liverpool Orchestral Society, the Welsh Choral Union, the Post Office Choral Society (Moscow has the only other of this variety known to me), and numerous 'celebrity' recitals kept a steady stream of Liverpudlians gravitating almost nightly to the doors of the beautiful hall during the winter season. There is a new hall now standing in its place, but nothing can properly replace the classic landmark which burnt to the ground in the 'thirties and took with it all the fine aura of years of distinguished music-making.

Henry Wood also came often to the Philharmonic with

his own Queen's Hall Orchestra; he appealed to me as a more sympathetic personality than the Doctor, and I admired the scintillating brilliance of his conducting, a brilliance reflected in the virtuoso quality of his orchestra. H.J.W. was a striking figure in those days, handsome, dynamic, and indefatigably energetic.

The autumn of 1904 was, for my father, a period of anxious problems and responsible decisions. The question of our education was soon solved. Within five minutes' walk of home were two apparently suitable schools: the Christian Brothers Institute (for Adolphe, Leon and myself) and the Convent of Notre Dame (for Marie and Sidonie). And there we all went. The discipline and atmosphere of the Institute were very different from those of the old school in Belgium. Study seemed mainly related to mathematics—my weak point—and I found no joy in difficult homework connected with something in which I hadn't the slightest interest. The lay teachers were unnecessarily vindictive when you didn't display acute intelligence in a subject, and as a result I developed a hatred for scholastic work and an acute self-pity. Every master in the school was a Squeers, and I a wretched Smike. But there were musical compensations in those drab days, even though my future career in music seemed to concern the school authorities but little. Music absorbed all my thoughts and a lot of my time; nothing else in life seemed of the remotest importance by comparison. So, at prearranged times, I studied violin and piano with Alfred and Charles Ross at the Liverpool College of Music, and my homework, which I had no stomach for, anyway, suffered still more severely as a result.

Two years later, Adolphe started French horn lessons with Otto Paersch, solo horn player of the Hallé Orchestra, and at the same time Leon began studying with Charles Reynolds, first oboe player of the Orchestra, and the only great English oboe player of his generation. Thanks largely to his influence, my brother possesses the tone which makes his playing so distinctive and personal. Paersch, too, represented that fine style of horn-playing often discarded to-day in favour of the coarse, blasting quality which many conductors demand from their horn sections. (I wish some of the people who think they know good horn-playing might have heard Paersch play the slow movement of the Tschaikovsky Fifth.) Like his colleague Reynolds, whose beautiful sensitivity was in vivid contrast to that of most London oboe players of the time (specifically Malsch, who ruined the tone-quality of the London Symphony Orchestra for years), Otto Paersch was a transcendent artist. Jaenecke, late of the New York Philharmonic, resembled him closest in style.

The College of Music in Liverpool boasted a sturdy student orchestra, and I became a member of it as soon as I entered the school. Old Carl Courvoisier, leader of the Liverpool String Quartet, presided over it, and helped us grind out Haydn and Mozart symphonies twice weekly. Courvoisier, to my delight, took a fresh symphony every week, and seemed less interested in our wrong notes than in covering the most ground possible in the shortest time. Haydn symphonies are usually played preciously and a bit condescendingly, but at the Liverpool College we played them with vim and gusto. Most of all I enjoyed Courvoisier at his quartet concerts. These were rather solemn affairs, given in a sombre hall and consisting usually of rather sombre music. There were invariably a late Beethoven quartet and one of the greyish Brahms ones in all the programmes, or so it seemed to me. The more introspective the music, the more I liked it. The concerts were usually held in the late afternoon: and as nobody bothered to light up the auditorium when dusk fell, the hall invariably took on a shadowy gloom which created for me an ideal atmosphere of romantic mystery. As a result, chamber music still induces in me the Gothic mood which fits well the hearing of great classics.

There was also in Liverpool at that time an amateur orchestra known as the Societa Armonica, conducted by Vasco Ackroyd, concert-master of the Liverpool Philharmonic. I applied for membership in it, fearing to be too young, but much to my surprise was accepted. The first

MY FATHER IN 1888

concert at which I played took place in the small St. George's Hall, where in the second violin section and a hired evening dress I helped render the *Hansel and Gretel* Overture and Wilhelm Berger's B-flat Symphony. These Liverpool amateurs took themselves very seriously indeed. The plush Victorianism of St. George's Hall made an appropriate background to the staid and very earnest group of socialites, shipping magnates, and professional men and women who made up the orchestra. I particularly recall the dowager with whom I shared the fifth desk, for she used a lorgnette at rehearsals to discriminate between sharps and flats. A member of the orchestra for many years was W. Dudley Johnstone, business-man and well-known amateur photographer. He played bass-clarinet and appeared to have developed a form of ophthalmic goitre through infusing the right amount of subdued passion into the chief motive of the *Liebestod*. When I left the orchestra for study in London my two brothers became members of it. After three years in the Societa, and much exertion on my part, I reached the post of principal second violin. The experience I gained from those early contacts with orchestral literature proved very useful, just as was that derived from membership in another group formed about then by John Blamphin at New Brighton. All three Goossens brothers belonged to it. We played light music in the Kursaal on the Pier, and enjoyed it enormously. My brother Leon surprised us all one day by playing the 'Ranz des Vaches' from *William Tell* on an English horn which he had acquired only two weeks before. Another time the three of us played a movement from a Reinecke trio. This imparted a decided 'tone' to the Pier concerts. Blamphin eventually became the New York passenger agent of the Cunard-White Star, and was always at the dock to wave farewell when in later years I left the shores of America for my annual summer vacation in England. It's a small world. . . .

CHAPTER X

THE three Goossens boys were soon inducted by Grandfather into the church choir at St. Anne's Benedictine Church, Edgehill. He showed no favouritism, and as a result we hated rehearsals, which represented an extension of home discipline to church hours. Adolphe and Leon had good soprano voices; my own quavering alto added little to the general effect. I was more useful on Sunday mornings at the children's Masses when given the task of accompanying hymns on the Gray and Davison organ with its three manuals, old-fashioned stops, and tracker-action pedals. Twice, as organist, I incurred the wrath of the Prior: once when my improvisation in the modern idiom extended through the Elevation, an unpardonable error, and once again when, having used the full organ for some five minutes on end, thereby consuming great quantities of wind at a prolonged stretch, the unfortunate organ-blowers gave up just as I needed a climactic sound for the end of a hymn. My performance on the organ was at best a sketchy affair, and the pedals were mostly untrodden ground, though I eventually evolved a makeshift left-foot technique which answered its purpose well enough.

About this time the Goossens Male Voice Choir made its last appearance before Grandfather's death. In October 1906 he went for his annual pilgrimage to Lourdes. A devout Catholic, he hoped always for a cure of his rheumatism, but this last visit to Lourdes proved fatal to him. He caught a severe chill on the return journey and on arriving in Liverpool had a sudden seizure, from which he never rallied. I stood with my father at his deathbed, shocked by the passing of the man I had always feared yet loved deeply. His early death (he was only sixty-one when he passed away) deprived England of both a colourful musician and distinguished pioneer in the field of opera in English.

Life in Liverpool was becoming increasingly irksome to me, and the unsympathetic attitude of my school towards music made what I was accomplishing there seem of little significance. Week after week I had stolen valuable study hours from homework time in order to attend orchestral concerts at the Philharmonic Hall. But one day, when things seemed intolerable, news came that the 'Liverpool' Scholarship at the Royal College of Music in London was open for competition. Here was a way of escape, if only I could pass the final examination in London successfully. Father having returned from one of his long tours with the Carl Rosa Company, I asked him to let me compete for the scholarship. He agreed, and I proceeded to end an inglorious scholastic career by taking the Oxford Local Examination, passing in all subjects except the one in which the school authorities hoped I might be conspicuously successful. That subject, was, needless to say, music! The examiner responsible for devising those questions was probably an expert contrapuntalist, but a boy of thirteen could hardly have been expected to cope with what was practically an examination for the degree of Doctor of Music.

One May morning in 1907, after bidding farewell to the school authorities with little regret, I set off for London with Father, determined to bring back the coveted scholarship. The day following our arrival, we journeyed by horse-bus to the Royal College for the examination. The beauty of Kensington Gardens, the bustle of traffic and exhilarating atmosphere of my new surroundings made it difficult to concentrate on the ordeal which lay ahead, and in my excitement I almost left my music on top of the bus. Fortunately, Father, who was carrying the violin-case and keeping a watchful eye on things in general, averted this near-tragedy, and we arrived on time at the College. Details of the actual ordeal are still fairly vivid after the lapse of years, and I remember the awesome row of examiners seated at a long table in the concert-hall when I walked on the stage to play. Among them were Sir Hubert Parry, Director of the College, Sir Charles Stanford, Sir Frederick ('Westminster') Bridge, Sir Walter Parratt, E. Fernandez Arbos, Achille Rivarde, and W. E. Whitehouse. This stern array might have thoroughly intimidated me had it not been for an encouraging twinkle in the Director's eye, which seemed to say, 'Go ahead; we're not as terrible as we look.' So I began with the Mendelssohn *Concerto*, of which the first half of the first movement seemed to be about all the listeners could stand. Then followed an unaccompanied prelude and fugue from a Bach sonata, in a sense an unfortunate choice, for the pianist in the Mendelssohn had at least given me some support. The Inquisitors allowed me to finish the fugue, and with a cheery 'Thank you' from Sir Hubert Parry I stumbled off the platform feeling rather like a criminal dismissed from the dock. After an interminable wait during which other competitors performed for the jury, the Registrar of the College, old Frank Pownall, came to the room in which we were all waiting to hear the results, screwed his monocle into his right eye, walked over to me and exclaimed in his bluff way, 'Congratulations, young man. You did splendidly.' It was some little time before it dawned on me that I had won the scholarship. I said goodbye to the Director, and, after filling up certain papers, Father and I returned to Euston Station, where I ate two pork pies to celebrate the event.

No sooner back in Liverpool than the significance of the ordeal I had undergone began to dawn on me. Not only did it mean the opening up of entirely new vistas, but, above all, the end of a provincial existence which, for a youngster, had begun to prove harassing and depressing. The thought of bidding farewell to the drudgery of school exhilarated me; even the prospect of severing family contacts for a long period of time failed to make me even a little despondent, though there were to be many lonely hours when the absence of brothers, sisters and parents would be all too real. But this London adventure was the prelude to independence, new hopes and ambitions, so I forgot my hatred of violin-practice, theory, and harmony, and really started to work in anticipation of the future. Then there was the excitement of buying new clothes and a big new suitcase, and even exchanging my violin for a slightly better one at George Byrom's violin shop (much to Father's perturbation), all of which couldn't make the time pass quickly enough. And there were the old familiar haunts to revisit— the Tower, the landing stage, the docks, familiar country walks on the outskirts of the city—always accompanied (inseparable as we were) by Adolphe and Leon. I remember one street in particular with shop windows filled with the mechanical things we loved: steam engines, model ships, electric motors, and all the things we coveted but could never afford. Suddenly everything in it seemed trivial in the light of the future, and so left me unmoved. . . .

We went for the summer to Llandudno in North Wales— as usual, by paddle-steamer, and, again as usual, with masses of egg and chicken sandwiches for the picnic lunch on board. A happy month there, and I bade goodbye to Chatham Street, the Philharmonic Hall, and the ships on the Mersey, and departed for a new home via the London and North-Western Railway's afternoon express from Lime Street Station.

CHAPTER XI

IT was a leisurely, prosperous, Edwardian London I came upon in September of 1907; a London of exaggerated fashions, hansom cabs, horse-buses, German bands, monster social activities, and (compared with the London of 1939) an exterior completely placid, complacent, and rather unctuous. When I arrived they were pulling down St. James's Concert Hall to make way for the Piccadilly Hotel; the violinist Joachim—as though he were unable to endure the destruction of the historic building with which he had been so long identified—died that year with it.

The Royal College being in ultra-smart Kensington—the heart of Victorian London, with its Victoria and Albert Memorial, Albert Hall, and Imperial Institute—the matter of finding reasonably priced lodgings in the neighbourhood threatened to prove at first rather a problem. But in the stucco-genteel vicinity of West Cromwell Road lived an elderly Irish spinster, who, with her eccentric sister and antique mother, conducted just the kind of establishment my father sought for me. At Miss Lynch's *pension* in Cromwell Crescent I therefore settled, comfortably and reasonably. With its atmosphere of somewhat straitened circumstance, it might have come right out of any stage play; but the food was good and the boarders congenial, so I didn't complain. From my bedroom there was a grand view of Earl's Court Exhibition and the West London Extension Railway, a mysterious line which started I knew not where, and ended equally obscurely. The roar of the roller-coasters in the Exhibition grounds and the puffing of the trains of the W.L.E.R. provided a night-and-day *obligato* to life at No. 11 Cromwell Crescent which perpetually delighted me. Fanny Lynch, in her way quite a *grande dame* among landladies, taught me chess, manners, and good reading, and tolerated no nonsense in the matter of late hours. Later, as we got to understand each other better, a slight initial mutual suspicion gave way to confidence and affection.

Professors at the R.C.M. were soon decided upon by the Director, so I found myself allotted to Rivarde for violin, John St. Oswald Dykes for piano, Dr. Ernest Read for theory, Dr. Charles Wood for harmony, and Sir Frederick Bridge for counterpoint—a distinguished, and, at that time, somewhat terrifying group. Rivarde, who, with Arbos, shared the chief violin professorships at the College, was a cross between an elegant Frenchman and a swarthy Latin-American, and I immediately regarded him with awe. In appearance he resembled a truculent Sarasate; certainly, in violin style and elegance, he was his double. His personality intimidated me so much at the outset that it was some time before I was able to hold my bow steady in his presence. He started by ruthlessly tearing my playing to pieces, making me unlearn everything I knew and re-learn exclusively his own system of style and technique. He spent seven or eight months trying to give me a bow-arm of the kind which was, and still is, the hall-mark of all Rivarde pupils, but at the outset we conceived a violent antipathy for each other. He judged me lazy and with no real talent for the violin (in both of which he was right), and I looked upon him as a surly, venomous, completely unsympathetic martinet. But in later years we became fast friends, and if he ever nourished any disappointment over my violinistic *carrière manquée* he never showed it. He died in 1940, an exponent to the end of the 'grand manner' of violin-playing. Never a virtuoso of great public repute (indeed generally little known save among his pupils, colleagues, and, in the old days, the Lamoureux Orchestra of which he was concert-master), Rivarde nevertheless left on his pupils the stamp of an impeccable style. There has probably never been a violinist who could impart to a student such fastidious elegance of playing as he did. Intolerant of any other school of violin-playing but his own, it was his fierce obsession for a flawless, stylized virtuosity which in the end resulted in his concentrating almost exclusively on technique rather than interpretation. In this regard he was the antithesis of his colleagues, Arbos and Sons, both formidable musicians for whose brusque nervous manner of playing he reserved a peculiar and icy contempt. Yet Arbos and he were real cronies. The sight of them engaged in heated gesticulation outside their adjoining class-rooms over some matter pertaining to fiddle-playing was a familiar one to us students. We liked them most when a prolonged discussion sufficiently disrupted the teaching schedule so that lessons were shortened, or even eliminated entirely. And when the colloquy took the form of an exchange of funny stories after lunch, we rejoiced. Both men were famous raconteurs: the stories of Arbos have become classics in the profession. . . .

With the piano, which was my 'second study', I was likewise none too brilliant. Dykes, anyway, was fairly affable and had sufficient insight to realize that, while it would ultimately be of great value to me, the instrument would never prove my strong point. He was a pupil of Madame Schumann, and a man of few words. My piano lessons invariably coincided with tea-time—professors at the R.C.M. are served with tea at 4.30 daily—and under the soothing influence of tea and muffins J. St. Oswald Dykes usually passed over my pianistic indiscretions with little more than an occasional grin and a puff of his walrus moustache.

In theory and harmony I soon forged ahead, thanks to an early grounding in *solfège* from my father and the Bruges Conservatorium. Considerably later, Dr. Charles Wood, my harmony professor, though he often winced at the 'modernities' of my five-part harmony exercises (and outwardly deplored them), secretly commended the 'daring innovations' which he insisted contaminated my work. But his pride in me knew no bounds when, for four consecutive terms, I figured at the head of the student body in harmony exams. Frederick Bridge, with whom I later studied counterpoint, wrote a text-book on the subject, but never quite seemed able to impart its contents to his pupils. His classes were comical, most of the time being taken up by sarcastic witticisms at the expense of his pupils; he had the reputation of being a wit, but I found his humour trying. He would fumble through our exercises at the piano, with the students perched on the table behind him, and kept so little count of our progress that I took the same counterpoint exercise to him on three consecutive occasions without his spotting the fraud. He was at that time organist of Westminster Abbey, a post which, as virtuoso, he filled none too brilliantly. Known as a 'left-footer' on the organ, his colleagues were wont to refer to the upper notes of the pedal organ at the Abbey as virgin soil. But he had few enemies, and his wit hurt no one. Later, in May of 1912, we sat together at a dinner of the Worshipful Company of Musicians when I received the silver medal of the Company, and he passed me the heavy, gold loving-cup to drink from at the end of the dinner with the remark, 'Here, young fellow, *this* stuff'll put you under the table!' And it practically did.

Of all the people I came in contact with during my years at College, the Director, Sir Hubert Parry, and his then secretary, Claude Aveling, were my favourites. The twinkling-eyed, debonair Sir Hubert, looking more country gentleman than erudite musician, had an encouraging word for everyone. No matter how much of a hurry he was in, he would stop and shake hands and ask how everything fared. His addresses at the beginning of term were masterpieces of fine English. Unfortunately, we never knew this until we read them in the College magazine, for he mumbled them, and the acoustics of the College Hall at that time were shocking. The only hall to equal it in this respect was the Memorial Hall at Eton. His music is—well, admittedly Victorian, but the sonorous phrases of *Blest Pair of Sirens* and the fine choral writing of *Job* are, in their own way, incomparable. As a musicologist, I think he was one of the most distinguished figures of his day. His studies of the great composers and their music are still little masterpieces of observation and erudition. Aveling, by contrast, was quiet, studious and self-effacing. He was a 'friend in need' to the students, and no problem existed with which he could not effectively cope. In the field of operatic translation, Aveling's work was extensive, and 'opera in English' is the richer for it. These two men did much to help steer me through a rather difficult first year at the R.C.M., for I don't hesitate to admit that, in contrast to the brilliant young virtuosi who surrounded me, my own natural facility as an instrumentalist had begun to show itself as somewhat limited. I started developing a serious inferiority complex, a handicap which the severity of Rivarde did little to dispel. Conducting and composition were my goals, and if there existed any short cut to them, I wasn't averse to exploring it. Much time was spent listening to the College orchestra at rehearsals when I should have been home practising the violin, and whenever there was an empty classroom with a piano in it I'd extemporize in solitude rather than return to Cromwell Crescent and Bach Inventions on a delapidated Collard and Collard.

CHAPTER XII

FATHER came to Covent Garden Opera House with the Carl Rosa Company a short time before Christmas, which considerably brightened those first weeks in London. As a special treat I took temporary leave of Cromwell Crescent, and shared theatrical lodgings with him somewhere in Brixton—one of many similar 'vacations' to follow. We stayed in one of those little yellow-brick houses situated in an endless row of other identical little yellow-brick houses. It formed part of a long, dreary street which echoed only to the calls of the milk-man, the coal-man, the cat's-meat man and the muffin-man, and a similar daily procession of vendors, whose characteristic yelps and squawks supply the final touch of melancholy to the drab South London suburbs. Our cheerful landlady was typical of the breed, and belied her rather mournful surroundings. The rooms and beds were comfortable, and the cooking unusually good. Those English landladies certainly can cook, and in later years when I went touring with travelling opera companies, Father's little black book of addresses containing the pick of 'rooms' throughout the country proved that one didn't have to stay at hotels to enjoy the best fare. There were, unfortunately, some exceptions to this, but you usually spotted them on arrival by the suspiciously dusty cruet on the sitting-room table and the fragment of rather tired-looking gorgonzola on the sideboard.

The repertory for the Company's two week stay in London was a familiar one, including the usual *Carmen*, *Faust*, *Cavalleria Rusticana* (its hundredth performance at Covent Garden), *Pagliacci*, *Marriage of Figaro*, *The Merry Wives of Windsor* (why isn't this charming work ever performed now?), *Trovatore*, *Lohengrin*, and *Tannhäuser*, and

67

a revival of Goring Thomas's *Esmeralda* (a better piece than the same composer's *Nadeshda*). All these were, of course, sung in English. I was a bit young to appreciate the subtleties of performance shown by the company, but when the London Press enthused about the opening night's *Tannhäuser*, I couldn't help but feel proud that Father came in for the lion's share of the praise. He was—and is—the most modest artist I have ever known. At the end of the operas he only appeared to take a curtain call after what seemed to be the use of considerable forcible persuasion on the part of the other principals to get him on stage.

Christmas brought with it a present from a friend which probably had as much to do with shaping my early creative tendencies as all the theoretical formulae acquired to date at the R.C.M. It consisted of a volume of Debussy piano pieces, the *Estampes*, which I had coveted ever since I spied the dark grey book in the window of my favourite Kensington music-shop. When I read through *Pagodes*—the first of the three pieces—the spell was cast, and from then on I steeped myself in all the music of Debussy I could find. This enthusiasm was no sudden hysteria; it was just a youthful reaction to something very new and very welcome. I wasn't much in sympathy with the heavy fare taught at the College, but I had come to think of it as an inevitable destiny. Something more exotic and highly seasoned seemed indicated, and my newly discovered Frenchman was the very thing: his music opened up new and alluring pathways. I took *Pagodes* to Dykes, whose moustache bristled at Debussy's impressionism. As an antidote, he prescribed Schumann. But the *Kinderscenen* sounded trite, so I returned with my newest discovery, Ravel's *Jeux d'eau*, antedating *Pagodes*. Those insidious harmonies were seemingly far more glamorous than any Brahms, Chopin, Dykes or anyone else could conjure up. And, considerably daring, I told him so. The result was that we arrived at a friendly compromise; I was to be allowed to bring to each lesson the latest importation from the Place de la Madeleine, providing I memorized by the end of the term a Beethoven sonata and

68

a lot of Schumann. The arrangement worked, and even Dykes grudgingly admitted his interest in the new technical problems presented by the whole tone scale.

Soon after my discovery of Debussy's piano music I read in the *Daily Telegraph* that my hero was coming, in person, to the Queen's Hall, to conduct two of his works with the Queen's Hall Orchestra. Henry Wood had gone especially to Paris to induce him to cross the Channel and appear before a London audience.[1] I borrowed some money from Miss Lynch and hurried to the Hall to secure the cheapest ticket available, only to be told all tickets were sold. So I rushed back to friend Aveling at the College, and by some magic he secured a gallery ticket which gave me a good view of the platform. The great day, 1 February 1908, arrived, and Debussy with it. He conducted *L'Après-midi* and *La Mer* (both of which Wood had rehearsed meticulously before his arrival) and though his manner of conducting was far from impressive (he held the stick as awkwardly as a flagpole), the performances were, as far as I remember, passably brilliant. The personality of the composer held me spellbound. I suppose the extreme pallor of his face, with its deep-sunken, burning eyes and that coal-black beard—a combination which gave him the air of a reincarnated Assyrian—struck me most at first. I noticed his disproportionately large head and, by comparison, his very small hands and short arms. When he started conducting *L'Après-midi*

---

[1] The following extract from Wood's *My Life of Music* throws an interesting light on Debussy's business sense: 'Speyer [The Queen's Hall Orchestra's good angel] and I had a good talk about the fee we were to offer . . . at last we decided on a hundred guineas . . . I tactfully approached Madame Debussy and revealed my mission. When she told her husband and mentioned the fee, he jumped up, furious. "What? A hundred guineas . . . for *me*? And yet you pay Caruso four hundred guineas?!" I corrected him immediately. "We never engage Caruso or any other singer at such a fee," I told him. Debussy calmed down and offered to think it over. I felt things were not too good, all the same; so I went out after lunch and wired to Speyer, suggesting two hundred guineas. Speyer wired back his agreement, repeating his assertion that we must have Debussy, whatever the cost. Fortunately, it did happen: Debussy agreed to come.' I quote this story to show that even in those early days the shy creator of *Pelléas* was anything but unrealistic in his business transactions.

69

I became fascinated and lost interest in following the full score lent me by the college librarian. The following year he came again to Queen's Hall and I again heard him conduct *L'Après-midi* and the nocturnes. In the second nocturne, *Fêtes*, the tricky changes of time-signature were too much for him, and at one point his beat became hopelessly involved. The orchestra refused to stop (much to the composer's astonishment), finished the piece impeccably, and an enthusiastic audience insisted on its repetition.[1] Shrugging his shoulders and with a helpless expression, he said to Wood after the first performance, 'Mais il ne *voulaint pas* arrêter!'

A few months after Debussy's first London appearance, I heard the début of a new London orchestra under its founder. (He, too, wore a beard, but very different to that of the Frenchman who preceded him.) Thomas Beecham was—in fact, still is—different in most respects from any of his colleagues. To say that he and his orchestra—a collection of the finest players in London—created a profound impression on the public is to put it mildly. Everything about Beecham was refreshingly unconventional. His deportment, appearance, programmes, and, in particular, his individual style marked him as a personality unlike any the London public had up to that time encountered. There was an electrifying something about his performances that evening, which, inexperienced though I was in the subtleties of interpretation, fascinated me. His stick technique, of an unusual kind, aroused much comment. So did his mannerisms, but certain exaggerations were discounted because of the superlative performance of the orchestra and the dynamic personality of the new star. The programme included the *Appalachia* variations of Delius and a Mozart symphony, and was in every way more characteristic of his taste than one he had offered four years previously with the

[1] At rehearsal he had insisted on the three muted trumpets *slurring* the triplet figure of the procession (just as the printed score has it) and in spite of the general practice nowadays of playing it *staccato*, the composer's phrasing seems to me indisputably correct.

Queen's Hall Orchestra. Few present that night anticipated the degree to which this dapper, self-possessed man was to mould the destinies of British music for the next thirty years. Little, too, did I foresee how much of my own future would be bound up with his enterprises, and how close would become our friendship through long association.

Progress at College was not up to expectations, and it wasn't until the end of the year that my professors' reports gave indications of any sort of improvement. I was discouraged. Violin lessons were a bi-weekly ordeal which only heightened my antipathy to Rivarde, and his to me.

A sample lesson would consist of an opening sally from the professor:

'Your bow arm is something abominable!'

'Yes, Mr. Rivarde.'

'Go on—*play!*'

A few quavering notes, whereupon Mr. R. bites his moustache, arranges his hair in front of a portrait of Joachim and sinks in a chair, the picture of desperation.

'Next piece.'

'Yes, Mr. Rivarde.'

I embark on a Vieuxtemps concerto, and after two staves: 'Stop! Have I not told you'—these words slowly and with horrid inflection—'that your *vibrato* is too slow?' (last lesson it was too fast.) 'Go on.'

'Yes, Mr. Rivarde.'

A few more staves, and Rivarde, inhaling to his boots an Abdullah No. 3, expels the smoke slowly and viciously in the direction of my chin-rest, as though to blot me and violin completely out of existence, once and for all. I choke violently, the lesson ends, and I leave the class. Rivarde says to the good-looking girl pupil who has been a witness of my ordeal: 'Is it not extraordinary? Each time I speak to Goossens, he trembles like a jelly. That is something *formidable* . . .!!' (His favourite expression.)

CHAPTER XIII

Just before the close of the year, someone (I think it was that last of the Victorians and close friend of great singers, Armine Bevan, whose Sunday afternoon *salons* were something 'out of the past') gave me a ticket for Kreisler's recital at Queen's Hall. I arrived at the hall to find my seat was in the front row of the stalls, almost directly behind Henry Wood. Kreisler played the Brahms concerto as he alone could play it. The inspiration I derived from this experience was such that, at the end of the concert, I left the hall convinced that if Kreisler, being a human being like myself, could work such miracles on the violin, I could anyway work a minor one for the benefit of my chagrined father. Next morning I practised four hours, followed by three hours more after lunch, and all the inhibitions and complexes I had acquired seemed to fall from me like magic. The following day Rivarde listened in astonishment to a completely transformed pupil. 'Yes,' he said gravely, 'I think you have decided to work, eh? That is *something formidable*!' And he grinned broadly, and I loved him for it. After that, violin classes were another story.

Among professional acquaintances at the College at that time was a member of the double-bass section of the London Symphony Orchestra—Claude Hobday, whose brother Alfred was leader of that orchestra's viola section. Meeting him one afternoon after a college orchestral rehearsal, at which he had reinforced the student group, I asked him why he was wearing evening dress. He replied that he had to go straight to Covent Garden to play in that evening's performance of *The Mastersingers*, and that it began at six. 'Can I go with you?' I asked. Puzzled, he replied that I could. On the way I confessed that I proposed to get into the theatre and somehow hear the opera that night. Knowing there would

72

THE AUTHOR, 1898

be no vacant seats, and not being able to afford one, anyway, I asked him to connive at getting me past the stage-door and into the dim recesses of the orchestra-pit, where, unseen, I might watch Richter. For a time Hobday refused to have any part in the matter, but by the time we got to Floral Street and the sacred precincts of the stage-door, he had weakened. 'Though Heaven knows what'll happen if you're discovered. . . .' Luck was with us and we slipped in unobserved. The next step was to get me into the orchestra. Fortunately, there is a dark alcove behind the bass players in the Covent Garden pit, and here, inconspicuously, I crouched on the floor, the phalanx of basses screening me completely from sight, so that when the 'Old Man' entered and took his place on the rostrum I was able to watch him, just as in the old Liverpool days. But this time my vantage-point had changed, and instead of contemplating him from a height I spent over five hours gazing *up* at him, and developed a stiff neck which lasted a week. The occasion was, in one sense, historic; the performance was being given in English, and Richter had always refused to conduct the Wagnerian operas in anything but the original German. For that evening's performance[1] he was persuaded, against his will, to succumb to the 'general request'. As usual, he conducted without a score, an easy matter for the man who, in his early horn-playing days, had copied the full score from Wagner's original manuscript. It was this link with a legendary figure and a legendary past, far more than what seemed, then, the miracle of Richter's conducting, which invested the occasion for me with considerable significance. He had known Wagner and had lived under his roof, and he stood that night as the incarnation of Wagnerian tradition. The logic of his tempi—the unhurried prelude (a lesson to some of our conductors to-day) the ease of the Pogner music (measured and dignified), the clarity of the second act finale (usually

---

[1] I remember Edna Thornton, Robert Radford, and Walter Hyde among the principal singers. They later sang the same opera under my direction in the Beecham Company.

a rout), the well-controlled flow of the quintet music (invariably scampered), and the balanced climaxes of the Finale (usually one huge shout)—left with me an indelible and impressive memory.

Early in 1909 the Lynch *ménage* moved from Earl's Court and installed itself on the cheerful heights of Campden Hill. The change pleased me enormously; I was getting a little tired of the respectability of Cromwell Road and the unvarying monotony of my daily walk to the R.C.M. via Gloucester Road and pompous Queen's Gate. But now, from the pleasant house in Berkeley Gardens, I followed more romantic paths. Down Church Street, Kensington, past the Carmelite Church, with the spire of St. Mary Abbot's in the distance, into Kensington Gardens past Kensington Palace, over the Broad Walk by the Round Pond, and on through the park to the Albert Memorial, and then, facing it, the Albert Hall and the flight of steps to the College; as lovely a ten minutes' walk as one might find anywhere in London, and as health-giving a one, too. I can think of no other suburb in which the dignity of London is so epitomized as in the Royal Borough of Kensington—a place of fine houses, stately trees, and historical treasures, with the air of a bygone day when well-to-do people lived amply and leisurely, when the arts and patrons of art flourished comfortably, and the business of living seemed spacious and unhurried. This atmosphere still survived in those tranquil pre-war days when I journeyed from my rooms to the College, every weekday—rain or shine—with a violin case, music, and umbrella. The Royal Borough, and with it the rest of the Empire, mourned that year the passing of its King, and London became for a time a sad, quietened city. I climbed a railing at Marble Arch to watch the funeral *cortège* on its way to Paddington Station. All the crowned heads of Europe rode behind the coffin, and I remember thinking rather blood-thirstily how a bomb hurled into that group of monarchs would have altered the whole course of history.

Progress at the R.C.M. becoming more marked at this

74

time, my father was relieved of a certain apprehension concerning my being able to 'make the grade' in my studies. Relations with Rivarde were almost cordial; he had admitted me to his 'ensemble' class, and in the autumn sanctioned my inclusion in the orchestra, where I started off among the second violins. I was proud of this, because membership in the orchestra automatically elevated one from the student *hoi polloi* to the ranks of the vastly more esteemed 'élite'. The year was one of crowded musical experiences. It began with the visit to London of Sibelius, whom I saw at Queen's Hall at a concert in which both *Saga* and *Finlandia* were on the programme. The first left the Londoners a little cold, but the ovation after the second was terrific. In this connection we are apt to forget the debt we owe to pioneers like Henry Wood and Granville Bantock, who in those distant years played the symphonies of Sibelius repeatedly to unenthusiastic audiences all over England. So, too, in a later day, Cecil Gray, (whose enthusiasm one might praise the more were it less one-sided), became his ardent hot-gospeller. In America, Serge Koussevitzky, Olin Downes, and others untiringly carried the Sibelian message to the American public, who, up to the time Finland joined forces with the Nazis, vociferously acclaimed any and every opus bearing the composer's name. Today, symphonies 1, 2 and 5 alone seem to evoke the old enthusiasm.

Sibelius did not impress me at first sight, as did, for instance, Debussy. I recall him as a military figure with chokingly high collar and a close-clipped, greying moustache—the antithesis, in fact, of the rather benign figure of his recent pictures. In later years, I saw a different side of the great man—the gastronomic Sibelius of five-course meals and good wine. It was in the 'twenties, when a few of us— Bax, Bliss, Ireland, and myself—met him at a luncheon party in his honour at Pagani's Restaurant given by Kling of Chester's. On arrival, the great man sat down and exclaimed, 'A very hot day, gentlemen!' Actually it was, and someone suggested an *apéritif*. '*Apéritif*? No! It is better schnapps!' The *maître d'hotel* produced the tall familiar brown stone bottle. Sibelius suggested we join him. Most of us unthinkingly did, whereupon the room seemed to get hotter for everyone except Sibelius. Prudently we all declined a repetition of this beverage, excepting a brother composer, who left early and failed to reappear. After the guest of honour had polished off numerous *hors d'œuvres* and more schnapps, followed by a juicy steak with burgundy, he asked to sample the *spécialité de la maison*, *pêche Melba* and Turkish coffee. This also necessitated a *fine cognac* as accompaniment, whereupon Sibelius with a happy sigh put down his napkin and exclaimed, 'Now we talk music, yes!' Few of us recall the conversation, which up to that point had been rather desultory. It consisted chiefly of a monologue by Sibelius in Nordic English about the Finnish countryside and people, with never a word about music. He declined to answer any questions about his own work and left exclaiming, 'Fine restaurant. I come back here!'

CHAPTER XIV

D URING the year's summer season of opera at Covent Garden I secured a gallery seat for three events. These were the first operatic performance in England of *Samson and Delilah*—it had already received frequent concert performances—and the English premières of Charpentier's *Louise* and Debussy's *Pelléas and Melisande*. Except for the magnificent singing of Kirkby Lunn as Delilah and the splendour of the temple scene (the collapse of the hall as Samson pushed the pillars apart was always one of the mechanical marvels of Covent Garden stage-management), my memory of the Saint-Saëns performance is vague. Not so with *Louise*; the acting and singing of Gilibert as the father were in themselves sufficient to make the occasion memorable. I saw the same artist in many later performances, and each time his interpretation had an affecting quality which in the end proved almost too harrowing to enjoy. *Louise* was, and still is, an extraordinarily vivid opera. Its properties of soup-tureens, fireworks, sewing machines, and strong melodrama put the average operatic recipe in a pretty tame category. Yet both from a musical and 'period' point of view it is the most dated of operas.

The transparent fragility of *Pelléas* left me hypnotized, so much so that even now I have only to hear those magical opening chords to recapture immediately the thrill of the first performance. Debussy came over to supervise the final rehearsals, and I haunted the theatre unsuccessfully for hours hoping to catch a glimpse of my idol. Campanini conducted the opera. It must have been a new experience for him, and probably necessitated an extreme disciplining of style to enable him to realize the subtler shades of the Debussy orchestra, since he was more at home with the 'blood and thunder' Italian operas than with French impressionism. I was disappointed by the extremely subdued lighting of the sets. As in most performances of this work, the producer seemed to forget that the stygian gloom of the grotto scene and the subterranean vault should be tempered somewhat to enable the audience to catch a glimpse of the singers. Unless this is done, their attention flags, and the beautiful work is set down as a 'bore'.

There was more opera in the autumn, when Father again came to Covent Garden with his company. He added *Tristan* to their regular repertory, and, as was usual with him whenever a new production came along, expended such an amount of energy and care for detail on the whole affair that I marvelled anew at his vigour and enthusiasm. Touring companies coming to London, on the heels of an international season of star artists and lavish productions, courted tremendous critical comparison. There was therefore need for augmented orchestra and chorus, so that none of the operas should bear a trace of the wear and tear of touring and constant repetitions. To Father's credit, it can be said that he was always meticulous about this.

Except for Carl Rosa seasons, I secured admission to performances at Covent Garden only by lining up with other galleryites about three hours before the opera began, and paying for my ticket. But when, in the spring of 1910, *Elektra* was produced there I got to the theatre at two o'clock on the afternoon of the performance, because of the crowd. *Elektra* was (and for some people, still is) pretty strong meat. Those who find it too discordant a dose of opera can imagine the feelings of the timid souls of thirty years ago. They raised howls of protest, babbling of decadent morals, outraged sensibilities, musical anarchy. . . . But others hailed it as a masterpiece, and I duly thrilled with them. One's blood congealed at the processional music, and turned to water when the double-basses helped Edyth Walker's mad digging into the canvas stage-cloth. I thought the Orestes music incredibly moving, and the final dance of Elektra more exciting than anything that had happened in Covent

78

Garden to date. Beecham whipped his hundred players into a lather of such excitement that we were often deafened and lost track of the vocal line quite frequently. I recall someone having provided me with sandwiches to munch during the performance, but such was the crush of people standing that I was unable to retrieve them from the tail pocket of my frock-coat for sheer inability to move my arms backwards or forwards.

Despite these operatic excursions, work at the R.C.M. now really absorbed me, and by the autumn of 1910 I had been promoted to the leadership of the second violins in the college orchestra. Shortly after this momentous event, the French composer Saint-Saëns happened to be visiting London, and at Parry's invitation came to the college one afternoon to conduct a rehearsal of his *Third Symphony*, which we were in the process of preparing. All went well until the finale, when the second violins bungled a lead. Saint-Saëns turned to our section, and, with the withering look of scorn he sometimes affected, addressed us in French:

'Play that by yourselves, second violins.'

We did, horribly. He looked at me.

'You. Show the others how it should go.'

I did, tremulously and ineffectively. Saint-Saëns glared at me for what seemed ages. Then he removed his pince-nez and apostrophized:

'*Gentil garçon, mais quel sacré violiniste!*' (Nice boy, but what an awful violinist!)

Then, to the orchestra (pointing at me), 'Vairy nervose . . .!' And we proceeded; but for the rest of the rehearsal I felt crushed and humiliated. When he finished and started to leave the rostrum, we stood up. At that moment, the great man caught my eye, and—winked!

A few weeks after this visit, we again enjoyed the presence of a distinguished visitor. He was Alexandre Glazounov, who arrived at rehearsal in a very morose state. Whether he found the college lunch insufficiently convivial or whether he was dyspeptic, we never knew. But his complete lack of interest in either his work (the *Fourth Symphony*) or us was embarrassingly evident, and it seemed at one moment that he would fall asleep from boredom. His aloofness had a quality of sullen indifference which made me wonder what would happen were he suddenly to become alive and the dull glow of his eyes smoulder into flame. Fortunately for us, it never did! He spoke no English, but as he didn't stop us once during the rehearsal, this handicap wasn't very noticeable. He waved a greeting after the last chord, mumbled something in Russian and made a lumbering exit.

Both Glazounov and Saint-Saëns were contemporaries whose musical make-up was practically identical. Both were prolific, academic, resourceful, and often inspired. But now they are both undeservedly neglected by conductors, and underestimated by the concert-going public. Their creative fertility stemmed from real genius, but I think that their chief claim to fame lies in their fine craftmanship. Both were cunning workmen. Saint-Saëns, economical of means and simple of expression; Glazounov wallowing in the luxuriance of an exotic but always well-controlled range of colour. Charles Villiers Stanford was their English counterpart, a fact which accounts for his constant references to both composers in his composition classes, and his obvious and intense delight in performing their music, for Stanford combined both the orderliness of Saint-Saëns and the romanticism of Glazounov. His music, little played nowadays, is a disciplined product of both qualities. He was also a great teacher, and it is hard to name any reputable English composer of the period between 1900 and 1924 who was not at one time or another a Stanford pupil. The photos of these men hang to-day in the sanctum on the second floor of the Royal College where C.V.S. used alternately to praise or castigate us twice weekly. Mine hangs there, too, for in this particular year (1910) I applied for membership in his class, and after a stiff test was duly accepted. He started me off on a theme and variations for piano, as he claimed that the supreme test of creative ingenuity lay in extracting the last ounce of variety from a good tune. With Beethoven, Mozart, and Brahms as models, I set out on what seemed a thankless task, but eventually succeeded in squeezing thirty-two variations from an utterly barren tune. Stanford liked them, and this gave me a feeling of great superiority. Some of the more 'modern' ones he erased on the ground of 'cacophony'—a subject which made him foam at the mouth. ('Damned ugly, me bhoy! Take it out!') From variations I graduated to sonatas, and string quartets, and by the time I left the College in 1912 I had turned out a creditable number of student efforts in many of the smaller forms, all of which bore the blue-pencilled excisions and comments of a strict and often intolerant mentor.

CHAPTER XV

STANFORD laid most of the blame for the wildness of
the young radicals on the pernicious influence of
Strauss and Debussy, though secretly he grudgingly
admired the more conservative efforts of both composers.
He was irritated when I told him of being present at the
Elektra performance earlier in the year, and that I considered
it thrilling and masterful. He said frankly that were I to
hear much more of that 'pornographic rubbish' he'd give me
up as a lost soul. So when I saw that the première of Strauss's
Salomé was announced for the end of the year at Covent
Garden, I was all the more determined to go.

The performance, given only after a long tussle with the
Lord Chamberlain, who objected to the head of John being
brought in on a platter (he gave his consent only when a loaf
of bread covered by a towel was substituted for it), realized
to the full the opera's colourful qualities, and its impact on
me was instantaneous. Aino Akté, by far the best—and
most personable—Salomé I've ever heard, gave an outstanding performance. She combined a lithe grace with
splendid singing, and looked the seventeen-year-old hell-cat
of the Bible in amazing fashion. The amount of epidermis
she displayed established a new record for Covent Garden
in this respect; beside it, the achievements of all previous
Delilahs and Thaïses seemed tame. Beecham once more
worked his customary spell over the fine orchestra, and, as
in the case of *Elektra*, again conducted without a score.
Even in these days of agile feats of memory by some of our
conductors, this sensational achievement established, in my
opinion, quite a record.

The year 1911 saw great pageantry in London. The
Coronation procession of George V, in June, I gazed upon
at Hyde Park Corner with some of my fellow students, in

joyful wonderment. Fortunately, we got there at 7 a.m., as did several thousands of other Londoners, all bent, it would seem, on occupying the same spot. The Coronation ceremony itself inspired much good music, though not included in this category was a march I dashed off in a fit of patriotic fervour. Stanford condemned it as barbaric. . . . Secretly, I cherished hopes of hawking my contribution to some publisher for a sum which might give me a measure of temporary affluence. Funds were low, for the allowance which I received monthly from my hard-working parent scarcely sufficed to give me the luxuries I craved for—particularly in matters of dress.

By the end of the year I took the bull by the horns and secured Parry's permission[1] to seek small engagements which would bring in extra pocket-money. At that time, there were no union rules forbidding a student accepting any kind of work he could get, so when the principal violinist of one of London's best-known hotel orchestras offered me a post in his 'ensemble', I accepted with alacrity, and bought a dinner coat. The work was interesting, though sometimes, when the leader was absent through illness, its responsibilities were heavy. The type of music we played ranged from operatic selections to 'cake-walks'. The repertory of one of these small orchestras (which usually consisted of two violins, 'cello, double-bass, and piano) was enormous, and we had to be ready to play anything from Liszt to Lehar at a moment's notice. We played in an alcove in the restaurant, and rejoiced when a convivial diner making his way past us, usually under 'full sail', would deposit a five-pound note on the piano with a request that we perform for his special benefit one of the latest musical comedy hits. I remember once a certain well-known member of the peerage coming over and depositing a fiver in my hand (mistaking me probably for a Hungarian) and mumbling in execrable French, '*Jouez-moi quelqu' chose de* très *moutarde*'! These perquisites were shared by the ensemble, and appreciably augmented our weekly salary in

[1] I had secured a year's extension of my scholarship at the R.C.M.

a gratifying manner. But all that was in the good old days. To-day, that same gentleman would probably think twice about spending a tenth of the sum for a couple of seats at a symphony concert—that is, if he liked symphonies. . . .

Owing to the tiring nature of hotel work and the late hours involved, I limited my operations during the year to three very-well-known establishments. At one of these caravanserai I had the experience of losing my post through the baneful influence of the *maître d'hôtel*. The leader of the orchestra, hearing that I was given to writing music, asked me to compose a short, tuneful (*sic*) number which might be played one evening during dinner, and possibly be added to the repertory. A few evenings later, I brought the parts along, but no score, so the leader couldn't possibly judge of its effect. On my assuring him that it was a completely innocuous effusion, and as it presented no difficulties of performance, and moreover as I had entitled it *Serenade d'Automne* or some such title, he consented to perform it without rehearsal. We embarked on it just at that magical time when the guests, having dined extremely well, are in a torpid condition induced by post-prandial digestive satisfaction. They were not long in becoming aware of the fact, however, that they were listening to a piece of very contemporary music. No sooner was the piece—mercifully short—over than the *maître d'hôtel* approached menacingly and announced his intention of summoning the Manager. He did, with the result that I was given a day's notice of dismissal on the grounds that I had played a practical joke on the establishment with my ugly music. So ended effectively my career as virtuoso at the Hotel—shall we call it Splendide!

Though grateful for the experience and new source of income derived from this work, I hated the atmosphere of hotels and their 'potted-palm' music. So I looked elsewhere and found a remunerative field in the orchestras of west-end theatres. Here conditions were better, as were the music and the hours. The little orchestras, too, were excellent; particularly that at the Haymarket Theatre, directed by the composer, Norman O'Neill. (How many remember his fine incidental music for Barrie's play, *Mary Rose?*) These engagements varied in length with the run of the play, so that up to the time I joined the Queen's Hall Orchestra, my next goal, I made the acquaintance of several theatres and their conductors. But the theatre I most wanted to visit professionally was the Royal Opera, Covent Garden. My wish came true that very year, but my début, unhappily, took place on the stage, in full view of the public. Beecham was producing *Don Giovanni* in English, and in the ballroom scene employed two orchestras which performed on wooden towers or balconies. These were wheeled on-stage by a crew of stage hands during the short black-out which preceded the scene. Dressed in a heavily brocaded costume, and carrying a violin, it was no mean feat, even for me, to climb to the top of my tower, which swayed precariously and seemed ridiculously insecure. One old member of the stage band—*entrepreneur* William Davin—was heard to exclaim that 'He'd be damned if he'd ever do this again for Beecham or any other — conductor!' The blackout occurred, but my tower stuck and refused to budge. Reinforcements appeared, and after frantic pushing and a totally unnecessary amount of blasphemy by the stage-hands, we rolled to our appointed places and the lights went up. But the swaying of the tower, and the vertigo induced by it (also by the bird's-eye view of the Covent Garden audience, looking highly amused) produced in me a nausea which I was only able to control until the end of the scene, when, having scrambled down from my eyrie, I knew for the first and only time in my life the misery of sea-sickness. I never again accepted a 'stage' engagement!

The year 1911 brought with it an event which constitutes a landmark in the musical panorama of those sumptuous days. Serge Diaghilev, with his Ballet Russe and a large retinue of secretaries, managers, Press agents, valets, and such-like, opened his first English season at Covent Garden during the Coronation celebrations, and provided Londoners with a taste of something unlike anything they had ever experienced before. Night after night I broke away from my prosaic jobs at different theatres to see the incomparable things Diaghilev had brought from Paris to offer his unknown London public. The half-crowns thus expended wrecked my slender budget, but in a good cause. *Scheherezade, Carnaval, Prince Igor, Lac des Cygnes, Sylphides, Spectre de la Rose, Cleopatra, Giselle, Pavillon d'Armide*, and, best of all—to me—the *Firebird*. Figures now legendary I saw on the stage—Nijinsky, Fokine, Bolm, Pavlova, Karsavina, and the master, Cechetti. Press and public swooned with joy at the novelty of these unimaginable performances. Their perfection can neither be described nor ever again equalled. The *Scheherezades, Carnavals*, or *Sylphides* of to-day convey only a small idea of what Paris and London were treated to in those years before 1914. When they played *Scheherezade* at Govent Garden, Diaghilev complained that the enormous stage wasn't adequate to accommodate the scores of dancers and supers who took part in the spectacle—a spectacle so daring that the blasé Parisians vowed they had never seen the like. So also with *Prince Igor*, when the legion of Polovtzian warriors threatened to leap into the audience, and their Georgian slave-girls filled the stage like exotic flowers. To-day's performances, by comparison, might grace the parish hall.

CHAPTER XVI

THE enthusiasm of Diaghilev for the newest forms of expression in painting and music had prompted him to start commissioning a number of new ballets in which choreographer, composer, and decorator worked together to produce an integrated unit, in contrast to a patchwork adaptation of already existing music with choreography fitted to it. (As, for instance, *Carnaval*, *Sylphides*, *et al*.) Diaghilev chose the young Stravinsky to carry out his first experiment, and gave him *carteblanche* to go ahead. The result was *Firebird*, which, so far as Western Europe was concerned, heralded the most challenging new influence since the magic of Debussy's *Faune*. There's no doubt at all but that nearly everyone who listened to it was spellbound by an idiom which immediately made Stravinsky the most discussed personality in music. When, later, *Petrouchka* succeeded it, the young Russian was hailed as a genius of the first order. His was not by any means a familiar modernity. It had nothing in common with Strauss, who, notwithstanding a bag of dazzling orchestral tricks, was still serving up a tolerably recognizable, though slightly decadent, romanticism. Nor had it any affinity with the sensuous pallor of the French Impressionists; neither did it anticipate the atonalism which was shortly to identify the music of Schönberg. Its roots were Russian, but its polytonal and rhythmic devices were arrestingly and uncompromisingly Stravinsky—which is to say that it was unlike anything else at that time. His craftsmanship and urgency of inspiration swept you along in a surge of dynamic realism. We youngsters imbibed draughts of this new creative tonic, and it went straight to our heads. But we couldn't ape it, and it remains a fact that even to-day Stravinsky's would-be imitators have, musically speaking, fallen by the wayside. Opinions to the contrary notwithstanding, the old master still towers head and shoulders above his contemporaries in significant and concise expression.

My visits to the opera became increasingly frequent. Covent Garden had the pick of European singers to choose from that year, and I heard some historic performances. *Aïda*, with Caruso, and *Tosca* with Giachetti, Zenatello, Zucchi and Sammarco, were two of the most outstanding. Sammarco was unquestionably the finest operatic baritone—except Scotti—I ever heard; his performance in the *Jewels of the Madonna*, a Wolf-Ferrari novelty (given the following year, 1912), was a feat of virtuosity unsurpassed by anyone excepting, perhaps, Lawrence Tibbett in my own opera, *Don Juan de Mañara*. Emmy Destinn, Bonci, and Battistini were other singers of that time whose singing made an indelible impression on me.

Hearing a great diversity of fine music, operatic and symphonic, stimulated my own meagre creative talents, and I determined to break away from class-room exercises in composition and try something a little more mature. In February 1912 I completed Opus 1, *Variations for Orchestra on a Chinese Theme*. At first Stanford expressed many misgivings, and blue-pencilled the opus freely. Many of his blue-pencillings I secretly erased, so convinced was I that the 'ugly' sounds I had written were vital to the colour of the work. Eventually the parts were copied by the college librarian, and at a rehearsal of the orchestra in June, Stanford asked me to 'take the stick' and read the work through. This was the first time I had actually faced a full-sized orchestra, but I had been secretly practising conducting, and, confident of myself, felt not a bit nervous. After what proved a fairly accurate preliminary reading, Stanford went upstairs to summon Arbos, Rivarde, Dr. Wood, and several other professors down to the concert hall to hear a repetition of the work. My own emotions at hearing for the first time the results of my first piece of orchestration were wholly and joyfully unique. The second reading proved still more successful, and the *Variations* were given their first semi-public performance at the final concert of the spring term some days later.[1]

In April 1912 father moved the rest of his family from Liverpool to London, and with their arrival I found myself once more happily reunited with my mother, brothers and sisters under the same roof. Adolphe and Leon were awarded scholarships at the Royal College of Music and promptly found themselves in the orchestra, thanks to their brilliant talents. My sister Marie started harp lessons with Miriam Timothy, as did later my younger sister, Sidonie. Now that we had all settled down together in London,[2] my residence with the Lynch family automatically ceased. In the quiet of the simple music-room at Edith Road, and with my beloved Bechstein grand (souvenir of Grandfather's era at Mount Pleasant), I began to feel a real urge for composition, and by the end of the year, I had turned out several experimental works, most of which I later destroyed. A *Miniature Fantasy for String Orchestra* and the *Old Chinese Folk-song* for violin and piano alone survived and are still played. The first fourteen of my published works[3] were written in the peace of our West Kensington home, and their untroubled character reflects its congenial and tranquil atmosphere. For almost seven years I worked steadily and without interruption there, thanks largely to the unselfish devotion of my family, who saw to it that no intruder came to disturb my youthful meditations.

[1] *The Times* critic was invited to this concert, and wrote as follows: 'In the middle of the students' orchestral concert, which Sir Charles Standford conducted at the Royal College of Music last night, came a set of *Variations on a Chinese Melody*, by Mr. E. Goossens, an "exhibitioner" of the College. This work had the rather unusual distinction amongst the compositions of being conducted by the composer, who evidently not only knows what to do with his orchestra when he is writing for it, but is well able to get it done when it is written. He took command with complete assurance, and yet without any ostentation, and his clear beat and simple indications to the players secured an admirable performance. The work, too, has the qualities of clearness and simplicity, and there is a quantity of certain melody, a vein of sentiment, which is not afraid of being obvious, and sufficient harmonic variety to suggest that plenty of it will come from him in the future.' This is dated 21 June 1912.

[2] 70 Edith Road, West Kensington.   [3] See Appendix C for full list.

In July came the realization of one of my chief ambitions
—membership of the Queen's Hall Orchestra. A timely
vacancy in the first violin section, together with Parry's
consent to my taking an orchestral engagement, secured an
audition. Wood was a bit ruffled when at the start of the
audition the D string on my violin snapped with a resounding bang, completely unnerving me for some time. 'Dear,
dear; a fine time to break a string,' he said. 'And I've *so*
much to do. Send in Mr. X, Brown.' I left to get a new
string; and returned just in time to hear through the door
the horrible sounds Mr. X was making in his attempts to
read at sight *The Ride of the Valkyrie*. He soon emerged,
pale and visibly shaken, and I took his place. First I played
part of a concerto, then: 'Read that' in a tone of voice
from Henry J. that boded ill for me if I failed. 'That' proved
to be something from *Parsifal*—hideously slow, so that my
bow shook. This was followed by a *scherzando* movement
with rapidly alternating changes of time, all to be played
spiccato, by some composer I can't think of. Then a manuscript piece which I flunked, causing Wood to murmur
'Dear, dear, dear!' And so on and so forth, until with the
perspiration pouring down and my knees shaking, and feeling like a victim stretched on the rack I heard:

'Are there any more outside, Brown?' 'No, Mr. Wood,
them's all,' and H.J. saying to me then: 'Go and tell Mr.
Newman you're engaged. First violin. Very good indeed.
But watch those MS. sheets. Dear, dear, dear: we constantly
play new works. All from MS. parts. Practise reading manuscript all the time. Dear me, watch those MSS!'

Thus began a four-year association with a fine conductor
and an outstanding orchestra. In the service of both I spent
invaluable years of apprenticeship, and got a first-hand
knowledge of practically the entire symphonic repertory.
Under no other conductor could a more thorough and
authentic grounding in the orchestral repertory have been
obtained, and certainly no conductor of that day combined
better musicianship with a finer stick-technique than did
Wood. Even though I played under other men with greater

ADOLPHE, LEON, MOTHER, SIDONIE, EUGENE, MARIE,
LISCARD, 1902

ADOLPHE, MARIE, EUGENE, LEON, SIDONIE,
EARLY VIOLIN STUDENTS, LIVERPOOL, 1904

'box office' names than H.J.W. (Nikisch, Mengelberg, Steinberg, Safonoff), I never encountered a sincerer artist or a more resourceful, experienced, and versatile conductor than the beloved head of the Queen's Hall Orchestra. The debt owed him by the last two generations of English composers alone is a fantastic one, and that of the British public to him is quite incalculable. It is largely due to his efforts that appreciation and understanding—such as it is—of that public for the meatier things in the contemporary symphonic repertory exist at all. In one sense, Wood had his reward in his own lifetime. One had to be present at his jubilee celebration in 1939 at the Albert Hall—as I was—to realize that. His death in August 1944 took place just after he had begun his fiftieth season of Promenade Concerts at the Albert Hall, and left England mourning the loss of its most picturesque orchestral figure.

My contacts in the orchestra were of the happiest, though the members of it were all considerably my seniors. Peppery Maurice Sons,[1] of the Royal College, Eric Coates, the composer, and Warwick Evans of the London String Quartet were the bright particular ornaments of the violin, viola and 'cello sections, while Fransella, de Busscher, and Alfred Brain were the virtuosi of the flute, oboe, and horn departments. The two latter, together with Alfred Kastner, harpist of the orchestra, eventually migrated to the Los Angeles Philharmonic, where in later years, conducting the Hollywood Bowl Concerts, I held happy reunion with them. A Rumanian named Weinberger with whom I sat at the fifth stand of the first violins supported a large family on an average of £3 per week, which comprised our weekly wage for the season (plus the proceeds from a little teaching and theatre work). Later, being promoted to the fourth desk, where I sat with Scipione Guidi, (who afterwards became 'concert-master' of the New York Philharmonic) I think our salary was increased by 10s. But those were the days when one really *played* for one's supper.

---

[1] That fine violinist, the late Arthur Catterall, took Sons' place as leader during the Promenade seasons.

CHAPTER XVII

MY first experience with the orchestra was at the Earl's Court Exhibition, where we had been engaged to give a series of concerts entitled 'Shakespeare's England'.[1] These functions took place in a depressing, barnlike structure, and, as far as I can recall, only once did we play to an even medium-sized audience—and that on the opening night. Wood, with typical industry, had hunted high and low for music based on the Shakespeare plays, with the result that much second-rate stuff was forthcoming, not only from second-rate composers, but great ones as well. He discovered most of it at the British Museum, but the concerts proved once again the immortal truth of the fact that people don't go to exhibitions to listen to symphonic music.

The season of summer Promenade Concerts at Queen's Hall which followed the Earl's Court experiment gave me my first sample of real orchestral high-jinks. Ten weeks of nightly three-hour symphony concerts, with three rehearsals a week (and Sunday afternoon concerts thrown in for good measure), is a back-breaking—but worthwhile—experience. Needless to add, we covered the whole gamut of the symphonic repertory during those sixty or more concerts, which invariably began punctually at eight and ended at eleven. And every night, seated behind a potted palm among the first violins, I'd watch that sea of upturned eager faces avidly drinking in everything we had to offer—through a thick haze of tobacco smoke. Only once that season did those patient 'standees' kick at the fare: the night we played Schönberg's *Five Orchestral Pieces* for the first time in England.[2] The work proved too much for them, and if ever

[1] In connection with the current exhibition of the same name.

[2] Concerning which the *Daily News* said the following morning: 'We must be content with the composer's own assertion that he has depicted his own experience, for which he has our heartfelt sympathy.'

Wood was suspected of playing a practical joke on his faithful adherents, that surely was the occasion. They hissed violently, and it required a whole fistful of familiar pieces to restore their usual equanimity.

Towards the end of this season, Robert Newman, manager of the orchestra, agreed to release Wood for the final two weeks to enable him to conduct the Birmingham Festival (at which Sibelius directed his *Fourth Symphony*); and Sir George Henschel, the Boston Symphony's first conductor, took his place at the Promenades. This genial, dignified musician immediately won the hearts of the orchestra by his unaffected approach to conducting, and some years later I had the privelege of becoming his friend. His charming daughter Helen inherited her father's tremendous gift for singing *lieder*, self-accompanied at the piano. (No one has really heard '*Ich grolle nicht*' properly sung unless they heard George Henschel sing it!)

The Promenade audience is probably unsurpassed in its vigour and enthusiasm by any group of concert listeners anywhere in the world. The stamina required for a person to remain standing during the performance of three hours of music (and that, in the case of many enthusiasts, every night except Sundays for ten weeks), is in itself no small matter. Add a knowledge of the orchestral repertory which would put many musicians to shame, plus again the fact that most of the audience at the Promenades are engaged in strenuous professional daytime activities, and you have a picture of a music-lover who makes the average listless, condescending patron of our concert halls look what the Americans call a 'piker' by comparison. It may be that there are still two or three individuals alive who have never missed a single concert of the whole fifty and more consecutive seasons, but I shouldn't be surprised to hear that by now this remnant of the 'Grand Army of the Promenaders' has departed to join its beloved Commander-in-Chief.

Thanks to a long student apprenticeship in chamber music at the R.C.M.—where I seem to have played most great classic quartets during my years there—I was gaining something of a reputation as a reliable ensemble player. At the beginning of the year I was invited to join the Langley-Mukle Quartet as second violinist, and did so. Beatrice Langley and May Mukle, both admirable artists, were respectively its leader and cellist and, with James Lockyer, the viola player, enjoyed a vogue among a clientèle which particularly prided itself on its love and encouragement of quartet-playing. So we played mostly at private houses in London and the country, but only after I had invested in some well fitting suits. In those days hostesses—and butlers —were beginning to look askance at ill-kempt specimens of the profession, and bohemian-minded musicians found it wise to cultivate the social graces. (Haydn and Mozart did the same, but with less effort and more inducement. . . .) Lockyer and I once arrived for an engagement at a house in Portman Square, and the raw footman who admitted us, having spotted our instrument cases and noting that our appearance put us in a different category from the *haut-monde*, blandly said, 'Good afternoon. There's tea for the band downstairs. . . .' This brings to mind the *nouveau riche* hostess who, having learnt from the leader of a newly-formed string quartet that its affairs were prospering exceedingly, remarked blithely, 'Excellent, Mr. H. Soon you'll be able to *add* to your numbers . . .!' But such incidents—or social gaucheries of any kind, for that matter— were conspicuously absent in our experience. We played often at the London parties of Lady Mond, most sympathetic and elegant of hostesses; Victor Beigel, most fashionable of singing teachers; Jim Baird, most sybaritic of London dilettanti; and numerous others. Somehow, too, there were usually to be found there the composers Cyril Scott, Roger Quilter and Percy Grainger; the painters Sargent, Glyn Philpot, and Harold Speed; the literati Yeats, Galsworthy and Bennett. It was as though this galaxy of creative talent rotated constantly in the orbit of our wanderings and became an integral part of the local scene. Cyril Scott in particular was in great demand at these functions. Wearing a high black cravate which made him

94

look like a good-looking reincarnation of Chopin, this exotic personality and lovable but aloof man played his delicate piano works as no one else since has been able to play them. There were joyous evenings, too, at Percy Grainger's flat in King's Road, Chelsea, where, over a tobacconist's shop, we made music far into the night. On almost every one of these occasions at least one novelty from his pen was forthcoming, and many of the jovial pieces which are associated with his name must have received their first quartet and piano performances at our hands in the long music-room. Percy's mania at the time was exotic percussion instruments, for he had just discovered the American firm of Deagan, whose staff-bells, marimbas, xylophones, etc., inspired a number of his works, and were always to be found in great profusion in his apartment. An athletic type, he could often be seen carrying some of these instruments on his back whenever they were needed at his concerts. Later, when he married, his wife, a dignified, handsome woman, often volunteered to relieve him of this chore. One day, meeting him at the train in Cincinnati, I asked, 'Where's Ella?' Glancing down the platform, he replied, 'She's coming right along with the staff-bells.' Sure enough, she was.

An affectionate and loyal friend, Percy Grainger; a sensitive composer with the greatest relish for sheer beauty in musical sound.

There were also those amazing week-ends at Sir Samuel Boulton's rambling country house at Totteridge. These were fantastic affairs, for his elderly daughter rarely invited fewer than twenty or thirty house guests on these occasions, and the amount of food consumed at the interminable breakfasts, lunches, and dinners would have fed an army. Grace Lovat-Fraser, Rosing, and Bertram Binyon usually supplied the vocal relief (after the Lucullan evening dinners) alternating with contributions by our own quartet. Sometimes the Sunday night supper was an elaborate fancy-dress affair, usually necessitating visits to the costumier Clarkson for some sort of outlandish costume. (Once I appeared at dinner as the Masque of the Red Death, creating a macabre sensation.) These functions were always the occasion for Miss Boulton to contribute some choice terpsichorean example, usually a veil dance à la Maud Allan. It was all inconceivably and remotely Babylonian—and at times slightly vapid.

Our travels as a quartet took us far afield, sometimes to Scotland, other times to Devonshire, and always to other people's big, warm, comfortable country houses. True, we earned our bread and board, and a fee: but in incredibly pleasant fashion. Where are the county folk to-day—in any country—who would invite a professional quartet to live in their midst for days on end, just for the pleasure of listening to music and enjoying their company? But such was England before the 1914 war, and doubtless will be again when happier days come to the world.

One day, Lockyer, our viola player, resigned, and the Langley-Mukle quartet automatically disbanded in the autumn of 1912. But it wasn't long after this event that my ex-student friends Beckwith, the violinist, Jeremy the violist, and Sharpe, the cellist, asked me to join forces with them in founding a new virtuoso quartet in friendly rivalry to the London String Quartet (Sammons, Petrie, Waldo Warner, and Warwick Evans), which held undisputed sway in the concert world as England's leading string quartet. We made a good début and soon found ourselves with quite a number of worthwhile engagements, and prestige. Membership of this group stimulated me to write two familiar works—the C major quartet and the Two Sketches, *By the Tarn* and *Jack o' Lantern*, which I think have been played by practically every internationally known quartet group. The last two pieces were written only a week before the concert at which they were performed, and *By the Tarn* was entirely rewritten the night before the concert itself—I being dissatisfied with it. The public liked the pieces, and, together with the *Phantasy Quartet*, they are actually sometimes heard to-day—that is, wherever the pathetically few quartets still functioning find a demand for their services.

The three movements of the C major quartet (No. 1) were written around the personalities and characteristics of my three colleagues, and are inscribed with the initials A.B., R.J., and C.S. Unfortunately, for those who never knew these delightful artists, any subtleties of characterization in the music must remain more or less buried.

Cedric Sharpe's father—a professor at the R.C.M.—was a friend of Arnold Bennett, and it was at the Sharpes' house in Putney that in 1911 I first met my future librettist. Bennett's favourite composer was Borodine, and in the days of our student quartet rehearsals at Putney he would often drop in to soothe his jangled nerves with a dose of either the Russian's A major or D major quartets. In a peremptory high-pitched stammer, he would demand, 'B-Borodine, p-p-p-please.' And he always got it. One day he was late getting to the house for a special rehearsal to which we had invited him. His wife told us afterwards that a passer-by had stopped him in the street with the request, 'Would you kindly tell me the quickest way to Putney Bridge?' Characteristically he had replied, 'There are e-e-e-e-eight million people in London; why the devil can't you ask somebody else?'

CHAPTER XVIII

ALL my chamber-music experience up to this time paled beside an event which transformed the middle part of 1912 and the two subsequent years into a sequence of musical thrills. One day a message from Aveling at the College sent me—with a viola—to No. 19 Edith Grove about ten o'clock at night. I had been told that some Americans named Draper were having a chamber-music session, and lacked a viola player. I was ushered into the dining-room on arrival, and was amazed to find Casals Thibaud, Bauer, Kochanski, and Muriel and Paul Draper just finishing dinner. Muriel was wearing a white turban with aigrette, a short brocaded jacket and a 'harem' skirt— considered then an extremely daring innovation.

Introductions were effected, and after some conversational preliminaries (rather halting on my part) we all went down some narrow stairs into the largest and most sumptuous studio I had ever seen. Built in the back garden of the house, its conspicuous features were a large Tudor fireplace surmounted by Gothic tapestry, an enormous Kien Lung screen behind an equally enormous sofa, a Bechstein piano, huge floor cushions, heavy candelabras, a dozen music stands, and stacks of chamber music. A nearby table held champagne and a large box of Corona Coronas, which the Spanish poet, Pedro Morales, self-constituted majordomo of the Draper studio parties, handed round to the guests.

Soon Casals suggested a little music, and called for a Brahms two-viola quintet. I was immediately requisitioned, and the five players, Thibaud, Kochanski, Rebecca Clarke, Casals, and myself launched into a *con amore* performance I shall not easily forget. My previous experience in chamber music at the R.C.M. proved its worth, and we didn't stop once to correct an error of *ensemble*. More music followed, and as the night progressed, more virtuosi came in to join our music-making—Arbos, Cortot, Persinger, Felix

Salmond, and the beneficent Rubio, a patriarchal, bearded Spanish cellist who by now has undoubtedly been canonized. Benign Henry James and portly Montague Chester of Vert's concert agency wandered in later. Between quartets Henry James held forth on the virtues and beauties of great classic music, and most of us listened intently to his quiet eloquence of speech. He ruminated rather than orated, which makes it difficult to recall his words over a stretch of years.

A pause for supper at 1 a.m., then more music; and the party started to break up only when the London dawn filtered through the skylight. Arthur Rubinstein announced he would close the proceedings, and gave a terrific performance of an unfamiliar Szymanowski fugue. Thibaud, who had been examining Kochanski's Stradivarius, tried a few passages on it and promptly at 4.10 a.m. commenced to play the Bach chaconne. I can't recall a nobler performance, nor a more atmospheric one. Surrounded by rapt listeners, and seen through the eerie, smoky haze of candles, dawn and fire-light, the superb artist became transfigured, and we were all incredibly moved. And when the taxis—which had ticked up enormous amounts while waiting for us to emerge—trundled off with their valuable cargoes, the night's events took on an air of complete unreality. On how many similar occasions did we not repeat these feasts! Always there were new faces, and unexpected happenings, as when one night Suggia and Casals took their 'cellos behind screens and made us guess which of the two was playing. Most of us failed in this. Or the time Arbos and Rubio regaled us for two hours with side-splitting stories (the Arbos classics, of course), capped by intricate Spanish dance tunes for violin and 'cello alone. Or when the beautiful Daisy Kennedy played the Franck sonata with Moisewitsch, and we discovered afterwards they were engaged to be married. And the inimitable Ruth Draper generously giving us monologue after monologue, and the descent of the infant Paul Draper, Junr., to the studio so that Beethoven quartets might build him into the fine artist of future days. And since mine is largely a family chronicle, it must be set down that the

Goossens boys were once together at those nights of music-making: Adolphe playing horn in the Schubert octet and Leon oboe in the Mozart quartet, to mention only two works from the repertory. One night in the summer of 1913 I conducted, perched on a soap-box, an improvised performance of the *Siegfried Idyll*; another night played in the Mendelssohn octet with Thibaud, Kochanski, Arbos, and Tivadar Nachez as the four violinists, Harold Bauer and myself as violists (Bauer played the viola excellently), and Casals and the beatific Rubio as 'cellists. Theirs was one performance, at least, where the divergent temperaments of the players were fully reflected in the execution! Equally true was it of a performance of the Brahms A major Quartet with Ysaye playing violin, Sobrino piano, May Mukle 'cello, and myself viola, at loggerheads throughout the entire work. The pianist didn't help matters by reinvigorating himself between movements with large glasses of champagne, having previously almost come to blows with Ysaye over a nearly catastrophic event. Sobrino, opening the lid of the Bechstein, failed to notice that Ysaye's Guarnerius violin reposed on top of it, with the result that the instrument slid off and disappeared on to what the horror-stricken spectators imagined to be the parquet floor of the studio. But there was no resultant crash: the fiddle had fallen gently into the soft cushions of the divan alongside the piano. For a while the air was filled with Walloon profanity of an unimaginable kind, and it seemed at one moment as though the big Belgian was going to strike the little Spaniard in stupefaction at a near calamity. Another night, considerably later, we were playing the Schumann piano quintet with Cortot when, during the slow movement, there appeared at the door the appropriately ominous and statuesque figure of Chaliapine with, in his wake, the pathetic, wan little Nijinsky. I was so fascinated by the sight of these extraordinarily well-timed apparitions that I lost my place in the second violin part, and fumbled for quite a time, much to Cortot's annoyance. Whenever I hear the viola theme of that movement, the Mephistophelean countenance of Chaliapine—standing in the dim shadows of the studio—is automatically evoked.

But these are incidents chosen at random, for the temptation is great to linger over tales of the elect who found their haven in the Draper studio; great artists who, escaping from their theatres and concert halls—not to mention their tenacious publics—met together only to experience again (under infinitely more ideal conditions and in infinitely more exquisite surroundings) the artistic emotions, sensations, and re-creations of their individual art. Muriel Draper herself, in *Music at Midnight*, has conjured up something of the atmosphere of her beautiful music-room, and the musicians who peopled it. Yet no words can ever adequately recreate the past glories of No. 19 Edith Grove. Its studio will stand as a relic of the days when great performers made music together just for the love of it.

The Spring of 1913 brought with it the English première of *Rosenkavalier* at Covent Garden, and Diaghilev returned to London about May with a whole collection of new ballets in his wake. These included *Petrouchka* and *La Sacre du Printemps*, which had just created a *scandale* in Paris. Londoners were equally bewildered, but genteelly so, and outside of considerable eyebrow-lifting and politely audible expressions of astonishment, the event passed off without anything approaching the tumult of the Paris première. *Petrouchka*, however, was the most original music I had heard and played to date: I acted as deputy violinist in some of the performances. Undoubtedly its freshness and originality is as great now as it ever was. Other Diaghilev offerings of that memorable season were *Tamar* of Balakirev, with the beautiful Karsavina; Nijinsky's version of *L'Après Midi d'un Faune* (a significant addition to stage erotica), the Debussy ballet, *Jeux* —a real stage tennis game, but a failure choreographically and musically—Tcherepnin's *Narcisse*, Reynaldo Hahn's *Le Dieu Bleu*, and Florent Schmitt's *Tragedy of Salomé* (my principal memory of which is Karsavina, marvellously made up, descending very slowly a fantastically steep flight of stairs). Chaliapine also made his English début this season in three Russian operas new to London: *Boris Goudonov*,

Ivan the Terrible, and *Khovantchina*. He became the idol of London in a single night when, after the mad scene of *Boris*, the audience vented its tribute in a mighty and hysterical ovation which shattered any previous records in intensity.

At the Queen's Hall Symphony Concerts,[1] Scriabine played the piano part in his *Prometheus*—looking the incarnation of Madame Blavatsky's theosophical theories, and wearing a Napoleon II beard and moustachios. Incredibly fragile he seemed, to have devised the enormous canvases of the *Divine Poem*, the *Poem of Ecstasy* and the hot-house *Prometheus*. But he was a sick man, and during one of the rehearsals he asked me—my chair was near him, and I spoke French—to go to the Hotel Dieudonné in Jermyn Street to bring back some pink pills which he had inadvertently left on the mantelpiece of his sitting-room. I retrieved them, and he seemed much comforted to have them. It was not until much later that we learnt he was slowly dying of cancer. Later that month I heard him play one or two of his fiendishly difficult last piano sonatas (Nos. 7 and 9, I think) and marvelled both at his nervous energy and miraculous technique. He took on at those moments an aspect of cold Satanic fury which seemed most appropriate for those particular works. He was a great man, and had he lived might have produced a lasting orchestral masterpiece. Nowadays his orchestral works assume a complexion of artificial hysteria which veils thinly their thematic poverty.

My orchestral career at Queen's Hall was beginning to show profits. Henry Wood, having heard that I had written those *Chinese Variations* for orchestra (dating from my Stanford days), asked me whether I would care to conduct them at that season's Promenade Concerts, and I eagerly accepted. The work was duly programmed for a Saturday night, and the Promenaders applauded quite startlingly when, after conducting the *Variations*, which went well, I returned to my place among the first violins to finish the concert. Bennett came to the concert, and said afterwards, 'Don't get a swelled head just because you've conducted the Q-Q-Queen's Hall Orchestra!'

[1] Carreno and d'Albert made their last appearances that season.

MY MOTHER, ANNIE COOK, IN 1914

CHAPTER XIX

By the close of the year the Goossens family had settled down in suburban West Kensington, and during practice hours the house provided a pretty fair imitation of a music-school. Father being on tour most of the year with the Carl Rosa Company, my mother reigned supreme over her musical ménage. Adolphe and Leon were already the star horn and oboe players of the Royal College, with Marie and Sidonie closely competing as harpists, while I divided my days between the Queen's Hall Orchestra, the Philharmonic String Quartet, and my Bechstein piano. Some early compositions[1] had already been publicly performed with some success, and I anxiously sought a likely publisher. London was an exciting place to live in during those musically hectic pre-war months; when 1914 appeared on the calendar it seemed as though all the concentrated activity of musical Europe was centred around Covent Garden and Queen's Hall.

The most conspicuous musical event of that fateful year was a Grand Season of Russian opera and Russian ballet at Drury Lane Theatre, lasting from 20 May to 25 July, or up to within rather more than a week before the British declaration of war against Germany. This season was remarkable, not only for its artistic opulence, but also because not once during the nine weeks of opera and ballet was there any deviation from the original prospectus, a tribute to the organizing genius of Beecham's general manager, Donald Baylis. Considering the numerous artists involved—principals, chorus, and orchestra—the tremendous quantity of scenery and costumes, the shortage of orchestral rehearsals and the unfamiliar nature of the works produced, this was no mean accomplishment. One glance at the programmes—made possible by the enterprise

[1] Suite for flute, violin, and harp and *Five Impressions of a Holiday* for flute, cello, and piano.

20 May. Wednesday. Opera. *Rosenkavalier.*

21 May. Thursday. Opera. *Der Zauberflöte.*

23 May. Saturday. Opera. *Rosenkavalier.*

25 May. Monday. Opera. *Der Zauberflöte.*

26 May. Tuesday. Opera. *Rosenkavalier.*

27 May. Wednesday. Opera. *Der Zauberflöte.*

28 May. Thursday. Opera. *Rosenkavalier.*

30 May. Saturday. Opera. *Boris Godounov.* Chaliapine Night.

1 June. Monday. Opera. *Boris Godounov.* Chaliapine Night.

2 June. Tuesday. Opera. *Rosenkavalier.*

3 June. Wednesday. Opera. *Ivan le Terrible.*[1] Chaliapine Night.

4 June. Thursday. Opera. *Rosenkavalier.*

5 June. Friday. Opera. *Ivan le Terrible.* Chaliapine Night.

8 June. Monday. Opera. *Prince Igor.*[1] Chaliapine Night.

9 June. Tuesday. First Performance of the Ballet. *Daphnis and Chloë.*[1] Thamar. Scheherazade.

10 June. Wednesday. Opera. *Boris Godounov.* Chaliapine Night.

11 June. Thursday. Ballet. *Antar.*[1] *Daphnis et Chloë.*[1] Petrouchka.

12 June. Friday. Opera. *Prince Igor.* Chaliapine Night.

15 June. Monday. Opera-Ballet and Ballet. *Coq d'Or.*[1] Scheherazade.

16 June. Tuesday. Ballet. *L'Oiseau de Feu. Antar.* Carnaval.

17 June. Wednesday. Opera. *Prince Igor.* Chaliapine Night.

18 June. Tuesday. Opera-Ballet and Ballet. *Le Rossignol.*[1] *Midas.*[1] Scheherazade.

19 June. Friday. Opera. *Boris Godounov.* Chaliapine Night.

22 June. Monday. Opera. *Prince Igor.* Chaliapine Night.

23 June. Tuesday. Ballet. *La Legende de Joseph.*[1] *Thamar. Antar.* Strauss Night.

24 June. Wednesday. Opera-Ballet and Ballet. *Coq d'Or. Daphnis et Chloë.*

25 June. Thursday. Ballet. *Midas. La Legende de Joseph. Cléopâtre.* Strauss Night.

26 June. Friday. Opera-Ballet and Ballet. *Nuit de Mai.*[1] *Petrouchka.*

27 June. Saturday. Opera. *Prince Igor.* Chaliapine Night.

29 June. Monday. Opera-Ballet and Ballet. *Le Rossignol. Midas. La Legende de Joseph.* Strauss Night.

30 June. Tuesday. Ballet. *Daphnis et Chloë. Cléopâtre. Le Spectre de la Rose.*

1 July. Wednesday. Opera. *La Khovantchina.* Chaliapine Night.

2 July. Thursday. Opera-Ballet and Ballet. *Coq d'Or. Les Sylphides.*

3 July. Friday. Ballet. *Nuit de Mai. Oiseau de Feu.*

4 July. Saturday. Opera. *Dylan.*[1]

6 July. Monday. Opera. *Ivan le Terrible.* Chaliapine Night.

7 July. Tuesday. Ballet. *Midas. Le Lac des Cygnes. Petrouchka.*

8 July. Wednesday. Opera-Ballet and Ballet. *Nuit de Mai. Cléopâtre.*

9 July. Thursday. Opera. *Dylan.*

10 July. Friday. Opera. *La Khovantchina.* Chaliapine Night.

11 July. Saturday. Ballet. *Thamar. La Legende de Joseph. Antar.*

13 July. Opera-Ballet and Ballet. *Nuit de Mai. Narcisse.*

14 July. Tuesday. Opera-Ballet and Ballet. *Le Rossignol. La Legende de Joseph. Les Sylphides.*

15 July. Wednesday. Opera. *Boris Godounov.* Chaliapine Night.

16 July. Thursday. Ballet. *Carnaval. Le Lac des Cygnes. Le Spectre de la Rose.*

17 July. Friday. Opera. *Dylan.*

18 July. Saturday. Opera-Ballet and Ballet. *Coq d'Or. Scheherazade.*

20 July. Monday. Opera. *La Khovantchina. Petrouchka.* Chaliapine Night.

21 July. Tuesday. Ballet. *Midas. La Legende de Joseph. Antar.*

22 July. Wednesday. Opera-Ballet and Ballet. *Coq d'Or. Narcisse.*

23 July. Thursday. Opera-Ballet and Ballet. *Le Rossignol. Daphnis et Chloë. Scheherzade.*

24 July. Friday. Opera. *Boris Godounov.* Chaliapine Night.

25 July. Saturday Ballet. *Petrouchka. La Legende de Joseph. Antar.*

[1] First Performance in England.

of Thomas Beecham, the capital of his wealthy father, and a superb assemblage of great artists—will attest to their sensational character. The list contained four English premiers of Russian operas, and three new ballets specially commissioned by Diaghilev. The operas were Borodine's *Prince Igor*, Rimsky-Korsakov's *Nuit de Mai*, *Ivan the Terrible*, and *Coq d'Or* (the latter mimed by dancers, with the singers placed in the orchestra and the chorus grouped on both sides of the stage, all very much against the composer's directions, but effective, none the less), also Moussorgsky's *Boris* and *Khovantchina*, and Stravinsky's *Nightingale*, this latter a hybrid work more effective in its later ballet form than as an opera. The first of the specially commissioned ballets was Strauss's *Legend of Joseph*, a vacuous piece. Young Massine, straight from the ballet school of the Imperial Theatre at Moscow, made a sensational début as Joseph, and the ladies of the audience followed the endearments of Potiphar's wife with the utmost sympathy. Ravel's *Daphnis and Chloe* was the second of the ballets, a great work, the finale of which has since become the test-piece of virtuoso orchestras. Diaghileff quickly antagonized Ravel by liquidating the off-stage chorus (an integral part of the ballet's tonal scheme) on the grounds that its members took up too much space and impeded the movements of the scene-shifters. This drastic piece of high-handedness created some rumpus, and permanently breached the friendly relations of the two men. Third of the commissioned ballets was the picturesque but comparatively tame *Midas*, by the Russian, Steinberg.

I enjoyed a 'worm's-eye view' of many of these operas and ballets from a place in the first violin section, and can testify concerning the prodigies of under-rehearsed performance we accomplished. Feats of sight-reading performed in a minimum of rehearsal time during that season have never been equalled anywhere, before or since. So, anyway, asserts Pierre Monteux, who conducted. We must remember that practically all the works listed were new and unfamiliar; no sooner was a new opera or ballet put into rehearsal than it was immediately followed by a still newer and usually more difficult one. Many of the works set forth in that 1914 prospectus have by now passed into the repertory of the great orchestras, and after long familiarity require little rehearsal to present them for performance. But in the distant days of 1914 much of this music was of an unusual idiom, and presented the players with ever-varying problems of style and technique. That picked group of British musicians, whose pre-eminence in sight-reading and virtuosity has, until recently, never been challenged by any other orchestra, set an all-time standard which, even among the high-precision orchestras of the American east coast, has never been exceeded.

At the termination of this Drury Lane season, I went to stay with some friends for a golfing holiday near Edinburgh. The golf-course commanded a splendid view of the Forth Bridge and the naval base at Rosyth, at that time crowded with the great battleships of the North Sea fleet. One morning I arrived on the course, to discover that practically the entire fleet had departed for a—to us—unknown destination, and under sudden emergency. The dramatic impact of this terrific exodus struck me so forcibly that concentrating on a mere game of golf seemed ridiculous. It was only later we knew that Winston Churchill, First Lord of the Admiralty, had acted promptly to forestall any German attempt to bottle up our ships in the Forth by sending the British fleet to battle stations in the North Sea. It also accounted for the absence from the course that morning of a caddy who limped, wore dark glasses, and spoke with anything but a Scottish accent. They say he later ended an otherwise promising career against a wall in the Tower of London.

The European political situation had been steadily fermenting since Sarejevo. Music was far from everyone's thoughts, and even the familiar opening concert of the Promenade season was postponed until further notice. 4 August, date of our declaration of war on Germany, came and went, and the directors of the Queen's Hall Orchestra finally decided to open a short season on 15 August. At this first concert we started with the national anthems of all the Allied Powers, an exhausting routine repeated at subsequent concerts. Strauss's *Don Juan* had originally been included in the programme, but at the last minute Wood wisely substituted Tchaikowsky's *Capriccio Italien*. Likewise a Franco-Russian programme took the place of the all-Wagner programme scheduled for the third concert, though certain newspapers, particularly the *Musical Times*, regretted this decision. Shortly afterwards we resumed the performance of Wagner's works, which were given in England steadily throughout the duration of the war.

During this season, my symphonic poem, *Perseus*, an extremely florid, Straussian work, was played under my direction. The audience received it in lukewarm fashion, and eventually I consigned it to the wastepaper basket, not before one of the critics had referred to my 'regrettable Teutonic tendencies'. (The same writer, in later years, accused me of being too partial to the French school.) This performance was marked by an over-zealous percussion player striking one of the tubular bells with such force that he sent it spinning into the trombone section, narrowly missing the cranium of our tuba player, Mr. Walter Reynolds. For the audience this incident created a happy diversion, and caused gales of laughter. For me, it occasioned embarrassment and considerable perturbation.

Some months after the outbreak of war, Adolphe, Leon, and I decided to enlist, and tried to join an officers' training corps. We were told that, not having attended a 'public school', we were ineligible for the rank of officer, but as my two brothers were immediately turned down because of their being under age, and I on grounds of poor health, this peculiar technicality didn't really count. The Goossens family therefore continued its musical activities uninterruptedly for some considerable time, a state of things marred only by my father's resignation from the Carl Rosa Opera Company early in 1915. Thus, after a period of some thirty years, the name of Goossens temporarily vanished from the English operatic scene, and a long tradition of close association with it bade fair to become a legend.

CHAPTER XX

B ACK at Queen's Hall, Henri de Busscher, a fine oboe
player, resigned in the spring of 1915 to take up a
position with the Los Angeles Philharmonic, leaving
the orchestra without a first oboist. Wood had already heard
of Leon Goossens (at that time just seventeen) as the most
gifted young oboe player of his time—the R.C.M. not being
backward in spreading the repute of its more brilliant
students—and sent for him to give an audition at Queen's
Hall. This affair, which I heard from behind a curtain, was
pretty grilling, but after exhaustive reading tests, during
which Leon showed no trace of nerves and also a bewildering
accuracy, Wood admitted to being thoroughly amazed, and
promptly engaged Leon on the spot. Sitting in the same
orchestra with Leon, I remember marvelling at his sang-
froid and musicianship when, confronted by a succession of
new works (many unrehearsed) he would give an immaculate account of all of them. Knowing the repertory, I always
anticipated with some trepidation his first encounter with
the oboistic high spots of the standard orchestral literature:
things like the slow movement from the Brahms violin
concerto (Kreisler used to say—and still does—'If there's
one thing more than another I enjoy playing in the whole
violin literature, it's the *andante* from the Brahms concerto
with Leon Goossens playing the oboe'), the cadenza at the
opening of the Beethoven *Fifth Symphony*, the *Second Branden-
burg Concerto*, and the *obligati* from the Bach arias, not to
mention the difficult passages of Strauss, Debussy, and
Sibelius. In those first three months of the season, Leon laid
the solid foundation of a great career, but no sooner had he
negotiated his first perilous season of Promenades, plus a
few symphony concerts, than he was seized by the prevailing
war fever, and enlisted in the Yeomanry. He remained in

the Army for three years, till the last month of the war, when he was returned home wounded after a miraculous escape from death.[1]

At the outbreak of war, all German professional musicians in Britain—and their number was legion—were sent back to the Fatherland, to the great delight of many British artists, who found themselves with increased work and considerably improved chances of livelihood. The public was soon to realize that in Albert Sammons, Felix Salmond, Lionel Tertis, William Murdoch, Myra Hess, and many other instrumentalists (and singers) England possessed the equal of the fine German artists who had up to that time almost completely monopolized the British musical scene. Activities of our Philharmonic String Quartet were also proportionately increased, thus ridding us of the inferiority complex under which all musicians of British origin had laboured up to the middle of 1914. Those were the days when we wore a khaki armlet over dress clothes at concerts as a mark of either induction in, or rejection by, the Army. No young male civilian dared appear in public in those days without that khaki armlet. . . .

In the autumn of 1915, the London String Quartet gave the première of my *Phantasy Quartet*. There was at this time a revival of the old English 'phantasy' form, in which an initial motto subject serves as the basis for the thematic material of a one-movement work. The idea was sponsored by a rich amateur, W. W. Cobbett, who offered cash prizes for the best phantasy, and who himself played the violin, indifferently but unremittingly! He edited the *Cobbett Cyclopedia of Chamber Music*[2]—a standard work of reference in which is to be found the following: 'Circulation of the Goossens string quartet in C major, Op. 14, written in dissonant vein, should in my opinion be confined to friends

[1] Ethel Smyth had presented me with a large silver cigarette case after I conducted her opera, *The Bosun's Mate*, in 1916. Home on leave in 1917, Leon borrowed it, and carried it in his tunic pocket. Together with his silver mirror, it deflected a machine-gun bullet which would otherwise have pierced his heart.

[2] Oxford University Press.

of the extremely talented artists to whom it is dedicated. It is little more than what in Germany is known as a *musik-alischer Spass*. But the *Phantasy Quartet* is on an altogether higher plane: a work in which one discerns the quality of genius.' (Cobbett either blew very hot or very cold!) 'It is not written for amateurs [*sic*], the ensemble being somewhat intricate, but it richly repays the expenditure of time in extra rehearsals needed by professional quartet players who desire to add it to their repertory.'[1] Some amateurs also added it to their repertory, usually with unfortunate results all round!

The quartet was very well received, and among the critics who praised it was a young man—Philip Heseltine—who, had he lived, might have exerted considerable influence on English music. He is best known as the biographer of Delius and composer of many exquisite songs and pieces for small orchestra, written under the *nom-de-plume* of Peter Warlock. I first met him in the company of Cecil Gray, when he had just been offered the post of music critic of the *Daily Mail*. His was an elusive, shy, intelligent personality, cynical beyond his years, and unaccountably bitter towards his fellow men. I saw something of him early that summer in the Cotswolds, where he had rented a bungalow on the slopes of Crickley Hill, overlooking the Vale of Evesham. Here, with Cecil Gray, most caustic of critics, Adrian Allinson, who painted Cotswold elms like no one else, and his East Indian mistress (whose dusky charm caused considerable comment among the neighbours), he spent the long relaxing days of an English summer. Sometimes Philip and I, on a decrepit motor-cycle, would explore together the neighbouring countryside for old parish churches and hostelries: the former to sketch, and the latter to sample the local Cotswold brew. Twice we

[1] Lovers of Delius may be interested in Edwin Evans' reference to this work, taken from the same volume: 'This is the first work which is really characteristic of the composer. Mr. Philip Heseltine records that "it was sent in MS. to Frederick Delius, who pronounced it the best thing he had seen from an English pen: and it is not improbable that the new resources revealed and suggested by it may have served to break down his apparent aversion to quartet writing, since his latest work (1916) has been cast in this form...."'

encountered staid county friends of mine on these trips, once nearly colliding with jovial Connie Rose—*dame du manoir* of Bourton-on-the-Water—in her hired Daimler, which screeched to a stop near a duck-pond. Later we sustained a puncture opposite Marie Corelli's home during a tea-party on the lawn, which we were promptly invited to join—and did. The charming, rather eccentric authoress of *The Sorrows of Satan*, whom I had previously met professed little love for contemporary music or musicians. Certainly, after harbouring two such unkempt specimens as Philip and myself, she could hardly have loved them more.

My early friendship with Philip might have done much to remove the lack of confidence he felt in his own powers as a composer had he carried out his intention of studying with me. But he procrastinated, and between his passion for Delius, his own misgivings about his ability to write worthwhile music, and his dabbling in literature—which was his real *forte*—he never got around to it. He had written to his friend Colin Taylor: 'In December I am going to begin a long and strenuous course of lessons with Goossens in the hope that I may be relieved of the fear which is hounding me that I have no musical bowels at all!' Successive Decembers came and went till the fatal day in 1930 when he was found dead (by his own hand) in a Chelsea apartment. A brilliant spirit was lost in his passing, and a handful of printed works bear witness to the talent which might have more considerably enhanced the lustre of English music had he survived.

Those early summer days in the Cotswolds, just referred to, were marked by further wanderings, this time with my former violin teacher Rivarde, whom the aforementioned Mrs. Rose had invited with me for a week's stay at her Cheltenham home.

I recall one day the charming and gifted virtuoso, Marie Hall, also a Cheltenham resident, played for us Vaughan Williams' beautiful violin piece, *The Lark Ascending*, dedicated to her, and still in manuscript. Rivarde pronounced her an outstanding artist; a more generous tribute than he was usually wont to pay those whose style differed as radically from his as did Miss Hall's!

Except for this episode, we forgot about music, and concentrated solely on holidays: the Promenade season was not far off.

Day followed day in this unspoilt countryside, which harbours all the loveliness that is England; magically-named towns and hamlets of Cotswold: Stow-on-the-Wold, Moreton-in-the-Marsh, Bourton-on-the-Water, Chipping Campden, Cirencester, and those exquisite twin pairs of Upper and Lower Swell and Upper and Lower Slaughter. We fished from the bridge at Burford, where you and your victim eye each other suspiciously through the transparent brown waters of the Evenlode. We stood in the nave of Fairford Church, where the setting sun bathes you in a hellish crimson as it streams through the stained-glass Last Judgement of the west window. And often we were at the Fish Inn, looking down on tourist-exploited Broadway, which trippers had considerably blighted. Best of all was the spot Housman tells of in the most magically evocative lines in all England:

> In summertime on Bredon
> The bells they sound so clear;
> Round both the shires they ring them
> In steeples far and near. . . .

Our native musicians were gradually coming into their own with the ousting of the foreigner from Britain. British composers, who, like their colleagues in other countries, had rightly nourished a grievance against conductors and audiences who found something to admire in the work of composers from every land but their own, began to share in this acclaim. Certain individuals, as, for instance, the brothers Isadore and Frederick de Lara, actually started 'promoting' the works of the lesser-known British composers, and in a series of 'War Emergency Concerts' presented a number of newly composed British works to enthusiastic audiences at the old Steinway Hall. My early works, trios, and quartets, all received a hearing at these concerts, though Isadore de Lara (who wrote *Nail* and

Messalina, lush spectacles for the old Paris Opéra audiences) must have quavered inwardly at sponsoring ultra-modern confections such as the Goossens works. But the series prospered, and the Queen's Hall Orchestra was engaged for a series of three concerts to present British orchestral works to an increasingly receptive public.

Wood conducted the first concert, which, among other novelties, featured the première of Elgar's *Carillon*, a musical background to a war poem by Cammaerts lashing German atrocities in Aerschot, Dinant, and other Belgian towns. (Buchenwald, Oswiecim, and Belsen await similar musical treatment to perpetuate their infamy.) The great French actress Réjane came over from Paris to recite the poem—Queen's Hall never witnessed such a demonstration as ensued after her delivery of the stirring lines. When she intoned '*Chantons, Belges, chantons!!*' the scornful fury of the poet's indictment fired the entire audience. The London public was in proper mood for the occasion—a Zeppelin had recently dropped bombs on London and had done no little damage. I saw the airship as it sailed along over Regent Street, after a Queen's Hall concert,—an impressive, sinister portent both of mankind's future plague, air war, and the eventual demolition of the beautiful Hall itself in the 1941 Blitz.

CHAPTER XXI

FOR the second of these orchestral War Emergency Concerts, about the middle of November, Mary Garden had been specially engaged, and only six weeks before the actual date de Lara asked me whether I had something ready, or nearly ready, for inclusion in the programme. I told him I was on the verge of completing a symphonic poem—which wasn't true. I also told him it would be ready in four weeks—which was equally untrue—but something urged me not to let the opportunity slip by. I immediately cast around for a subject, and lit upon a fragment from one of the poems of Ossian. It was an apocalyptic thing, full of thunder, earthquakes, and disaster, but I thought it appropriate to the times, and immediately set to work on the sketch. This was completed in eight days, and the orchestration three weeks later. The *Symphonic Prelude*, which lasted about a quarter of an hour, employed a very large orchestra, an organ, and the enormous mushroom-bells of Queen's Hall up in the organ-gallery, likewise a thunder-machine. I used such a big orchestra that de Lara, looking at the score, remarked, 'Are you *quite* sure you haven't forgotten something?' The din of the climax created a great effect, and while the musical content of the piece didn't bear too close scrutiny—though it wasn't too bad in spots—the public seemed enraptured. Some years later, when I conducted *Carmen* for Mary Garden in Rochester, N.Y., she recalled this concert with impressive accuracy. Said she: 'There are only two things I remember about that concert, Eugene. One was a damnably noisy piece of yours and the other was a simply awful hat I wore which cost me fifteen guineas!'

I was still a member of the Queen's Hall Orchestra at the time of that concert, and, as had often previously been the case, left my seat among the first violins to conduct my piece, and returned to it at the finish. On my way back I spotted Thomas Beecham in the audience, but thought little of it until the end of the concert, when a message came to the band-room that T.B. wished to see me at the stage-door. He offered his congratulations, and asked me to meet him the following morning at his home in Cavendish Square. 'Shall I bring my violin, Mr. Beecham?' 'Heaven forbid,' replied T.B. characteristically, which made me wonder what he wanted. During the interview next day, at which he appeared clad in an exquisite mauve silk dressing-gown and pink pyjamas, Beecham said he had promised to produce two new English works, *The Critic*, by Stanford, and *The Boatswain's Mate*, by Ethel Smyth, but that, feeling rather tired, he had decided on taking a holiday in Italy instead. Then he sprang the question which caused me to veer to the nearest piece of furniture for support. 'Would you care to take over these two works?' 'Certainly,' I replied quickly. He turned to the piano, took two scores from it and handed them to me. 'Very well; there's a piano rehearsal of *The Critic* at the Shaftesbury Theatre to-morrow morning. Just tell the producer and the singers you're taking my place, and go ahead!'

With only a few precious hours ahead of me left in which to master the details of a new opera, I was still fully confident of being able to tackle the job, so, ushered out by the suave Larner, Beecham's valet, I left, walking on air, sat up half the night, and by 3 a.m. had absorbed all I needed of the score's contents to enable me to take the first rehearsal.

By ten o'clock that morning, after a short sleep, I was at the theatre, being introduced to George King, the stage manager, and my future associates and singers: Mullings, Ranalow, Austin, Heming, Langley, Russell, Chapman, Heather, Wynn, Ayres, Caroline Hatchard, and Lena Maitland. I told them I had come to conduct the rehearsal, an announcement which they seemed to take quite calmly. A smooth rehearsal ensued, followed by a short pre-lunch visit to the bar across the road to celebrate this first of many more equally enjoyable gatherings. Later, Stanford himself attended orchestral rehearsals, but interfered remarkably little with them, though he seemed surprised at finding his twenty-two-year-old former pupil in control of affairs. About a week before the actual production Cairns James, the producer, informed me I'd have to conduct all performances in the disguise of Mr. Linley of Bath; readers of Sheridan's comedy will recall the character. I protested violently on the grounds that my 'dignity' might be impaired, but when Stanford rather tearfully beseeched me to make-up for the sake of the artistic effect, I acceded. It was a tiresome business, for it meant arriving at the theatre an hour before each performance to have a white perruque adjusted, and put on an elaborate eighteenth-century costume with lace ruffles. On the opening night, having submitted to this procedure, and after a short final rehearsal with the actors (for some spoken lines fell to me during the performance) I went ahead and conducted my first opera without mishap. Press and public enthusiastically praised the work and its performance, and dear old Stanford literally shook with excitement at the end of the evening when, hand in hand with his erstwhile pupil, he took many curtain calls. Sir Hubert Parry, Director of the Royal College, sat in a stage box, and seemed to relish Stanford's quotation from his *Blest Pair of Sirens*. It was all a bit like what the Americans call 'Old Home Week'!

That this witty and beautiful opera should have passed so completely out of the current repertory shows how unsafe it is to prophecy about matters operatic in England. Ethel Smyth's *The Boatswain's Mate*, which I conducted two weeks later, seems to have shared the same fate. The composer herself elected to conduct the première of her work—much to my annoyance, as I had taken all the preliminary orchestral rehearsals. At the last moment she took over the baton, thinking herself the Heaven-sent conductor she was not. This necessitated additional last-minute rehearsals, which she directed with a maximum of fuss, pomposity, and ineptitude. The men had the utmost difficulty in following her beat (she always rolled the sleeves of her blouse well beyond her elbow, so that 'the gentlemen of the orchestra could see the beat plainly!'), and the ensemble at the première suffered severely from her inability to convey accurate indications to orchestra and stage. This performance followed precedent: the crisis which ensued when she interfered with the final rehearsals of Beecham's production of her opera, *The Wreckers*, was still fresh in everyone's memory.[1] A peppery woman, if ever I knew one!

The conducting staff of the Beecham Opera Company at that time consisted of Beecham, Percy Pitt, Julius Harrison, and myself. Pitt, the genial and popular Musical Director of the Royal Opera, Covent Garden, who counted a host of friends among European operatic artists, and whose knowledge of opera and operatic routine was equalled by few of his contemporaries, showed himself from the start a helpful, friendly colleague for whom I soon developed a real affection. In fact, he often made me feel more like an adopted son than a professional colleague. Very frequently— especially in later touring days when I was called upon to conduct an unfamiliar work at short notice—he would go through the score to point out those danger spots where for the conductor to be forewarned is to be forearmed. During our long professional association this particular loyalty toward me never wavered. Julius Harrison, a novice like myself, won his spurs during this same season, and his background as pianist and composer, not to mention his sympathetic collaboration, created a friendly bond between us.

Scenery and costumes for both *The Critic* and *The Boatswain's Mate* were designed by Hugo Rumbold, nephew of Sir Horace Rumbold, Ambassador to Turkey. Hugo was an irrepressible character with a fine feeling for stage design and period, a devastating sense of humour, and an incurable stutter. The spectacle of Hugo, immaculate in Anderson and Sheppard clothes, paint-brush in hand, arguing about colour with Ethel Smyth from the top of a

[1] Readers of Beecham's *A Mingled Chime* will recall the episode.

step-ladder during rehearsals was something to be remembered. Maurice Baring, the writer, present on that occasion, recorded the conversation to me later:

'Mr. Rumbold.'

'Yes, Miss S-S-Smyth.'

'Could you manage to deepen that red on the walls?'

'What red on w-w-what walls, Miss Smyth?'

'The wall you're working on now.'

'W-w-what's the matter with it?'

'Not dark enough!'

'How much d-d-darker d'you want it?'

'Oh very much darker.'

'How about the setting sun on it?'

'What setting sun?'

'Why the s-sunset you've got in your s-score. How about it?'

'I don't remember anything about a setting sun.' (*etc., etc.*)

CHAPTER XXII

In May we left London for six weeks at the New Queen's Theatre, Manchester, a large house admirably suited for operatic performances. *Boris Goudonov* opened the season. The chorus, short of rehearsal, improvised parts of the revolution scene in the grand manner on the opening night, but improved at later performances after closer familiarity with the music. (The tenors and basses actually rehearsed in a large 'saloon car' *en route* from London to Manchester, much to the astonishment of the passengers and crowds on the platforms at Rugby, Stafford, and Crewe.) After the first performance, conducted by Beecham, the opera was handed to me, together with several other works—*The Magic Flute, Phoebus and Pan, Madame Butterfly, Aïda*, and *Pagliacci*—all of which I did without orchestral rehearsal. You can dispense with the latter only if you have a good knowledge of the score and a strong nerve, both of which I had; but it was a grilling test of apprenticeship.[1]

After Manchester we returned to London to open a season at the Aldwych Theatre with a repertoire and singers much benefited by out-of-town performances. Beecham conducted *Othello* on the opening night with Mullings—reputed by many as good an Othello as Tamagno—Austin and Licette in the chief roles, and a fine new setting done by a timid Russian named Polunin, who used the entire stage floor on which to paint his back-cloths. This opera (together with three or four others new to me) was also confided to me after the opening night. By a strange coincidence, the conductor's scores at these performances (loaned by Ricordi) were those used by my grandfather and father at the productions they conducted with the Carl Rosa

[1] As a matter of cold record, out of the sixty or seventy different operas I conducted during my English operatic years, forty or more were without orchestral rehearsal.

Company respectively fifteen and twenty-five years earlier, both also in English. It always gave me a strange emotion to encounter their two familiar pencil markings; often I was constrained to add my own to keep the three-generation record straight.

After two months of nightly performances, the season ended with Mozart's *Seraglio*, and the company looked to a well-deserved holiday, with Beecham in his curtain speech reminding the audience: 'Thirty weeks of opera in English so far, with a war going on, and more to come before the year ends.'

In August we received word from the War Office that my brother, Adolphe, had died of wounds received in the first Somme offensive of the British Army. He was only eighteen, and had enlisted when some recruiting Gordon Highlanders with their band passed the hall in Glasgow after a Scottish Orchestra rehearsal at which he had been playing. He impulsively fell in step behind them, still carrying his horn-case, and marched off to his fate. My intense grief on receiving the news of his death wasn't lessened by the thought that Leon was also shortly to leave for France, and so I went up to London to enlist again, and was again rejected for service on medical grounds. Leaving the recruiting office, I met Edmund Burke, the Canadian baritone, who had just been made C.O. of the massed divisional bands of the Canadians, numbering about three hundred and fifty players in all. He had little difficulty in persuading me to take over the job of preparing them for a concert they were to give in Paris three months later. I agreed only on condition that I should be allowed to choose the programme for the concert, and that I should be allotted two rehearsals a week before it took place. The Canadians were quartered at Folkestone, and I arranged my bi-weekly trips there to fit in with rehearsals and performances of the opera in London, which resumed activities at the Aldwych Theatre in October. The season had barely got under way when very early one morning Beecham telephoned, asking me to pack a bag and take a taxi immediately to his father's home in Hampstead. I arrived there about 7.30, and found T.B. looking pale and harassed. He said: 'My father died two hours ago. Take these scores, catch the 8.30 from Euston for Liverpool and conduct the concert there for me to-night. The rehearsal is this afternoon at two. You can just make it. Then go on to Manchester to-morrow and take over my concert with the Hallé Orchestra in the evening. Rehearsal in the afternoon. There's a third concert in Bradford with the Orchestral Society the day after to-morrow. Rehearsal in the morning. Forsyth[1] will meet you at Liverpool to-day. Good luck!' I left immediately for the station, having expressed my condolences. Four hours on the train and I arrived at Liverpool, after absorbing the contents of more than half a dozen unfamiliar works during the journey. Forsyth met me as arranged. He had previously broken the news of the substitution to the Directors of the Philharmonic, who received it with some misgiving—as well they might, this being my début as a symphony conductor. I had three hours rehearsal in which to prepare the evening concert. The experience I had gained in the opera-house served me so well that by 4.30 everything was in order for the evening, and, to me, the worst part of the ordeal was over. Orchestra and chorus, most of whom at the outset appeared sceptical about my being able to tackle the job efficiently in one rehearsal, had shown themselves increasingly co-operative as the afternoon wore on, and, now that it was successfully over, beamed their appreciation and gave me a heart-warming reception. The concert passed off without a hitch and with the greatest enthusiasm. Even the previously apprehensive Board of Directors appeared *en masse* in the green-room after the performance to offer congratulations. Old Riley, the Secretary, remembering me as a schoolboy, burst out in good Lancashire, 'Eh, lad, there's nowt you couldn't drink now,' and promptly opened a historic bottle of claret which had graced the mantelshelf of the green-room for I don't know how many previous Philharmonic concerts!

[1] Manager of the Hallé Orchestra.

The Manchester and Bradford concerts went equally well, with the fine Hallé Orchestra playing on both occasions. Meantime, my Canadians down in Folkestone were beginning to show the good results of constant rehearsal. There being no hall in the town big enough to accommodate a band of 350 soldier-musicians, the local armoury had been requisitioned for rehearsals, and my fifty or sixty piccolo and flute players, eighty clarinettists, sixteen oboists, sixty cornet and twelve bombardon players, plus numerous other brass players and not to mention a goodly body of string basses and percussion, lifted the roof rehearsing Bizet's *Patrie*, Tchaikovsky's *Nutcracker*, Elgar's marches, and other showy pieces.

The time finally arrived when we were due to start from Folkestone for the Paris concert organized by Leon Bailby of *L'Intransigeant* for the purpose, it was said, of smoothing out relations between Canadian and French authorities—reported somewhat strained at that time. With the rank of honorary lieutenant, I got to the boat, having mastered a smattering of Army rules and regulations, and found that it was reserved exclusively for staff officers, while my Canadians were relegated to a second steamer, which followed us across the Channel. It seems to me that had our ship been torpedoed, the British Army would have lost a good third of its high-ranking officers! All went well till lunch-time, when, going down to the dining saloon, I felt a sickening tug at my knee, and pitched headlong into a group of colonels, brigadier-generals, and full generals, who followed me in a heap to the bottom of the stairs. What ensued was a nightmare of cursing 'brass-hats' extricating themselves from endless lengths of a puttee which, I was blissfully unaware, had become unravelled at the top of the staircase, and had been stepped upon unknowingly by some Very Exalted Officer indeed. Helped to my feet by a steward, I fled to the bowels of the ship and emerged crestfallen only when we reached Boulogne. The journey of the band and its officers from Boulogne to Paris took from 5 p.m. until 6 a.m. the following morning, owing to air-raids at Abbeville and consequent re-routing. We were met at the Gare du Nord by the Governor of Paris and a deputation of the famous 'Garde Republicaine' Band. Being the only French-speaking member of the trio of officers in charge of the Canadians, it fell to me to reply to the speech of welcome—an ordeal, under the circumstances. This little ceremony over, the entire party adjourned to the station bar, where we were hospitably plied with hot rum in such quantities that the events of the next few hours remained a complete blank for most of us. Eventually we landed up at one of the oldest and dirtiest barracks in Paris—La Pépinière. Next day, when it came to the time for our departure for the Trocadero, the buses which were to take us there failed to turn up. So I was put in charge of three hundred and fifty Canadians with instructions to get them to the concert hall by Metro. This operation temporarily disorganized the schedule of the Underground, especially when I asked the ticket-seller for three hundred and fifty tickets for the Étoile Station. Some of the men managed to board wrong trains, with the result that two or three were still circling around Paris long after the concert had started.

CHAPTER XXIII

SEVERAL incidents contrived to delay the start of the concert, as, for instance, when it was discovered that the Band of the Garde Republicaine, which was supposed to perform the 'Marsellaise' in conjunction with us, used a pitch several vibrations lower than the Canadians, a fact which automatically made their co-operation impossible. Marthe Chénal, the temperamental *prima donna* of the Paris Opera, on hearing of this, absolutely refused to sing the 'Marsellaise' unless both bands accompanied her, and as she couldn't be made to understand that this was out of the question a substitute singer had to be found. At the sight of her rival, however, Chénal promptly underwent a change of mind and consented to appear with one band only. Just before going on the platform to conduct Bizet's overture, *Patrie*, the same puttee that had caused the *fracas* on the channel crossing started to unwind itself, and I had to unbend sufficiently to make temporary repairs. The band proved a sensation; the Parisians acclaimed us so much that some of the selections had to be repeated. A second concert followed that same evening in the Cirque Médrano, and here we occupied the sandy arena in place of the usual performing lions. Then back to La Pépinière, from whence half my Canadians were drafted to the front lines. The rest, luckier than their brethren who saw heavy fighting, returned to England with me.

The following Sunday I was ordered to Folkestone to direct a camp concert with the remnant of my Canadians. The concert was due to start at 8 p.m., and the last day train left London at two in the afternoon. Beecham telephoned in the morning, asking me to call and see him at the Albany before leaving. Our business accomplished, he started showing me some newly acquired walnut furniture—his latest enthusiasm—and then insisted on my staying to lunch. I reminded him that my train left at two, but he waved aside this objection by offering his car and chauffeur to drive me to Folkestone, which I accepted. About three in the afternoon I decided to leave, as the wintry day was ominously dark. No sooner arrived at the outskirts of London than a pea-soup fog descended over the landscape—a fog so impenetrable that the chauffeur was compelled to creep along the country roads at a snail's pace. I realized then that there was no hope of arriving at Folkestone in time for the concert, so decided to stop at a wayside house to telephone news of my predicament to the authorities. Suddenly, at a fork in the road, a signpost loomed up dead ahead through the fog. The car ran straight into it; there was a nasty crash—and a still nastier silence. The chauffeur was knocked insensible, but came to after a few minutes. The peak of my cap saved me from disfigurement from broken glass, but the car was a total wreck, and I had the questionable pleasure of informing its owner of the fact by telephone. His comment on hearing the news was characteristic: 'Splendid! I've wanted a new one for a long time! . . .'

By Christmas, 1916, despite the war, opera in English was in a comparatively thriving condition. London, which had always seemed rather to turn up its nose at opera in the vernacular (compared with the provincial cities of England), began to show a gratifying interest in our activities. Mayfair and Belgravia particularly rallied to the cause, a source of wonder to those who always associated diamond tiaras with the spring Grand Season at Covent Garden. The indefatigable and enthusiastic Lady Cunard nightly held court in her box during the opera seasons, and daily summoned to her home in Carlton House Terrace for teas, lunches, and dinners as varied a group of musical enthusiasts as was to be found anywhere at the time. At one of her luncheons at the beginning of 1917—heaven knows how *I* got there, but I think T.B. and I had rehearsed together that morning— I remember Lord Balfour, Herbert Asquith (whose régime as war-time premier had just given way to the coalition of Lloyd George), the Duchess of Rutland, Lady Diana Manners, Duff Cooper, Sargent the painter, Yeats, Delius,

Beecham, and Eddie Marsh (Mr. Churchill's secretary) all seated at an enormous table presided over by the picturesque Emerald herself. However large the gathering, the querulous voice of Delius always managed to make itself heard over a general conversation, and this occasion was no exception to the rule. Even England's two senior statesmen lapsed into silence when the Delian tones were heard asking why it was that the British public displayed such abysmal ignorance of opera as compared with other European peoples. 'Don't talk like that,' answered Beecham. 'Just you wait till we produce *A Village Romeo and Juliet*.[1] That'll disprove what you say.' 'Bah,' said Delius. 'The public here doesn't know a note of my music, and cares less!' 'Perhaps,' slyly observed Eddie Marsh, 'that's because they don't like it.' 'Don't like it? Don't like it?' shouted the irate Delius. 'Tell me what they *do* like!' A quiet voice interrupted with: '*Dear* Mr. Balfour, *do* tell us how the Lloyd George Coalition is working,' and Maud Cunard had steered the conversation into safer channels. Her gift, too, for silencing the entire company whenever one of its members talked about something in authoritative fashion was never better seen than on that occasion. Thus, without interruption, we heard first Mr. Asquith—as he then was— making the frankest off-the-record observations on current political events, and the usually shy Sargent giving his candid opinion on contemporary painting. One blamed the newspapers for capitalizing on political distortions, and the other the natural gullibility of the people for accepting artistic ones. Both arguments had, as I recall, a specious, familiarly plausible ring. . . .

Operatically, 1917 was a crowded year. Seasons in London, Birmingham, and Manchester monopolized its first five months and both *Tristan* and *The Tales of Hoffman* were dropped into my lap—at short notice—almost at the outset of the Aldwych season. Needless to say, no orchestral rehearsal for either work was forthcoming, for I came by them, in the usual fashion, on the day of the performance!

[1] Delius's last opera.

Fortunately, I'd coached the principal singers in their roles on many occasions, and, strange though it may seem, the last-minute direction of *Hoffmann* proved an infinitely more perilous experience than the conducting of a sweeping, straight-forward *Tristan*. Two other conductors had imposed their strange tempi and stranger cuts on Offenbach's lovely work, so that the business of maintaining rigid contact between singers and orchestra in this opera, without previous rehearsal, proved a hair-raising experience. No orchestral score being available, I was left with a vocal score, which gave no instrumental cues. This did little to lessen the tenseness of the evening, especially in the last act, where one of Dr. Miracle's magic flasks flew from his hand, and caught me a resounding whack on the temple. The *Tristan* performance was memorable for something else beyond Mulling's and Rosina Buckman's really great singing of the principal roles, for Adrian Allinson, whose painting of Cotswold elms, while outstanding in its way, hardly qualified him as a stage designer, had executed new settings of the opera which not only quarrelled violently with the Wagnerian idiom, but in their highly stylized ineptness shocked practically everybody in the theatre. So when the curtain rose on Act I to reveal a back-cloth depicting a single enormous wave in the style of Hokusai, threatening to engulf Tristan's ship and all aboard her, a great gasp rose from the audience. The second and third acts afforded equal surprises, and the scenery was withdrawn at subsequent performances, though, in justice to Allinson, it must be said that he made amends later in some beautiful settings for *A Village Romeo and Juliet*, where he could paint elms and silver birches to his heart's content.

In Birmingham the bill-boards showed the names of both Eugene Goossens, Senr., and Eugene Goossens, Junr. My father had been suddenly engaged to reinforce the conductorial staff, with the result that standard works like *Aïda*, *Trovatore*, *Pagliacci*, and *Faust* felt the grip of his experienced hand, and singers who had lapsed into complacent ways were rudely shaken out of them every time Father appeared in the orchestra pit to take over these 'chestnuts'. It can't be said that this added to his popularity; for in the Carl Rosa days his severity had been a byword, and the old leopard saw no reason to change his spots at this late date. His presence reacted beneficially on my own self-criticism, or lack of it. The facility I had acquired in the ways of opera—I think I was born with it—hadn't really been accompanied by a proportionate depth of interpretative powers. The example of my father's conscientious approach to his work finally brought this about, plus a growing realization of the competitive professionalism which surrounded me. Thus we settled down together, with the happiest results, into the touring existence which Father knew so well, and the taste of which I had only just begun to sample. We abandoned hotel life in favour of homelier theatrical lodgings, with their nourishing meals and affable landladies.

In Manchester *Samson and Delilah* and Mozart's *Abduction from the Seraglio* were added to my repertory, and (miraculously) I was allotted a short orchestral rehearsal for the latter, but not for the former. A sumptuous production of *Figaro* was the chief event of a nine weeks' London season at Drury Lane Theatre, ending in August. That *Figaro*, with its Nigel Playfair production, Rumbold scenery, and Beecham's most fastidious Mozart conducting, surpassed any similar production I've seen in an opera house before or since. Witty dialogue—most authentically Beaumarchais—took the place of the unintelligible gabble which usually passes for Mozartean recitative, and gave the work a dramatic continuity usually lacking in the average performance. Playfair, the best available authority in London on eighteenth-century theatrical style, infused a degree of vivid finish and subtlety into the production and acting, and Hugo Rumbold produced settings and costumes more wondrous than any I've ever seen elsewhere. Such a lavish production was bound to set the seal on its promoter's efforts to give Londoners opera in English on a scale hitherto undreamt of. The public flocked to our performances as never before; particularly, too, since the vocal standard of these was of an extremely high order.

CHAPTER XXIV

(*Interlude*)

AFTER a few weeks' holiday in the Cotswolds I went fishing in Devonshire with Rivarde, my former violin professor, and Arthur Bent, a fellow violin teacher at the R.C.M. With Lynmouth as our headquarters, we set out to fish the River Lynn, and with much expensive tackle arrived early in the morning at a spot a mile upstream, where it was said the salmon were plentiful. Obviously, we were not the only ones who had been told of this. On arrival there the place looked like a fisherman's convention. Grimly we staked a claim near an old stone bridge, and settled down to wait for a 'strike'—something the other fishermen had apparently been doing without result ever since dawn. Suddenly Rivarde, dressed in immaculate blue serge, an old Burberry, and a magnificent black sombrero *à la* Sarasate, was seen to be playing an evidently big fish right in the deep rapids under the bridge. Excitement among the spectators was intense, as it was obvious from Rivarde's strenuous efforts to reel the fish in, and from the rod bent almost to breaking point, that the catch would prove a weighty one. After a period of unbearable suspense, he collapsed on the bank with a jolt as a large Huntley and Palmer biscuit-tin, which had become anchored in some stones, and to which the current had imparted a simulated activity down among the weeds, hurtled through the air at the end of his line, reducing all his subsequent operations to the level of farce.

Later that day, at the local inn, we decided to abandon fly-fishing for deep-sea fishing, and accordingly set off early next morning in a large-sized rowing-boat, which required the full force of our united efforts to bring to a point at least half a mile from shore to avoid the long-distance swimmers of the locality, with their sarcastic remarks. We must have presented an astonishing appearance to them. Rivarde had brought an umbrella, as a thin drizzle was falling, and Bent was in bright yellow oilskins, which gave him the appearance of a lifeboat skipper. I was foolishly and optimistically wearing a battered panama. This having absorbed a certain amount of moisture I discarded for a cap and sweater, the latter inscribed across the front 'Mersey Docks and Harbour Board' and bought second hand from a ship's chandler. It also became so waterlogged that it soon joined the panama.

The morning was depressingly calm, with none of the exhilarating breezes or lively movement one usually associates with the sea. Arrived at our chosen location and beginning operations, we started hauling in dog-fish with monotonous regularity. Ugly and sharp-toothed, they kept us in a constant state of nervous apprehension; snapping and whipping about at the bottom of the vessel, they retained a vitality unlike any fish I had ever seen. Irrespective of whether we used rod or line, and immune to changes of bait, they kept on coming, till the boat seemed a nightmare of lashing dog-fish. There was only one thing to do, and we did it. With boat-hook and oar, we jettisoned the entire cargo, and at Rivarde's suggestion rowed straight out to sea to put as great a distance between ourselves and that fatal school of dog-fish as possible. We also hoped to encounter something slightly more edible and prepossessing to take back as evidence of the trip.

Nourishing this hope to the exclusion of everything else, and with a new vigour born of it, we rowed the heavy boat a good two miles from shore before noticing that the wind had freshened and the sea had become considerably more obstreperous than in the early morning. The rain had ceased and a threatening formation of clouds looked ominous, so we judged it high time to resume operations. Shipping oars, we baited the lines and awaited results. (Rivarde had brought an odoriferous cod's head to use as bait, from which he expected the best results.) The forward movement of the boat, since we had stopped rowing, had given way to a wallowing motion, accompanied by spasmodic heaves as every now and then an increasingly large wave would catch us broadside on. Using an oar to steady the boat, Arthur Bent relinquished his fishing efforts, whilst the colour of Rivarde's face began to take on a greenish hue under his black sombrero. Up to now he had held forth and discoursed with great animation and characteristic gestures on the technique of deep-sea fishing and its subtleties. I remember it went something like this:

'The rod should be held lightly, just like a violin bow. Careful now; watch the position of the thumb and first finger. As soon as you get a strike, bring the rod back sharply, as with the bow in "flying *spiccato*". So!'—suiting the action to the word, and whishing an imaginary rod into the air. 'The fish will bear down on the rod and give a sort of nervous vibrato to the arm, just like in violin-playing, by which you will be able to sense its exact weight and stamina. But that is where most fishermen *go to pieces*, just like a nervous violinist on the concert platform.' Here Rivarde gives a graphic imitation of this, at the same time tugging at the line he's holding to see whether the cod's head is still there. '*My* system of complete muscular relaxation—*just* as in my violin-playing—will avoid all that.' (I thought of the biscuit-tin under the bridge.) 'Never be brutal to a fish. *Insinuate* it towards you, as though you were inviting it to be caught. Reel in gently—*legato*, with a light bow-arm' —a slight pause, during which his change of complexion begins to be painfully apparent—'then, at the climax, *conquer* the fish, *dominate* it'. He pulls at the line as a tremendous tug signifies a strike. Great excitement, during which his sombrero falls to the bottom of the boat, and is swamped by a wave which threatens to engulf us. The line is hauled in, minus the cod's head, but plus an extra-sized dog-fish. A torrent of profanity from Rivarde as he hacks it from the line. His complexion is now a bilious yellow. 'Is it not something *formidable* that we can't be rid of these —— dog-fish?' A long pause. The weather is now very squally, and it has started to rain in torrents. 'But to-morrow we'll teach these fish!' A very long pause. Rivarde's hue is now a deathly pea-green. 'Do you happen'—this rather feebly—'my dear Arthur, to have brought that cognac with you?'

Dear Arthur, eyeing our distance from shore apprehensively, is busy heading the boat homeward—'Come on, Goossens, lay on those oars'—and, oblivious to Rivarde's now heart-rending plight, we strive our utmost to make port as rapidly as possible. But a strong rip-tide and an increasing force of wind and rain are proving too much for two oarsmen to cope with, and it looks, after a few minutes, as though we aren't going to make it. The worst has now happened to Rivarde, and, groaning, he subsides into the stern sheets.

Suddenly the miracle happened. The boat, now almost out of control, shipped a large wave, most of which concentrated its icy force on our seasick passenger. It was a douche that instantly revived him. He shook himself. 'Goossens'—reproachfully, as though we were back in his class-room at the R.C.M.—'don't *feather* your oars when you're rowing at sea. One would think you were using a *flautando* bowing. No, idiot; watch *me*.' And suddenly, with a newly found vigour, he seized his oar, and, his back to us, started rowing energetically like a Varsity stroke. This drenched elegant was saving the ship with a vengeance, and over the sound of the storm—a real storm by now—his voice rose exhorting us, 'One, two—one, two,' as the three of us, with a fair attempt at unison, fought our way, backbreakingly, into Lynmouth Harbour. Soaked through and exhausted, Rivarde spoke as we moored the boat: 'Just look at this fellow Goossens, Arthur! It's just as of old in my class—he's trembling like a *jelly*!'

I was, but a hot toddy averted severe chills that night, and next morning (and for many subsequent mornings, to the great joy of the natives) we set forth on further deep-sea expeditions, and encountered, according to the varying instructions of local fishermen, different species of fish, from mackerel to conger eel (large size). These horrors we released as soon as they appeared; they put the best efforts of the dog-fish to shame, and induced such violent nausea in Bent that he threatened to jump overboard and bequeath his entire violin class to both of us if any more than the first two were shipped.

No further storms appeared for the rest of my stay, but the day before leaving we had another narrow escape. An excursion paddle-steamer being about to pass by, I headed the boat straight for it, and got caught in its wash; all for the sake of listening to the strains of a harp and violin playing 'I'll be Your Honeysuckle if You'll be My Bee', a contemporary ditty on which I had devised some rather trite variations. Casualties from the heavy wave shipped aboard were three packets of sandwiches, two bottles of ginger ale, and Arthur Bent's yellow oilskins, which floated out on the Bristol Channel as though glad to be restored to the grave of the Ancient Mariner from which they were obviously originally filched. As a result of this little contretemps, my stock as a navigator considerably declined, and departure for London next day seemed aptly timed. Yet I could not forbear, on my last morning in Lynmouth, from paying a secret pilgrimage to the old stone bridge up the river to see whether, in place of the biscuit-tin, a fat salmon had taken up its abode there. Needless, to say, it hadn't. . . .

CHAPTER XXV

My father opened the Drury Lane autumn season of opera that year with Rimsky-Korsakov's *Ivan the Terrible*, a tribute from Beecham to seniority and experience which I think he appreciated not a little. I conducted a newly furbished production of *Tannhäuser* in English at Drury Lane on the same date in March 1918 as the Germans launched what was to prove their last major offensive. At no time during the war did the public protest against the playing of Wagner's works, even when, during a later performance of the same opera, a Gotha dropped bombs on an air-raid shelter in the vicinity of the Opera House, killing a hundred people. A chunk of shrapnel fell through the glass roof of the stage on that occasion, narrowly missing Tannhäuser (Mullings) just as he was returning to the Venusberg. The audience, with considerable phlegm, sat unperturbed, and Mullings hardly batted an eyelid.

By July I had been handed the *Valkyrie*, *Louise*, and *Coq d'Or* (in a fine translation by Edward Agate),[1] and half the standard repertory, and felt that a change of scene was indicated after almost forty consecutive weeks spent in the opera house. So I went to Harlech, on the Welsh coast, for a month's rest as the guest of George Davidson, known to his friends as G.D., former Chairman of the London branch of the Eastman Kodak Company. George was an elderly idealist whose unconventional ways and socialistic views had so alienated him from the business world that he had retired to Harlech to build himself a home in which he might welcome his friends—those, that is, who felt like facing the eight-hour trip from London to see him. The house, called 'Wernfawr', was built on the slope of a hill leading to romantic Harlech Castle, and had a sort of neo-medieval

[1] Viola-player in the orchestra.

character. A lofty main hall (containing a fine Aeolian pipe-organ and a large concert grand piano perfectly tuned to it) was the chief feature of the house, and at least two hundred people could, and sometimes did, gather there for concerts. Alvin Langdon Coburn, American camera-portrait artist resident in London, spent his summers close by in a small house filled to the ceilings with esoteric books. He was indispensable to any music-making at 'Wernfawr'. His hobby was the pianola; not only did he possess a large modern library of rolls, but, with the aid of a cutting machine, added from time to time the choicest selection of contemporary works to his collection. The pianola, in Alvin's hands, was uncannily human. One night G.D. asked Alvin and myself to give an informal pianola and violin recital at 'Wernfawr' for a few friends. I said, 'What about an accompanist?' 'Right here,' replied Alvin! 'Since when have you learnt to play the piano?' said I. 'I haven't,' he said. 'But I've cut pianola rolls of the piano parts of the Franck sonata, two Brahms, three Beethoven, and two Mozart sonatas. What'll you have?' I chose the Brahms C minor, and was astonished to find when we played it together that Alvin's accompaniment was as sensitive as any human hands could have contrived it.

I found Cyril Scott at Harlech, living in a house on the golf-links. He was in the throes of composing a tone-poem to be called *Disaster at Sea*, or some such title, based on the sinking of the *Titanic*—a happening Cyril had long wanted to depict in music. I couldn't somehow associate the composer of the two *Passacaglias*, *La Belle Dame sans Merci*, and the delicate songs and piano-pieces with such a morbidity. Discordant strains of 'Nearer my God to Thee'—the hymn played by the ship's orchestra as the vessel was sinking —interwoven with a great volume of sound depicting the *Titanic* foundering, issued from the window as Cyril pounded his tinny Welsh piano and sang in a high, ecstatic voice—his invariable habit when composing—moved even nearby golfers to look around in wonderment. I don't know whether the piece was ever played, but the score, in

ADOLPHE GOOSSENS

LEON GOOSSENS

spite of the unpleasant subject, was an impressive one. Cyril was, of course, requisitioned for the 'Wernfawr' evenings of music and, as he had mastered all the intricacies of the Aeolian organ in the hall, contributed twenty-minute improvisations as beautiful as any I have ever heard. Once we played together his *Talahassee* suite for violin and piano, and another time improvised crazily on violin and organ against a background of pieces by Ornstein which Coburn had cut for the pianola.

Another musician lived on the hill near the castle in a thatched cottage—none other than the redoubtable Josef Holbrooke, the most prolific, and alas! to-day the least played of all that older generation of living British composers. 'Joe', like his younger contemporary Peter Warlock, rode a battered motor-cycle, to the terror of the country folk, who regarded it and its rider with superstitious dread. Mounted on that noisy vehicle—he rode with no 'cut-out', at a terrifying pace—Joe could be seen and heard, day and night, rushing on some innocuous errand (usually to Mr. Parry, the town druggist, who sold everything from postcards to paregoric): a bearded demon in goggles, roaring and echoing among hills and down cliff-roads. That he never collided with anything more substantial than chickens, of which he invariably left a long trail behind him, was a constant source of wonder to us all. Sometimes he'd come down to 'Wernfawr' and join our music-making, when he could be torn away from his work-table at the cottage. G.D., our host, used on those occasions to preside at the Aeolian organ, the only times it was ever used mechanically, and would regale us all with symphonic excerpts from Joe's operas. 'The Flight of the Wild Fowl' from *Dylan* and the Overture to *Bronwen* were my favourites, for G.D., having little musical capacity and being slightly hard of hearing, would play both at fantastic speed, producing unheard-of effects from the organ. This bewildered everyone, including the composer, who would rush to the organ and pull the control lever hard over to decelerate the head-long pace of his opus. A selection from the third opera of

Holbrooke's trilogy, the *Children of Don*, which G.D. would occasionally play as a quiet antidote to the two afore-mentioned, was invariably performed so slowly that you could sleep comfortably before it came to an end.

Last of the musical colony at Harlech was Granville Bantock, head of the Birmingham School of Music, who, the reader may recall, first introduced me to orchestral concerts at New Brighton years before. Bantock being an ardent lover of the Orient and its philosophies—his choral setting of *Omar Khayyám* is the only one I know—found in Cyril Scott, with his profound knowledge of occultism and Eastern mysticism, a man after his own heart. Their chief interests, at that time, were herbalism and Yogi. Their mentor in the first was already in Harlech—a Lancashire enthusiast called Foster who claimed to, and did, cure most diseases by a system of herbal emetics. (The fine details of this treatment, which I successfully underwent for a time, may be passed over discreetly. Enough that it was drastic, and unaesthetic, but sufficiently effective to cure a diabetic local villager suffering from a gangrenous leg.) Their knowledge of Yogi was derived chiefly from books, though it was whispered that Cyril had found an 'adept' who had imparted a number of the cult's secrets to him, all of which, the pupil claimed, had benefited him vastly. Walking among the sand-dunes one morning, I came upon the two men, one heavy and bearded, the other slim and ascetic, sitting cross-legged, Oriental-wise, in the hollow of a dune—and in a state of nature. The first was seemingly endeavouring to tie knots in the muscles of his abdomen, and the second was trying to swallow a length of solid flexible rubber tubing—Bantock and Cyril Scott, practising Yogi. I cursed the luck that caused me to forget my camera, and withdrew quickly and silently, leaving the two disciples to their Oriental pursuits. Later, as a neophyte, I tried to emulate them—unsuccessfully.

To complete the artistic colony at Harlech, there arrived at that time Margaret Morris and her School of the Dance. This consisted of a group of young women and men whose plastic posing and 'self-expressive' callisthenics in short Grecian tunics were the pride and joy of the locality. 'Meg' Morris and her assistants held classes on the seashore and in the courtyard of 'Wernfawr', imparting an Attic flavour to Harlech that surprised—and occasionally shocked—the elders of the town. The aesthetics of the group, typified by page-boy haircuts and multicoloured Liberty clothes, were sufficiently exalted to be classified as 'expressionist' by lovers of the unusual, and as plain 'arty' by the common man. However, the descent of the school on the community resembled a locust-like invasion in which such matters as lodgings (Miss Mordaunt) and commissariat (Mrs. Morris) contrived to dissipate temporarily, by their very extent and urgency, the aura of 'High Art' which ordinarily suffused the school's activities.

John Fergusson, eminent Scottish painter, a source of inspiration and help to the Morris clan, came along as usual to supervise the rather Cézanne-ish efforts of the School in its afternoon painting work, which took place outdoors, unless the weather was too bad. The students adored 'Fergus' for his patience and efficiency and his faculty for linking up in his lectures the twin plasticities of paint and body movement. The rhythmic improvisations of the dance —in which Meg and her pupils excelled—he translated into terms of colour and brush stroke, so that, at Harlech, the two arts were synonymous in theory and practice. I helped to add a smattering of music to the curriculum by an occasional lecture on rhythm and form; these led to debates into which the more daring spirits among the students waded—most times out of their depth—and the meetings would end in hopeless confusion of thought and subject-matter.

Over this diverse assortment of musicians, painters, dancers, and writers (Robert Graves and family were nearby, too) frowned the sombre ruins of Harlech Castle. Perched high on the steep rock, washed centuries ago by the sea, it formed that summer the scene of the Pageant of Harlech, a spectacle in which, with the aid of a specially written script and costumes imported from London, we all participated, to the intense joy of the townspeople. Cyril Scott's quavering performance as old Father Time, Foster the herbalist disguised as a medieval bowman, and my impersonation of Edward II, with Mr. Parry the chemist as Simon de Montfort, were highlights of an impressive performance—that is, when we didn't forget our lines! And through it all, the schedule of the Margaret Morris School of Dance continued uninterruptedly.

CHAPTER XXVI

Blackpool, Glasgow, Edinburgh, Leeds, Manchester, London (Drury Lane), Birmingham, and Bradford were the principal stopping places for our operatic caravan during the next twelve months—months which saw the close of what we fondly believed was the war to end all war. Shortly after the Armistice the Goossens family—minus one of its sons—came together again in the house on Edith Road. My brother Leon, after his miraculous escape just before the war's end, proved that three years' battle service had failed to impair his artistry and sensitiveness as an oboe player. Rather the contrary. My sisters Marie and Sidonie had finally embarked on professional careers as harpists, to the tune of a prodigious consumption of harp strings. Father now knew for the first time in many years the joys of staying at home, save when isolated operatic tours called him from the shelter of retirement. At such times, his flower garden languished grievously for lack of care, none of the members of the family feeling qualified to do justice to it. My dear mother cared proudly for her house, its occupants, and its visitors.

Spring of 1919 saw the resumption of Covent Garden's Grand Season, and, just as in pre-war days, fashionable London turned out in force in top-hats and tiaras to applaud the galaxy of international stars which gave the season its *éclat*. Unexpectedly, and by a strange coincidence, I found myself one evening part of it. During a performance of *Falstaff* in Manchester one night in May I received a telegram which called me to London next day. I arrived at midday, accomplished my business that afternoon, and decided to spend the night at Edith Road. No sooner there than I was called to the telephone by Percy Eales, Manager of Covent Garden, who seemed much relieved to find me in

London. He asked me to change into evening clothes and go straight to the theatre to conduct *Faust* in place of Coates, who had become suddenly indisposed. Melba was to sing Marguerite, and the opera, of course, would be performed in French.

I found some dress clothes—my evening things being in Manchester—and went early to the theatre to refresh my memory from the full score of *Faust*, as I hadn't conducted it for some months. At 7.15 I went up to Melba's dressing-room and knocked at the door. Knowing she had been told of the substitution of conductors, I felt no hesitation about entering as soon as she said 'Come in', but I wasn't quite prepared for a vision of the diva *en negligée*. I must have shown some embarrassment. 'You're Mr. Goossens. Please sit down.'—Melba reached for a *peignoir*. 'Have you ever conducted *Faust* before?' I replied, 'Frequently.' 'But in French?' she asked—as though that made a world of difference. 'No; but I speak French fluently.' 'Excellent' said Melba. I asked whether she made any changes in the traditional tempi, so that I might be forewarned. 'None whatsoever. I sing it exactly as Gounod wrote it. And I hope,' she added suspiciously, 'you conduct it the same way!'

During the actual performance she was as good as her word, for her singing of the role turned out to be a most refreshing musical experience. With none of the kittenish tricks and simperings elderly *prime donne* usually indulge in when they're playing a youthful role, the incomparable singer realized Gounod's Marguerite to perfection, and made our task in the orchestra pit easeful and unapprehensive. Only once, in the quartet, when Mephistopheles' *rubato* threatened to get out of hand, did she help the other singers—and myself—restore a normal ensemble by giving that gentleman a baleful glare which carried a warning not to be ignored. At our final curtain-call together, she plucked a rose from her bouquet and thrust it in my shirt-front with a spontaneous gesture which carried as pleasant a tribute as I shall ever know. Nellie Melba was the *grande dame* of singing, unaffected and charming. The purity of vocal style which was her great characteristic remained always unimpaired to the end. When she came to sing *La Bohème* with the B.N.O.C., her performance was unforgettably touching. . . .

A few weeks later I returned to London to conduct what we all hoped would be a successful (though necessarily limited) run of Lecoq's *opera comique*, *La Fille de Madame Angot* at Drury Lane. Beecham had decided on it as a summer venture, with principals, chorus, and orchestra drawn from his company. Hugo Rumbold carried out scenery and costumes and the production was on a lavish scale, with a slick, up-to-date translation, but the public tired of it after three or four weeks, so the run was brought to a close. The opera's topical implications and political subtleties were lost on the Londoners—a generation fed on vacuous operettas and trashy musical comedies could hardly be expected to relish the sparkle of Lecoq's music and the nineteenth-century gallicisms of the libretto, however much modernized! So Madame Lange (Gladys Ancrum) sang her political couplets at the close of the second act to a splatter of applause, instead of to the demonstrations which, in the Paris of '73, nightly greeted the song, when the opera ran for four hundred consecutive performances. I found it a relief to play this lively score with a virtuoso orchestra of thirty players, after the dose of grand opera I'd absorbed in the previous two years. Considerably refreshed as a result, I returned to Harlech to write the incidental music for the Plough Society's production of Verhaeren's *Philip the Second*, effectually obliterating all traces of Lecoq's champagne in the depths of Inquisitorial melodramatics. Ernest Newman used to say at that time that the overture to the play was the only piece of my music he enjoyed. . . .

Lest the reader tire of operatic peripatetics, enough to mention that after a short visit to Scotland the company came in November to Covent Garden, where both *Prince Igor* and *The Nightingale* found their way into my Russian repertoire under, for me, the usual circumstances. I didn't

mind taking over *Igor*—previously well rehearsed and produced by Coates—at a few hours' notice, especially as my
old friend, Edmund Burke, former C.O. of the Canadian
Massed Bands, was singing the part of Igor. But when
Percy Pitt brought me the score of Stravinsky's *Nightingale*,
saying that a certain conductor-colleague had changed his
mind about directing it and would I like to prepare and
conduct it in the course of the next three days, I judged the
moment ripe for some plain speaking. I said that for three
years I had shouldered some pretty risky assignments at
short notice, cheerfully and willingly. I said, of course, there
might be quite a number of other people besides myself
willing and able to conduct unfamiliar operas without
rehearsal at a few hours' notice, but that so far I hadn't
noticed them in this vicinity. I said that this last minute
'pinch-hitting' for other people—usually indisposed—over a
period of three years was quite a stimulating experience
(though a trifle hard on the nervous system) and appealed
very much to a certain sporting venturesomeness in me; also
that the gospel of *bisogne vivere pericolosamente* found no
more literal exponent anywhere than myself. But I expected
a colleague to be equally sporting, and not to hand over a
complex work like the *Nightingale* three days before the
production, after zealously retaining the score till the very
last minute. To Pitt's astonishment, I declined to take it on
—not alone for the sake of Stravinsky's music, but for my
own reputation. Percy, perturbed, was in a quandary, for
there was no one else to do it, and I was in no mood for
yielding.

But I had bargained without one Theodor Komisarjevsky,
a volatile Russian straight from the Moscow Art Theatre,
who had been engaged to produce the opera. That gentleman alternately cajoled, flattered, wheedled, and generally
put on such an 'act' with me that the most hard-boiled
veteran (which I was not) would have succumbed to it.
My heroics were unavailing, and there was little else left but
to forget hurt feelings and give in to *force majeure*. The opera
is one of Stravinsky's most difficult; so with an orchestral

rehearsal scheduled for the following afternoon, preceded by a morning piano rehearsal with the singers, I had to do some intensive studying overnight to become familiar with the score. Komisarjevsky, knowing little English, produced the opera through a species of sign language, while chorus and principals tried hard to act like primitive Chinese, suspiciously in the old Savoyard manner of *The Mikado*. The performance was good, in spite of everything, but the work left the public rather chilled and bewildered. Later, in an orchestral version played as straight ballet, and with the first act eliminated, Diaghilev gave us an utterly transformed work, stunningly effective.

•

CHAPTER XXVII

THE day of the *Nightingale's* second performance a week later coincided with my first excursion into matrimony. Neither my future wife, the former Dorothy Millar, known to us as 'Boonie', nor I, planning a short Riviera visit, could have foreseen such a Stravinskyian interpolation in the blank fortnight we had originally set aside for the honeymoon; so, though we made an early morning trip that day to the ecclesiastical authorities, the journey to Antibes was indefinitely postponed. A slight delay in the ceremony was occasioned by my meeting the volatile Rivarde on his way to the College that morning, when he insisted on explaining at length a new and revolutionary method of *vibrato* he had just devised. He tucked the crook of my walking stick under his neck and leaned the end of it against a lamp-post as though playing an imaginary violin, much to the astonishment and bewilderment of passers-by and bus-drivers—always ready with a bright word! A mental picture of my bride and guests waiting at the church forced me to put an end to Rivarde's dissertation, which he none the less resumed later by telephone.

Early the following year—1920—Casella, the Italian composer, and I gave a joint concert of our works in Brussels, with the violinist André Mangeot[1] and Georges Pitsch, Belgian 'cellist, collaborating. Except for the respectful apathy of the Bruxellois and a sudden failure of the lights during my trio, the concert was chiefly and painfully memorable for a pair of patent-leather shoes I had bought that afternoon, my old ones having been left behind in London. At first reasonably comfortable, their true nature only became apparent as the concert started, and by the time

[1] Leader of the International String Quartet, of which Sir John Barbirolli was at one time a 'cellist.

the interval arrived I was hardly able to walk. In addition, as time went on, they developed an excruciating squeak, so that I played *Kaleidoscope* almost entirely without pedal effects. It remained for Casella, in his concluding trio, to atone for my deficiencies in this respect! A reception held afterwards at a restaurant next door was sufficient of an ordeal, but when at 1 a.m. no cabs of any kind were revealed on the streets, and we were faced with returning to the hotel on foot, I defied convention and walked back carrying those Belgian patent-leather horrors in my hand. A fine chill from the cold pavements resulted, but the relief was worth even that.

Later, Mangeot and I left for Paris to give the first performance of my *Lyric Poem* before an audience of the S.M.I. at the Salle Gaveau. Milhaud and Ravel appeared in the same programme, but the young radicals in the audience found all three of us boring, so reserved their chief plaudits for a vocal *scena* by a certain Oubouhov—all about a disembodied spirit, in the best Vorticist tradition. The composer both sang and played his *opus*, the vocal part consisting chiefly of moans and groans and ululations, culminating in a prolonged whistle. The lively audience, which had grown increasingly restless, took their cue from him and let go with a chorus of whistling and catcalls, much to the annoyance of the radicals, who started a near riot requiring the efforts of three *agents* to subdue—plus the stage electrician, who kept switching the house lights off and on to clear the hall. Erik Satie and Florent Schmitt, complete with pincenez and red ties, both lent a hand to the claque for Oubouhov, so much so that, with a mob of adherents of 'Les Six'[1] and 'L'Ecole d'Arceuil',[2] they ended by completely turning the tide in favour of the composer. It was all typically Parisian of the early 'twenties. The thought of it makes one wish that present-day audiences might show an equal zest for expressing their likes and dislikes. American and British concert halls could do with a lot of this sort of

[1] The composers Poulenc, Durey, Honegger, Milhaud, Auric, and Tailleferre.

[2] Principally the composer Sauget, who wrote like Gounod.

thing to counteract the lethargy which hangs over most of them whenever controversial music is played.

There was nothing controversial about the first of an annual series of Sunday afternoon concerts I conducted early in February at the Royal Albert Hall with the New Symphony Orchestra, but the audiences were apathetic, though polite. Indefinably depressing was that rather meagre public in a hall seating ten thousand, and not even Josef Hoffman playing the Rubinstein concerto—after a long absence from London—succeeded in arousing it from its Sunday stupor. He said to me after the concerto, 'They sleep well after their roast beef!' One missed the 'live' atmosphere of the old Queen's Hall Sunday concerts, and even though popular Landon Ronald had built up a loyal following at the Albert Hall, his ultra-conservative programmes made it difficult for others to perform novelties with any chance of success. The complacency of that South Kensington audience was—and for a long time continued to be—maddeningly irritating, a condition which the Victorian atmosphere of the hall did little to mitigate. I succeeded in arousing some degree of interest in a few new works at later concerts, but unlike Queen's Hall, the red plush upholstery and vast expanses of this public monument to the Prince Consort seemed more conducive to sleeping off a heavy Sunday lunch than absorbing fresh meals of contemporary music. As I write, the Proms, transferred there from the pathetic bombed-out skeleton in Langham Place, have changed all that: Henry Wood's pioneering spirit has finally ousted the ghosts of a stuffy past. . . .

Parsifal and Bizet's *Fair Maid of Perth* were the new productions in a spring season of opera at Drury Lane; Coates directed the first and Beecham the second, after which both operas were handed over to me (naturally, without benefit of orchestral rehearsal) for their third and fourth—and subsequent—performances respectively. I was somewhat nervous about conducting Wagner's masterpiece without having run through it with the orchestra; but at the actual performance, once through the prelude and into the first

148

act, my fears vanished, as the sumptuous work unfolded itself through the drama of its three wonderful acts. Though this opera had always deeply impressed me, I was unprepared for its moving nature, a quality which it seemed only someone actually conducting the work could possibly realize to the fullest extent. Stanford sat behind me during the whole evening, and afterwards came back to tell me how much he'd enjoyed the performance. So affected was he by the music that he burst into tears—something I'd never seen him do before! (I was much moved by the sight and had difficulty restraining my own.) 'Damned beautiful, me bhoy, but ye took the Grail march a mite too fast. Maybe though 'tis myself's been playing it too slow these last years. The Old Man's spirit surely hovered over ye this night.' And he wiped his glasses, took up his hat, and left. That was the last time I saw him.

My absorption during the performance was such that I hardly noticed the mishaps that befell some of Wagner's stage directions that evening. The stuffed swan killed by Parsifal that careened down on to the head of a super in the first act, necessitating the immediate removal of both swan and super. The spear, too, launched by Klingsor at the end of Act II, which remained quivering in the centre of its invisible wire, mid-stage, and had to be further impelled towards Parsifal by a forcible jerk till it came within his reach. But from the standpoint of sheer eventfulness, the *Parsifal* performance paled by comparison with that of Bizet's opera. Just prior to my taking over, Beecham (somewhat capriciously, it always seemed to me) decided to divert the overture to the middle of the opera and make sundry other cuts and alterations, concerning many of which—but not by any means *all*—I was only informed just before curtain time. Most important change of all—the transposition of the overture—was by a mysterious over-sight not communicated to me at all. The result was that I started conducting the overture at the beginning of the opera and the orchestra started playing something totally different. To those not 'in the know' this can best be likened

149

to the sensation of treading on a stair that isn't there, something we've all experienced at one time or another. I quickly recognized what the orchestra was playing (the prelude to the third act), and adjusted my beat accordingly, the concert-master meanwhile rising to give me a rapidly whispered explanation of the situation. But it was an unnerving experience, and I vowed to have Beecham's blood at the end of the act. Enquiry elicited, when I arrived backstage, that he had left ten minutes previously for Brighton, having remained in the theatre long enough to enjoy his little joke at my expense. . . .

CHAPTER XXVIII

THAT Drury Lane season carried a memory of other incidents, both potentially disastrous, in which I played an embarrassing part. *A Village Romeo and Juliet*, the beautiful and in some ways strangely un-operatic masterpiece of Delius, was having its second performance, and we had reached the last act, in which the lovers write *finis* to earthly suffering by scuttling their boat in the middle of the lake. This effect was extremely realistically achieved at Covent Garden by the simple process of lowering a portion of the stage, with the boat on it, at a given musical cue. The procedure had to be accomplished very slowly in order to give the lovers ample time to sing the concluding part of their final duet while the boat was going under. I promised Beecham, who was conducting, that I would give the stage-manager the cue at the right moment, whereupon the vessel would slowly start disappearing from view. It did, but four pages of score too soon, owing to my mistaking an identical phrase occurring earlier for the real stage-cue. Moreover, it seemed that once the process of lowering the hydraulic stage-bridge had started, there was no possibility of arresting it. It also seemed that never before had the bridge moved so quickly, so that, to the dismay of everyone concerned, the lovers were compelled to sing at least two pages of their duet from the submarine depths of the lake. This episode earned me a peppery rebuke from T.B., who, incensed by other mishaps —principally musical—during the performance, said, 'Next time, you conduct the damned thing yourself.' I did, and someone else gave the stage cues. Out of excessive caution, however, that person gave the fatal cue much too late, with the result that the boat started sinking only with the final curtain. I'm not at all sure but that my way wasn't dramatically the more effective! . . .

Two weeks later, during a performance of *Trovatore*, there occurred another contretemps, for which I disclaimed all responsibility. Strolling back-stage during the convent scene, I was suddenly confronted by the stage-manager, George King—usually a rather phlegmatic type—shouting, 'The organ! the organ! There's nobody to play the organ!' Unfamiliar with this opera, and not having been present at any of its rehearsals (mainly because I never did, and still don't, care very much for it), I was at a loss to account for King's sudden hysteria. He didn't leave me wondering for long, but just dragged me over to the Covent Garden organ and propped an open vocal score on the desk, from which I soon perceived that a resounding organ chord was due to be played in about five measures' time. I quickly pulled out all the stops in sight, and at what I judged to be the right moment, embarked on my Covent Garden début as organist. I was quite unprepared for the result. No sooner did the great sound issue forth than there appeared, from all quarters of the stage, *répétiteurs*, assistant conductors and all manner of lesser underlings who hurled themselves upon me and literally tore me away from the instrument. What George King hadn't known (and what I obviously couldn't possibly have been aware of) was that this particular section had been cut out that morning! Everyone in the orchestra pit—including T.B.—was convulsed with mirth at the accident, Mullings and Buckman on stage were completely nonplussed and for a time unable to continue their duet, and the audience gave itself up to loud merriment. King and I, both very red-faced at the end of the act, received a merciless 'ribbing' from all concerned. This eventually centred on the unfortunate stage-manager, after it was found that I had had no intention of deliberately sabotaging the act. But it taught me to stay miles away from back-stage operations of an unfamiliar opera, however great the inducement to participate.

Some weeks following the end of this season, Albert Sammons and his colleague, the late William Murdoch, played my new violin and piano sonata at Wigmore Hall.

MARIE GOOSSENS

SIDONIE GOOSSENS

These two lovable men and unequalled artists (never could England boast greater virtuosi) launched the work on a career of popularity which happily still continues, and they played it *con amore*: Sammons, with that luscious tone-quality which made the folk-tune in the slow movement sound so beautiful that I despair of ever hearing it played that way again. Murdoch, who had such feeling for ensemble-playing that he could be as self-effacing as a wraith and as assertive as a lion, put such warmth of colour into his playing that the blend of piano and violin fused them as one instrument. On countless occasions I have listened to these two men in a repertory ranging over the whole sonata literature, and I think there will never again be on any platform, anywhere, a more perfectly matched team, or one that reached artistry and depth of feeling in performance greater than did those unassuming, modest players. I have listened to all the great virtuosi, with names more famous than these Englishmen, teamed together for sonata appearances. With one or two exceptions, their performances have been haphazard, some-times slipshod, and almost invariably fortuitous. Sammons and Murdoch made the business of sonata-playing a thing of intimacy, long association, and constant study. A sonata for violin and piano isn't a violin piece with piano accom-paniment, nor a welter of pianism through which the violin barely penetrates; but alas! at the hands of many virtuosi who ought to know better, that's what you often get. A thousand pities that these Englishmen didn't leave a sheaf of recordings for posterity. Lionel Tertis, the man respons-ible for having brought the viola from ignominious obscurity to its present status as a virtuoso instrument, and Felix Salmond, who can put greater depths of meaning into a Brahms 'cello sonata than any living player, are two other Englishmen of similar calibre.

Opera having temporarily come to a halt, one or two of the principal members of our company decided to fill up the time before operatic activities were resumed in the autumn by putting on a production of *The Beggar's Opera*—chosen with no implication as to its title! Frederick Austin, one of our leading baritones, and a versatile, intelligent composer of much fine music, had taken the old songs of Gay's little classic eighteenth-century opera, and discreetly and tastefully devised beautifully harmonized accompaniments for them, to be played by a harpsichord and a handful of string-players. Frederick Ranalow was cast as the highwayman, McHeath; Austin himself and a small group of principals played subsidiary roles. A dozen highly attractive young women formed the picturesque collection of Mc-Heath's 'doxies', and Nigel Playfair produced the opera. Lovat Fraser's scenery and costumes set what in the U.S.A. is called an 'all-time high' for authentic eighteenth-century atmosphere. I promised to conduct the first four weeks of the production—if it ran that long. All concerned shared misgivings that the London public might find the opera little to its taste, especially as the diminutive Lyric Theatre, Hammersmith, which had been chosen as most suitable for the intimate character of the work, lay miles off the beaten track of West End theatreland. We opened on 5 June, and the piece ran for two and a half years. The first night ovation was such that it took half an hour to clear the theatre after the performance. The Press raved next morning, automatically setting in motion a great public pilgrimage that eventually became compulsory for every lover of beautiful theatre. The natives of Hammersmith gaped with wonder at the nightly influx of fame and fashion to their unpretentious suburb, and all connected with the venture found it impossible to believe that Fortune had so smiled on them. Admitted that good wine needs no bush, it all established beyond a doubt the unpredictability of the theatre. . . .

After a few weeks I relinquished my little orchestra to another conductor and went off to Harlech to finish a symphonic poem on which I had been busy for some time past. Called *The Eternal Rhythm*, it was one of those long, metaphysical things (scored for an enormous orchestra) which, in retrospect, seemed to combine all the worst clichés of Scriabine, Strauss, and the newer French school. I looked on it rather as a grandiose experiment in florid orchestration, but when it was produced at the Promenade Concerts in September it registered a big hit—much to my surprise.[1] I was curious to get the reaction of the newspapers, which all showed some caution in expressing definite opinions. Such comments as 'harmonically, we have to tread water a good deal' (*Daily Express*), 'Strange and often lovely orchestral effects produced with a minimum of noise' (*sic*) (*Evening Standard*) were almost noncommittal in their vagueness, and I concluded that the work had failed of its prime object—to *épater le bourgeois*. I therefore destroyed it six years later, and have regretted doing so ever since.

After this concert I returned to a winter routine of operatic touring, including eight weeks in Scotland, where I concentrated chiefly on improving my golf-game instead of writing music. The frugal atmosphere of Scotch theatrical lodgings was not in any way conducive to stirring up my exotic Muse. Besides which, the keen air of the Braid Hills course, near Edinburgh, and the Clyde country around Glasgow are a wonderful restorative after morning rehearsals in the stuffy atmosphere of theatre bars. (That's where you always have piano rehearsals in travelling companies when you can't get the stage. . . .)

[1] The Berliners, too—on a later occasion—liked it.

CHAPTER XXIX

SHORTLY after building his Harlech residence, G.D. acquired a London one. It was one of those large bright, detached houses on the north side of Holland Park,[1] of the sort known as double-fronted, with the main entrance giving into a hallway between two very large-sized front rooms. G.D. demolished the hallway, and turned the entire ground floor into a well-proportioned music-room. The street door opened directly into it; but, caring little for convention and having few visitors, the owner didn't mind that. His visits to London were so rare that when I asked him early in 1921 whether I might rent his studio-apartment over the mews at the end of the garden, he agreed. He also gave me the key to that big music-room in the main house, so that I might use it whenever I chose—which I often did.

Behind the Chinese light wood panelling of the room was installed an Aeolian pipe-organ, not as large as the Harlech one, but equally beautiful in tone quality. A concert grand piano and some chairs, all of the same wood as the wall panelling, comprised the only furnishings of the room. It should have been an inspirational place for composition, but, like all beautiful, large rooms, wasn't a good 'workshop', and I preferred my studio over the mews. The big room was the scene of many gatherings. One night I invited congenial friends there to meet Ravel, who was in London for a short visit. He had hardly been in the room two minutes before he spied the organ console, headed straight for it, and started experimenting with every sonority he could extract from the instrument. Celesta, chimes, harp and 'echo-organ' effects were his favourites, and he spent a good half-hour absorbed in what was for him a completely new revelation. Not even the arrival of Adrian Boult—pushing a bicycle through the front door from the street—roused the great little man from his absorption, and only later, when the Hardings brought

[1] Arthur Bliss lived nearby.

156

Manuel de Falla, Malipiero, and Jean-Aubry with them to join the party, could he be induced finally to abandon his new love. *'C'est épatant; inouie. Mais, mon cher, vous devez gagner un argent fou pour pouvoir installer une si belle orgue dans une pièce si magnifique.'* I quickly disabused him of this, reminding him that struggling musicians usually lived in back-garden studios, and that only a very generous landlord made possible the use of the music-room and its appurtenances. Malipiero, the Italian, and de Falla, the ascetic timid Spaniard (with his English Boswell, J. B. Trend, always in tow), also succumbed to that Aeolian organ. Malipiero in particular came back to Holland Park on several later occasions to sample it.

De Falla found its mechanics a little awesome, and in his meek Castilian French observed that it had *'une sonorité très sinistre'*. Looking at him, one wondered how he could have conceived such full-blooded music as that of *The Three-cornered Hat*, and, still more, how he ever left his peaceful home in remote Granada for the excitement of big cities like London and Paris. His second visit to Holland Park a few weeks later took place shortly after the birth of my eldest daughter, Anne. He insisted on seeing the baby and was so excited that he drank a toast to her in sherry, and called her Anita.

The month of May arrived and with it the crystallization of a daring idea. Operatic comings and goings for some months past had been less frequent and exciting than formerly, and I was beginning to realize that the routine of opera and concert touring was hampering my chief ambition —namely, to perform important contemporary music with a fine orchestra. Grateful for the experience and remuneration this routine had afforded me, I couldn't help but feel that the opportunity to enliven London's concert halls with some rousing performances of 'modern' music had finally arrived, if I could but find means to avail myself of it. The only stimulating musical event since the end of the war two years previously had been the return of the Diaghilev ballet to London with a handful of new ballets, such as *The Three-cornered Hat, Chout, Rossignol, Pulcinella*, and a revival—with new choreography by Massine—of *Le Sacre du Printemps*.

Listening to the scrappy, under-rehearsed playing of this last ballet at a performance early in the year, conducted by the sorely handicapped Ansermet (a superb musician), I resolved that Londoners should soon hear it played in the concert hall as it *should* be played—by a fine, adequately rehearsed orchestra of virtuosi. The time seemed ripe to give my scheme a trial, and after discussing it fully with Ibbs and Tillett, the concert agents, I decided to go ahead and find some backing for what would certainly prove a costly début in the field of concertizing. Recalling a previous promise of support for a similar idea from a well-to-do and musically enthusiastic business friend of mine in the North, I wrote an outline of my project to him, and asked for his support of it. To my intense surprise and gratification, he wrote immediately guaranteeing the whole affair—with the proviso that his part of it should receive adequate publicity if the concert proved successful! Armed with his letter, for the gentleman bore a reputable name, I showed it to my agents, and we decided to proceed with the venture. Queen's Hall was booked for 7 June, and the pick of London's orchestral virtuosi (one hundred and five of them, including my brother Leon and my sister-harpists, Marie and Sidonie) was engaged for the concert. There were five rehearsals. The posters and programmes—for which Edwin Evans wrote classic notes— were printed, and I secured full rights to the orchestral material of the works to be played at the concert. They were, in order of succession, first performances of a Spanish fantasy by the versatile Lord Berners; a prelude, *The Forgotten Rite*, by John Ireland, most fastidious of British composers; the now famous *La Valse*, by Ravel; and, finally, *Le Sacre du Printemps*[1].

A week before the concert I began to get a little uneasy about my Yorkshire friend's reluctance to send me the necessary cheque, which, according to our agreement, was to have been deposited in my bank ten days before the start of rehearsals. After repeated telegrams, I finally received—

[1] I had originally intended to make the programme an all-Stravinsky one, but in deference to my friend, Serge Koussevitzky, who had planned to feature Stravinsky's new wind-instrument symphony at a concert three nights after mine, I relinquished the idea.

two days before the first rehearsal—a letter from him stating that unforeseen circumstances and adverse business conditions suddenly compelled him 'with much regret' to withdraw his support from the venture. This laconic document gave no hint that the writer had any idea into what consternation and embarrassment I would be plunged by a last-minute cancellation which would deprive over a hundred musicians of a lucrative engagement.

It was a rather desperate situation, but not entirely hopeless, for I still had the better part of two days in which to borrow sufficient funds to meet the huge orchestral bill. My own slender budget certainly couldn't have stood any additional strain, and in those days I didn't even know the definition of 'collateral'. Only a rich, music-loving patron of the arts might possibly have been mildly interested in coping with this kind of emergency, but I was not on sufficiently intimate terms with such an individual. And, anyway, I mused, the eighteenth century—not the twentieth—was the era of musical patronage! Suddenly, in this connection, the name of Lord Howard de Walden occurred to me. I had heard of his interest in music and musicians, and, though I had never met him, impulsively and with a crushing sense of urgency decided to write to him. As eloquently as I could, I told him of my dilemma, and, with a fervent prayer that he might not have gone to the country, despatched a District Messenger with my letter, post haste to Belgrave Square. Within three hours another messenger returned with a note. It read:

My DEAR GOOSSENS,—Here is a cheque. Best of luck. DE WALDEN.

There must be a special word in the dictionary to describe an individual who will send a comparative stranger a cheque for five hundred pounds within two hours of being asked for it. I've forgotten what the word is, but I remember vowing at the time that, irrespective of whether the noble Lord cared if his generous impulse remained anonymous or whether he didn't, I would one day make it my business to put his deed on record. I herewith do so as grateful tribute to a gesture the like of which, in these days of loud-mouthed patronage, one could rarely hope to meet again.

QUEEN'S HALL.

Sole Lessees: MESSRS. CHAPPELL & CO., LTD.

An Orchestral Concert
of Contemporary Music

CONDUCTED BY

EUGÈNE GOOSSENS

TUESDAY, JUNE 7th, at 8.15.

PROGRAMME.

Spanish Fantasy - - -	*Lord Berners*
Prelude "The Forgotten Rite" - -	*John Ireland*
Choregraphic Poem "La Valse" - - -	*Ravel*

AND

FIRST CONCERT PERFORMANCE IN ENGLAND OF

"Le Sacre du Printemps"
STRAVINSKY.

(Tableaux de la Russie Païenne, en deux parties).

SPECIAL ORCHESTRA OF ONE HUNDRED & FIVE PERFORMERS.

TICKETS (including Tax) **Reserved, 24/-, 12/-, 5/9; Unreserved, 3/-, 2/4.**

May be obtained from Chappell's Ticket Office, Queen's Hall, and 50 New Bond Street; usual Libraries and of

Telephone: 4156 Mayfair.
Telegrams: "Organol, Wesdo, London."

IBBS & TILLETT, 19 Hanover Square, W. 1.

BAINES AND SCARSBROOK, LTD., PRINTERS, SWISS COTTAGE. N.W.6.

CHAPTER XXX

THE happenings of that summer evening at Queen's Hall a quarter of a century ago have passed into legend. An orchestral concert in June was, in those days, an unheard-of happening, so my big group of picked virtuosi was a tempting bait for an audience sated with the under-rehearsed pedestrianisms of winter orchestras. The current vogue for Stravinsky and the ballet made attendance at Queen's Hall that night almost a compulsory social event; and, going out on the platform to start the concert, I was greeted by that dream of all concert-givers—a full house. Word had gone around that the composer of the *Sacre* was expected any minute from Paris, but by the 'interval' he hadn't appeared. So after a successful first half, I decided to prolong interval time, hoping that the boat train wouldn't have been too long delayed. The audience forestalled my decision: to quote the facetious Mr. Philip Page in the *Evening Standard*:

Celebrities were three-a-penny, Mrs. Asquith, Bernard Shaw, Diaghileff, Arnold Bennett, Iris Tree, Sir Alfred Mond, and Karsavina were all admiring and admired. Before the main event (Stravinsky's *Sacre du Printemps*) people in funny clothes met in the corridor just to greet each other and the coming catastrophe [*sic*], Lord Berner's *Spanish Suite*, and Cyril Scott's velvet suit, were comparatively minor happenings.

After a twenty-five-minute break, during which the missing composer failed to appear, the audience finally resumed its seats, and, not daring to hold things up any longer, I returned to the stage to start the chief event of the evening. Just as I raised my stick to give the bassoon player his cue for the opening phrase, a movement in the dress circle caught my eye, and a trio of weary travellers—Stravinsky, Diaghilev, and Massine—crept into their seats. The suspense was broken, and the orchestra settled down to give

161

Londoners twenty-five minutes of ensemble-cum-virtuoso fireworks more dazzling, I venture to think, than anything so far heard in Queen's Hall. The last explosive chord of the 'Danse Sacrale' had barely erupted before the audience sprang to its collective feet and gave an exhibition of hysterical enthusiasm which put the fiercest demonstration of the Parisians quite in the shade. Next morning Robin Legge of the *Daily Telegraph*, in a long column, noted that—

since *Ein Heldenleben* first shocked a London audience many years ago, no such first performance has been heard in Queen's Hall. . . . The momentum of the second section is irresistible and terrifying. Apparently the young conductor is one of the coolest musical brains in England [In a previous issue I was the youth who wrote with cool efficiency!], and his control of this epic dance, the building up of his climaxes [etc., etc.] marks him out as a conductor, *pur sang*. [Father bristled with pride at this.] Belgium has given us a precious hostage in this young Londoner [and still more of this!] . . . The eleventh-hour arrival from Paris of Stravinsky was a happy accident, appreciated by everybody, and the ovations at the end of the performance were in keeping with an occasion which will surely be regarded as historic. . . . Bernard Reillie was the leader of the hundred and five performers who comprised the glorious orchestra.

Richard Capell, who later succeeded Legge on the *Telegraph*, wrote in the *Daily Mail*:

The orchestra [in the *Sacre*] gave an example of what really superior orchestral playing can sound like, an example rare and useful. . . . The performance was delayed for the presence of its composer, who arrived from Paris in the course of the evening and came at once to the hall. He was called to the platform, cheered and cheered again, a slight man of forty, the most innocuous exterior to house such dark powers of wizardry.

Mr. Fox Strangways, a rather narrow-minded type of Victorian critic that London at that time seemed unable to dispense with (they used to be either that or young things just down from Oxford who 'knew it all'), paid grudging tribute to the work in the august *Observer*. At the end of his piece, this occurs:

I asked Mr. Bernard Shaw, who had been indefatigable in attendance at performances and discussions of modern music all the week, to give the *Observer* readers the view of our oldest music critic, and he replied regarding this particular work: 'Mind, I am not to be understood as condemning it, but if it had been by Rossini, people would have said that there was too much "rum-tum" in it.'

162

This profound remark was only equalled by the same distinguished gentleman's observation at a lecture I gave on the *Sacre* the following week, when, after I invited questions, he stood up and asked, 'Why, Mr. Goossens, when I bought a seat for your concert last week, did you make me pay a guinea for a shilling's worth of music and twenty shillings' worth of noise?' I replied that whatever his opinion of the *Sacre*, I appreciated his contributing a guinea to my £600 bill of expenses. The exchange of courtesies thereupon came to an end, but not our friendship.

The reaction of all the other critics, including Messrs. Newman and Evans, those perennial sparring partners, was on the whole very laudatory, both concerning the works and their performance. Several papers commented on the fact that there were four members of the Goossens family on the platform—Leon playing first oboe, and Marie and Sidonie the two harps. They failed to mention the fact that several more were in the hall, including Father and Mother, who by that time had both acquired a startling taste for everything new in music. Mother indeed was heard to remark afterwards that this newfangled stuff acted like a bottle of champagne on her spirits. And it invariably did!

Only Peter Page in the *Standard* inferred with a slight flavour of sour grapes that—

the much-discussed concert of the season owed its prominence to the fact that a large section of the public seems to like to have its ears shocked as well as its legs pulled. . . . Stravinsky, who appeared at the close of the concert in a brown suit, and was hectically applauded, is a clever fellow. . . . Presumably no mistakes were made, but had the performance been a mass of errors, the result would have been no more ugly and no more beautiful. . . . I am aware that the catch-phrase of the twentieth century is 'beauty is only a relative term'. This is an argument used most frequently by those who find the most difficulty in creating anything beautiful. Starting crazes and startling fools are both easier jobs.

Mr. Page, a 'clever fellow' who frequently had to eat his own words, was obviously more 'startled' than he had realized!

My own emotions during the actual concert were strangely detached. I was aware that it was a success, that the public was reacting as I had hoped it would, that the orchestra was behaving like a high-precision aeroplane engine, and that I personally seemed to be functioning in an unusually responsible capacity very much as I had anticipated. (At no time did any thought of doing otherwise occur to me.) Only when our merry family supper party at the Eiffel Tower Restaurant had ended and the other members of the Goossens family had gone home did I begin to lose that sense of objective exhilaration which had stayed with me during the whole evening. And only then did the thought of further adventures into the exciting territories of the evening begin to suggest themselves to me.

Next morning the spontaneous telephone messages of a friend offering to back a second concert on the strength of Press reviews and the general enthusiasm of the public got a quick welcome from me, and three days later the *Daily Telegraph* announced the following:

It is pleasant to hear that in response to urgent requests Mr. Goossens will repeat the programme of last Tuesday at Queen's Hall on the 23rd of the month.

So a fortnight later, with the same orchestra and a slightly altered programme—*La Valse*, Stravinsky's symphony for wind instruments, my own *Eternal Rhythm*, and *Le Sacre*—the second concert took place at Queen's Hall. Again *Le Sacre* worked its spell, and though the attendance was rather smaller than before, the same scenes of enthusiasm followed the closing event of the evening.

CHAPTER XXXI

IT was only natural that I should now begin to investigate the possibilities of in some way keeping intact the great orchestra I had suddenly brought into being. The personnel of the London orchestras had suffered considerably during the war; moreover, the baneful 'deputy' system of old days still handicapped most of them. Under this system, a player could send a substitute player if he found it inconvenient to attend a concert or rehearsal himself. My own group included not only the élite of the other orchestras, but also a new, hand-picked younger element which imparted to it a zestful, more brilliant sonority than that of any of its older rivals. Partly, therefore, because of my reluctance to contemplate its disbandment, and partly because of my zeal to give Londoners the bigger and better doses of contemporary music I felt they should be getting, I sought ways of financing a projected series of 'modern' concerts to be held in the autumn of the year at Queen's Hall. At first the problem seemed insurmountable, and the sum required to guarantee such a series too astronomical to contemplate. Yet a week later the solution cropped up without my having lifted a finger about it.

An invitation to spend a week-end at Lord Lathom's Lancashire home arrived just as my wife and I were on our way to Harlech for a vacation. 'Ned' Lathom, whose passion for the theatre and whose financial ventures in it made him one of the best-known figures in London theatrical life, had impulsively telephoned me the day after my first concert offering to guarantee the expenses of a second one. I accepted with alacrity, and, as already recorded, duly gave the concert; not, however, without some wonderment at his sudden interest in highbrow music as contrasted to West End revues. And now, over the breakfast table at

Blythe Hall, he suddenly said, 'Why don't we give some more concerts with that orchestra of yours?' I was alone with him, and, overcome with astonishment, said, 'What do you mean by "we"?' 'Well,' he said, 'I think I could interest a sufficient number of friends to guarantee a short season, and see whether the London public wants the sort of thing we could give them. That orchestra simply mustn't disintegrate!' I said, 'I thought you were only really interested in theatrical shows.' 'I am,' replied Ned; 'but after being at Queen's Hall the other night I thought I'd like to try my hand in the concert field.' Thereupon, the generous though by no means over-wealthy Earl of Lathom, armed with pencil and paper, and fired with a new enthusiasm, proceeded to write down a long list of subscribers to his guarantee fund, thereby launching himself—and me—into a scheme fraught with many and varied perils. A few weeks elapsed before he assured me that sufficient progress had been made in the matter of securing guarantors to warrant our proceeding with arrangements for the series.[1] Four concerts were therefore announced, to be given on the following dates and with the following programmes:

QUEEN'S HALL CONCERTS

Programmes

27 October 1921

Fanfares (selected from a series of Fanfares specially composed by contemporary musicians for the revue *Fanfare*)

De Falla, Satie, Prokofiev, Harty, Goossens, Milhaud, Roussel, and White

Fugue in C Minor	Bach-Elgar
Tone Poem: The Garden of Fand	Arnold Bax
Pastorale	Arthur Honegger
Suite: Beni Mora	Gustav Holst
Symphony No. 1 in C Minor	Brahms

(Substituted for Stravinsky's *The Song of the Nightingale*.)

9 November 1921

Overture: The Siege of Corinth	Rossini
Mêlée Fantasque	Arthur Bliss

[1] He was over-optimistic, as events unfortunately showed.

166

Symphonic Poem, *The Builders of Joy*	F. R. Heath
Alborada del Gracioso	Ravel
Five Orchestral Pieces	Schönberg
Tone Poem: Thus spake Zarathustra	Strauss

23 November 1921

Fugue in C Minor	Bach-Elgar
Fantasie: The Wild Sea-Fowl (from *Dylan*)	Holbrooke
Symphonic Poem, Prometheus	Liszt
Aubade	Cyril Scott
Suite: El Amor Brujo	Manuel de Falla
Rondes de Printemps	Debussy
Symphony: Antar	Rimsky-Korsakoff

12 December 1921

Further Selection of Fanfares	Bax, Harrison, Milhaud, Malipiero, Poulenc, and Wellesz
Suite in G for Organ, Oboe, and Strings	Bach-Wood
Symphonic Rhapsody, Mai Dun	John Ireland
Oriente Immaginario	Malipiero
Symphonies d'instruments a vent	Stravinsky
Le Sacre du Printemps	Stravinsky

Those introductory fanfares at the first concert were written for a short-lived periodical called *Fanfare*, edited by my friends Philip Heseltine and Leigh Henry. The suggestion of securing original fanfares from contemporary composers for inclusion in each number was one for which I must now modestly claim credit (Mr. Leigh Henry notwithstanding), just as I then claimed priority of performance. The fanfares played were as follows:

1. Manuel de Falla, *Fanfare pour une Fête*, for two trumpets, tympani, and side-drum.
2. Eric Satie, *Sonnerie pour reveiller le bon gros roi des singes* (*lequel ne dort pas*), for two trumpets.
3. Serge Prokofiev, *Fanfare for Three Trumpets*.
4. Hamilton Harty, *Fanfare for a Revel*, for four trumpets.
5. Eugene Goossens, *Fanfare for a Ceremony*, for four trumpets and side-drum.
6. Darius Milhaud, *Petit Fanfare*, for trumpet behind scenes, viola, cello, and percussion.
7. Albert Roussel, *Fanfare pour un Sacre Paien*, for four trumpets, and tympani.
8. Felix White, *Fanfare for a Challenge to Accepted Ideas*, for full wood, brass, and percussion.

The following appeared in the programme as a footnote:

The idea of the present series of fanfares originated with Leigh Henry, who, noting the more condensed forms of drama and choreography, desired to experiment whether or no the varied contributions of contemporary musicians in the given shape of a fanfare could not at least produce the germ of a type of sympathetic prelude capable of use as an introductory piece at the commencement of a concert, spectacle or ceremony, and which would approximate to the character of an epigram or an aphorism in literature, and which would avoid the extended nature of the accepted overture form with its architectonic development which was generally of too portentous character to be suitable for use in a programme of, for instance, the modern chamber orchestra type.

(That sentence, devised by Mr. Leigh Henry himself, undoubtedly takes a prize as one of the longest non-stop pieces of English on record.)

In spite of all anticipation, it must be said that neither preliminary guarantees nor subscription lists for my series of concerts were very encouraging. Indeed, the hall was barely half sold before the first concert, though I was hoping against hope that there would be a considerable box-office sale for the first night. Here I was again disappointed. Ned Lathom had obviously been over-sanguine. Nevertheless, Queen's Hall was about three-quarters full for the opening concert, which passed off with great enthusiasm, and at which Elgar and one or two of the other composers represented on the programme came on to the stage to receive ovations from the audience. The programme was to have concluded with the first concert performance of Stravinsky's *Song of the Nightingale*, but to gild the pill of overmuch contemporary music, and to bolster the sagging subscription list, I substituted at the last moment the C minor symphony of Brahms. Next morning R.C., in the *Daily Mail*, commented on the concert:

Mr. Goossens and his picked orchestra gave us a wonderful concert last night at Queen's Hall—the first of a series, the rest of which ought to be overcrowded, else Londoners indeed will prove themselves slow to know a good thing. After a bright, challenging opening with some fanfares came Sir Edward Elgar's new orchestral version of a Bach organ fugue. . . . The audience demanded it twice over, and Sir Edward, for the second time this week, was called to the Queen's Hall platform and acclaimed. Bach's career has taken a new turning! Superb performances and the cunning arrangement of the programme gave ideal relief both to the profuse and dreamy beauty of Mr. Arnold Bax's *Garden of Fand*, its author's master work, and to the extraordinarily bold, brilliant *Beni Mora* of Mr. Gustav Holst.

The *Evening Standard* said:

> Almost the only fault in the concerts given by Mr. Goossens is that they provide too much to be taken in at one time, not so much in quantity—this is considerable—as in quality. The experiment of the Fanfares was a mixed success, but it was an amusing opening to a great concert.

The second concert coincided with a thick fog—a real 'London particular'—which prevented half the audience even *finding* Queen's Hall, leave alone occupying a seat in it. What should have been one of the biggest crowds of the series turned out to be a painfully thin one, which didn't prevent R.C. heading his *Daily Mail* notice, 'Lively night at Queen's Hall'. It proceeded:

> The Goossens concert last night at Queen's Hall—such music-making, and some music, too—so that when it is all talked about to-day, 'Why didn't I make the effort to chance the fog?' hundreds of back-sliders will be saying. For this is an orchestra. . . . The music: Rossini, *Siege of Corinth* Overture proved not at all dead and buried, but the biggest bit of gaiety, laughing at time (it is eighty years old) and fog. Arthur Bliss's latest *Mêlée* thrusts and parries with a Russian weapon held in a good English fist, a bold, well practised fist, and this time there is the beauty of serious strokes in the mêlée. John Heath's *The Builders of Joy*. These builders are children of sorrow, with a Celtic aphorism. Their joy, according to Mr. Heath, is granite built on hills, but scantily sunlit. But again, a fist, an undoubted fist. Schoenberg, *Five Orchestral Pieces*. Nature's music: wind in the trees, stockbrokers, someone being run over by a bus; there is music in this, this is music, says Schoenberg. Rhetoric go hang! The five pieces give you in twenty minutes the music of most events mentioned in to-day's *Daily Mail*, without artistic titivation. And Strauss, *Zarathustra*? A man of gifts, and the greatest of these is cheek though he can score a C-major chord, and then would have us believe that his cheek keeps the rest really going. No nonsense with soloists last night, . . . etc.

By the third concert of the series, that small minority, the 'musical public', showed signs of really paying us some attention. The 'nobility and gentry' had so far shown a disappointing interest in proceedings, much to Lord Lathom's (and my) chagrin, for we had counted heavily on their subscriptions to atone for an alarmingly small guarantee fund. My late June symphony concert had intrigued them, but those fashionable and sporadic enthusiasms of the London summer season weren't quite hardy enough for transplanting to the murky winter months. So that while the pit and gallery were thronged, circle and stalls showed depressingly empty spaces. With all society's vaunted interest in the new, that eternally small coterie of cheap-seat enthusiasts was the only one which showed any concern for my contemporary exercises. Like my grandfather on a much earlier and similar occasion, I was for bringing the series to a premature conclusion, but other counsels prevailed, and with a varied programme the concert took place before a small, enthusiastic audience. Both Elgar and Howard de Walden were present, the one to hear a repetition of his orchestration of a Bach fugue, and the other to hear an excerpt from his opera, for which Holbrooke had composed the music. I had resurrected the *Prometheus* of Liszt for the occasion, a work described by a gossip-writer in the *Daily Sketch* as 'a novelty by the Ungarian Liszt'. Cyril Scott's *Aubade*, Debussy's *Ronde de Printemps*, and the Bach fugue were the hits of the concert, proof of the eclecticism of the audience.

A repetition of the *Sacre* and some additional publicity brought the largest crowd of the series to the fourth and last concert in early December. The programme opened with the following selection of Fanfares:

1. Arnold Bax, *Fanfare for a Hosting at Dawn*, for wood, brass, and percussion.
2. Julius Harrison, *Fanfare for a Masked Ball*, for four trumpets.
3. Darius Milhaud, *Petite Fanfare*, for trumpet behind the scenes, viola, cello, and percussion.
4. Malipiero, fanfare for four horns, four trumpets, tympani and side-drum.
5. Poulenc, fanfare for the fifth act of *Romeo and Juliet*, for clarinet, bassoon, brass, contrabass, and percussion.
6. Wellescz, fanfare for six trumpets and tympani.

The programme followed with the suite in G by Bach, arranged and orchestrated by Sir Henry Wood; the first performance of John Ireland's symphonic rhapsody, *Mai Dun*; some little pieces called *Oriente Imagginario* by

Malipiero; and the *Wind Instrument Symphony* by Stravinsky. After the intermission, the *Sacre* (which the orchestra could now practically play in its sleep) rang the curtain down, to a tumult of cheering, on as eventful a series of programmes and as fine an orchestra as I ever hope to conduct. Twice, on subsequent occasions, and under other auspices, the Goossens Orchestra appeared at Queen's Hall, but except for the major portion of its personnel being later incorporated into the newly re-conditioned London Philharmonic, it permanently ceased to function in the cause for which it was primarily conceived—the virtuoso performance of great contemporary music.

If those who had first spoken fair words of support to us had kept their pledges, both a worthwhile idea and a worthwhile organization might have been permanently added to the none too crowded panorama of London's music.

CHAPTER XXXII

Years ago, as a small wide-eyed boy, I sat behind my father at a Carl Rosa Opera rehearsal in the Shakespeare Theatre, Liverpool, watching the musicians in the orchestra pit, when suddenly Father rapped on his desk, and something like this ensued:

'A flat, first clarinet!'

'It's B flat in the part, Mr. Goossens.'

'Excuse me, Mr. Gomez, it should be A flat.'

'When I played this opera under your father, I always played a B flat here.'

'I don't care what you played under my father. I want an *A* flat!'

'But Mr. Goossens ———'

'*Sacré nom d'un chien! Qu'est ce que vous . . .*' etc.; and Father's voluble French drowns out the Spanish imprecations of Señor Gomez. The rehearsal proceeds, and later, good friends, the two emerge from the stage door arm-in-arm, and Father introduces the waiting young Eugene III to the clarinet player.

'Well,' says Manuel Gomez, patting my head, 'so *this* is the youngster! And what are you going to be when you grow up?'

'A conductor, of course!'

'*Mon dieu!* To think that I might live long enough to curse a *third* generation of Goossens!'

He did—in October 1921. Shortly before the first of my series of concerts the management of the still active Carl Rosa Company invited me to 'guest-conduct' certain performances during their autumn season of opera at Covent Garden. My father having long since severed his connection with the company, and opera elsewhere being temporarily in a state of suspended animation, I accepted; and agreed to direct all the Wagner performances, *Tristan*, *Mastersingers*, *Lohengrin*, *Tannhäuser*, and two complete cycles of the *Ring*, plus a revival of a prize-winning work by Dr. Naylor called *The Angelus*, with *Butterfly*, *Aïda*, and *Pagliacci* thrown in for good measure. Except for a well-trained chorus, the singers failed to equal in calibre those of the Beecham company, and, like the Carl Rosa orchestra (considerably augmented by London players), were hardly up to Covent Garden standards.

The season opened with *Lohengrin*, and during the dress rehearsal I stopped to adjust the wood-wind balance.

'Too loud, clarinets.'

'It's marked *mezzo-forte*, Mr. Goossens.'

'Excuse me, Mr. Gomez, but you're playing it *forte*.'

'Well, I've always played it that way. . . .' (I waited for the ominous words, 'for your father', but a merciful Providence halted them).

'Now, this time—*just for me*—give me a real *mezzo-forte!*'

'But Mr. Goossens. . . .'

'Gracious Heaven!' I shouted. 'Let's get on with the rehearsal!'

History had repeated itself, almost verbatim. I'll even wager the crusty old man and I walked out of the stage-door arm-in-arm just to keep the record straight. Manuel's brother, Francis, the bass clarinet player, was also in the orchestra, and playing under the third generation. The performance of *Lohengrin* was adequate, but the amount of rehearsal time allotted me throughout the season was definitely not, and when the *Morning Post* critic wrote next morning that 'the efforts of Mr. Goossens at the conductor's desk were a stimulating influence', I was at a loss to know whether he was indulging in masterly understatement or plain sarcasm. The season evoked some of Ernest Newman's choicest invective in the pages of the *Sunday Times*, usually at the expense of the singers, and invariably of the orchestra. I remember that his remarks regarding the Rhine-maidens and the horn players in the *Rhinegold* (though no longer extant) caused great consternation, and put one horn player to bed with a nervous breakdown.

Mention of the *Rhinegold* brings to mind a typical incident connected with its Carl Rosa performance. A certain Mr. B., a wealthy young amateur with a tolerable voice, and anxious for operatic experience, was 'engaged'—at his own urgent request—by the company's manager to sing a small part. This character only appears towards the end of the opera, and his contribution towards the general ensemble is almost negligible. Mr. B. always arrived at rehearsals in a large silvery Rolls-Royce, a heavy fur coat, and armed with a variety of nasal sprays. He was pompous and invariably late, but in view of his insignificant musical contribution to the evening this was overlooked, specially as the C.R.O. officials hoped he might help out with the deficit at the end of the season. The night of Mr. B's début arrived, and the opera had progressed to the point where the public could appraise the newcomer's worth, when, on looking up to give him his musical cue, I quickly saw that he was not among those present on the stage. (Froh's lines therefore went unsung.) Wondering what mishap had befallen him, I proceeded, and it was only when we reached the final pages of the 'Entry of the Gods' that I noticed he had finally joined his brother gods on the rainbow bridge—too late to be of musical help and comfort. Asked afterwards to account for his absence, he calmly said, 'I thought I had much more time before my cue came, so I went upstairs to the treasurer's office to get my salary!' It should be noted that he did so on that occasion for the first—and last—time!

Other similar low-lights of the season hazily come to mind: three frowsy stage trumpeters in *Aïda*, all wearing pince-nez; the steamy breath of the *Siegfried* dragon condensing over the orchestra pit; an over-age Tristan trying to disguise his lack of voice by singing up-stage into the back-cloth; Wolfram gazing raptly at the dowdy chorus and singing, 'How beats the heart to see such beauty rare!'; the Cockney supers in the finale of the *Mastersingers*, and last, but not least, the dreadful, dreary platitudes of Naylor's Christmas-card 'Angelus'. (It won a prize!)

On the whole, though, the principal performers were well up to the standard of certain Continental opera houses, though rehearsals were of the sketchiest and results, therefore, not of the most polished. The older members of the chorus, some of whom had sung under Grandfather's baton in the 'eighties, made up in routine enthusiasm and training what they lacked in voice. One veteran, after a performance of *Pagliacci*, told me he had sung in well over a thousand performances of that opera since its first production in English by the company. (His automatic gestures epitomized those of every chorister in the world.) Yet though in many respects this was not the Carl Rosa of palmier—and sterner—days, there was something rather thrilling and a little touching in the spectacle of the old company braving the critical atmosphere of Covent Garden, impervious to the ravages of time and the competition of younger organizations. I felt privileged to have been allowed to have a hand in the workings of a group so long identified with my family, so that, going on stage for my curtain call after *Götterdämmerung* on the final night, I linked hands, not with Siegfried and Hagen, but with the shade of my Grandfather and the spirit of his son—the latter being corporeally present to witness the performance.

Besides opera-conducting and concert-giving there were other activities that autumn which made it in many ways a memorable one. The Albert Hall Sunday afternoon concerts had resumed their sleepy course, and on the occasion of one of these, which I conducted in November, London was visited by a repetition—only worse—of the terrific fog which so obliterated my second Queen's Hall concert a week or so earlier. Because of the thickness of the fog, at least a dozen members of the Albert Hall orchestra failed to appear in time for the concert, and the audience of a mere five hundred —in a hall seating ten thousand—were barely visible from the stage. Noel Coward came to the concert with me, and after a perilous journey on foot all the way from Earl's

Court, we arrived at the hall, choked and blinded, to discover we couldn't find an entrance door to it. Two complete circuits of the enormous building were necessary before we were able, by tapping with a cane, to find the orchestra door. Those familiar with a real London fog will know I don't exaggerate. Noel sat in a box and, lulled by the strains of a practically invisible orchestra, gave himself up to a little creative work, emerging from the concert into the Stygian night with words and music of his song, 'Russian Blues', practically complete. Sung to the tune of the 'Maiden's Dance' from *Prince Igor*, the original, 'My heart just loosens when I'm listening to Mr. Goossens', rhymes prettily—but the published version was altered, for the better!

About this time Vaughan Williams resigned from the conductorship of the Handel Society, a body of amateur ladies and gentlemen who publicly two or three times a year sang and played, usually with more zest than accuracy, choral and orchestral works by almost any other composer than Handel. (I *did* once conduct *Acis and Galatea* with them.) I was offered, and of course duly accepted, the vacant post, which entailed some pleasantly informal weekly rehearsals with a group of very charming people and the conducting of some rather nerve-racking concerts. At the latter, usually given either at Queen's Hall or the Royal College of Music, chorus and orchestra would suddenly be augmented by a number of strangers (absentees from earlier rehearsals), whose lack of familiarity with the matter in hand led to blemishes of performance, caustically commented upon in next morning's papers. The Earl of Balfour, who was President of the Society, once observed in his charmingly languid way, after a performance of the *Spectre's Bride*: 'A great pity, a *very* great pity, Mr. Goossens, that the sartorial elegance of the chorus wasn't better reflected in its rendering of Dvorak's little masterpiece!' My former dentist, Samuel Timms, was an active member of the tenor section, and often took me along to meetings of the Westminster Glee Club, another organization in which he enjoyed membership. At these meetings we sang at sight madrigals and catches—as lustily as they ever did in the good old days.

Amateur activity in all musical forms has always been one of the characteristics of a country ignorantly dismissed as unmusical by the superior persons of other nations. For if the number of amateur choruses, glee clubs, orchestras, band and string quartets existing in England up to the outbreak of the war were computed, they would be found to outnumber easily those of any other land. Not for nothing did the English inherit a centuries-old tradition which proclaimed an ability to take part in consorts of viols, part-songs, rounds, glees, and the rest as one of the outstanding virtues of gentle living.

CHAPTER XXXIII

ONE evening in October I went to dine with Mrs. Mathias, a strong champion of the ballet, to meet W. A. Propert, who was just completing an expensively designed and illustrated tome called *The Russian Ballet in Western Europe*. (He persuaded me to contribute a chapter to it on 'The Music of the Ballets' and re-wrote some of it himself, on the ground of my unpolished literary style!) After dinner, Diaghilev came in, and either by design or accident immediately buttonholed me on the subject of conducting his forthcoming production of Tchaikovsky's *Sleeping Princess* at the Alhambra Theatre. The idea was appealing, but I reminded him that I was already committed to a great deal of concert, opera, and choral conducting at that particular time. He waved aside the objection, however, by promising to engage a second conductor who would direct alternate performances with me. On learning that he had in mind the admirable Gregor Fitelberg, I agreed, though it seemed a pity that Ansermet had ceased to be the Ballet's regular conductor, and couldn't therefore collaborate.

It must be said that many of Diaghilev's friends viewed his coming venture with some misgiving, for the good reason that the London public had been accustomed to hearing three different ballets an evening rather than one long work. But Diaghilev argued that his departure from tradition was justified. This was the most classic of all ballets, lasting a full evening, with the world's greatest dancers, new scenery, costumes of unparalleled splendour, and a large orchestra. Altogether as lavish a spectacle as London would ever witness —greater, said Diaghilev, than the original 1890 production in St. Petersburg. The classic Petipa choreography was to be used; a sign-record of it had been faithfully transcribed and preserved by Sergeef from the original production.[1] Nijinsky's sister Bronislava was engaged to devise some interpolated dances (including the 'Three Ivans') and some of Russia's greatest dancers—Trefilova, Spessivtseva, Egorova and Vladimiroff—were imported to thrill London's balletomanes. Leon Bakst, in spite of contract difficulties with Diaghilev, finally consented to design the scenery and costumes; they still remain among the best examples of great stage *décor*.

As the first night approached, Diaghilev, who had experienced heart-breaking delays and difficulties over the production, became tensely apprehensive about his experiment of giving Londoners a long run of a single ballet. He was also deeply committed financially, as the proprietor of the theatre had advanced a large sum which was to be repaid weekly out of receipts. The preliminary expenses of the production had been staggering. 2 November arrived, and with it a brilliant audience for the première. Everything went well up to the end of the second act, where a great effect of scenic transformation, the growing of the magic forest, was to provide the thrill of the evening. On this occasion the forest started to grow, and almost immediately there was a horrible sound of splintering, rending wood. I looked up to see painted canvas and wooden frames hopelessly snarled, and instead of a scene of incomparable beauty the curtain fell on meaningless wreckage. An outburst of applause from the audience spoke volumes for its sympathetic reaction, and, although things proceeded without incident after the débris had been cleared, the mishap created an ominous effect impossible to dispel for the rest of the evening.

After the performance I found Diaghilev completely inconsolable over what he looked upon as an ill-fated occurrence. In spite of everyone's reassurances, he refused to believe that the accident, which need never have happened had the theatre possessed up-to-date machinery,

[1] Much of the divertissement, *Aurora's Wedding* (dances taken from the *Sleeping Princess* and familiar to all Ballet lovers to-day), consists of Petipa's original choreography.

boded anything but ill for the future. In this he proved right, for the attendance began to fall off at the end of three weeks, and, in spite of everything Diaghilev could devise to stave off the inevitable, it steadily declined, until by the end of January it had dwindled to a mere handful. What feats of financial legerdemain he and his managers performed to keep the enormously expensive show operating over a period of thirteen weeks few of us ever realized at the time. I remember how my heart sank as, at each of my successive performances, I counted the meagre audience before starting the ballet, and marvelled at a public that could spurn such an artistic feast. How different things were ten years later, when the mere name 'ballet' brought the fans flocking to the most trivial entertainment!

At the beginning of February 1922 I conducted the last performance—ironically enough, before a capacity audience, which, to atone for the sins of omission of its absent brethren, gave ovations to all concerned. On stage at the last curtain-call, tiny Lopokova plucked roses from her bouquet for me, and the stalwart *régisseur*, Grigoriev—still today the veteran of old Diaghilev days—hugged me, with tears in his eyes. Diaghilev never heard those last-night plaudits. He was in Paris, seeking means to avert the threatened disintegration of his company. He found them in the shape of a good sized cheque from his generous supporter, the Princesse de Polignac, just in time to give him enough pocket money to enable him to eat at his favourite restaurant instead of a cheap *bistro*, but too late to save his favourite black pearl studs. . . . I said '*Au revoir*' to the ballet and to my colleague, Fitelberg, with mixed feelings of regret and mild exhaustion.

A string of varied activities had proved rather too arduous for comfort, as a list of ten consecutive conducting days taken from my diary will show:

October

    Thursday 27: First Goossens Concert at Queen's Hall.
    Friday 28: *Tannhäuser* at Covent Garden.
    Saturday 29 and Sunday 30: Rehearsals at Covent Garden.
    Monday 31: *Mastersingers*.

Tuesday 1: *Lohengrin.*
Wednesday 2: Opening night, Russian Ballet.
Thursday 3: Ballet.
Friday, 4: Lecture on Contemporary Music.
Saturday, 5: *Carmen* matinée, Covent Garden. At night, Russian Ballet.

It continued this way till Christmas, and though my ballet performances had averaged only four a week, the saccharine strains of Tchaikovsky had distinctly begun to pall long before January 1922 came along.

Robin Legge, in the *Daily Telegraph*, summed up the old year as *annus mirabilis* for young British musicians. Only a few weeks prior to this I had conducted a concert of the British Music Society in an all-British programme, consisting entirely of works by Holbrooke, Scott, Holst, Vaughan Williams, and this writer. The house was full, but before 1914 you could not have sold a single seat for such a programme. Even the august Musical Association, a stronghold of conservative opinion, if ever there was one, swallowed my paper on 'Contemporary Developments in Music', which I read to its members at Novello's publishing house in Wardour Street. It wasn't easy for them to digest some of my arguments, but when Sir Ivor Atkins, organist of Worcester Cathedral, observed that 'he, for one, would never be able to swallow half this modern rubbish', he echoed the reactionary point of view of all the church organists in the room. When I remarked that the impressionism of the day could be laid chiefly at Debussy's door, the Rev. H. Cart de Lafontaine acidly observed that he had always attributed it to Mendelssohn!

Those of us who were in the know had been anticipating a statement which appeared in the London Press about this time concerning a new enterprise launched by former singers of the now defunct Beecham Opera Company. (The activities of the latter had unavoidably terminated some eighteen months previously, to the intense regret of every admirer of Beecham's great work in the cause of English opera.) The new company was known as the

British National Opera Company, and the *Daily Mail* observed:

> It will be of deep interest to see how far they manage to repair the sad gap that was made in England and English musical affairs by the cessation of the Beecham enterprise in 1920. . . . The company will command the sympathy of all beholders on this ground; that its members, the pick of English singers, acquired operatic technique and a wide repertory by great talent and persevering labour, only to be disappointed of the full proofs of success by an occurrence which was not in any way their fault. The performances in the North next month will show how far is justified this daring project of running opera by a committee rather than by the one despotic head always heretofore considered necessary in the opera house."

Three months later I conducted the opening *Tristan* of the company's London season at Covent Garden, a performance which should have set at rest any misgivings the *Daily Mail* might have entertained regarding the new company's standards. Meanwhile, Covent Garden had become the centre of strong rumours. Chief of these was that—horror of horrors—it was to be turned into a movie-theatre. Lovers of the dignified old house quailed at the mere idea. True, the theatre had been used for nothing better than a storehouse ever since the start of the war, but it was hoped that the syndicate would have it revert to its original uses as soon as a suitable tenant was forthcoming. When the latter turned up in the person of Mr. Walter Wanger, head of United Artists—of Hollywood, U.S.A.—who announced through the Press his intentions of opening a short season of super-films at the Royal Opera House, Londoners knew that the rumours had been well founded. And when he announced that the music for the films would be furnished by no less a body than the august London Symphony Orchestra they knew that the old order was indeed going to undergo a change!

CHAPTER XXXIV

THE day after the Press interview with Wanger, I was surprised to receive a telephone call from him, requesting a meeting. Over lunch at the Berkeley he explained that he wanted me to arrange and conduct the musical setting for two or three full-sized pictures, beginning with the first London showing of *The Three Musketeers*, with Douglas Fairbanks, Senr., as star performer. There were to be two performances daily, and sixty-five members of the London Symphony Orchestra were to be engaged. The music was to be drawn exclusively from the symphonic repertoire, in the best traditions of the great orchestra engaged to perform it. The idea was a novel one, not without possibilities, and I consented.

It must be remembered that up to that time, long before the coming of the sound film, the average movie orchestra was a diminutive and rather pitiable affair, even in the largest English cinemas. As for the type of music used to accompany films, the less said the better. The possibilities of combining symphonic music of the highest quality with the best contemporary films seemed therefore endless, and even the somewhat questionable taste involved aroused no scruples whatsoever in my mind, especially in the light of contemporary practice. So with the help of my late brother-in-law, Frederick Laurence, then in charge of the amazing Goodwin and Tabb music library, I started to devise a continuous eighty-minute accompaniment to the exploits of Mr. Fairbanks and his dashing companions. This led to the discovery of much little-known, and, in some cases, undeservedly neglected music. (I consistently tried to avoid using the familiar symphonic repertoire, though such things as a fragment of the finale from Tchaikovsky's *Sixth*

Symphony fitted a duelling sequence to a T. and Saint-Saëns *Phaeton* is the classic prototype of all horse-back chases.) My happiest and most useful discovery was one August Enna, a prolific—and soporific—nineteenth-century composer whose music provided an inexhaustible reservoir of tedious but appropriately varied symphonic accompaniments. It fitted anything, and also conveyed a spurious impression of great emotional depth, making it very suitable for my purpose. It also proved completely anonymous and unidentifiable in performance. If, at any future time, the 'grand manner' of orchestral movie accompaniments returns to relieve us of the clichés of Hollywood's film composers, let me commend—in the Breitkopf and Haertel edition—Mr. August Enna's numerous, indescribably weary, completely unknown symphonies.

Walter Wanger's courageous venture duly opened to a medium-sized house. My sixty-five players, the flower of the L.S.O., produced a noble, well-rehearsed sound from the pit, providing in the process a miniature anthology of much of the world's great music. Special racks had to be provided to accommodate the mass of music performed during the show. The 'deputy' system flourished untrammelled, and Covent Garden became the Mecca of those musicians periodically at liberty for an occasional afternoon's or evening's engagement. It is safe to assume that by the end of the run very few orchestral players in London had not seen Douglas Fairbanks in *The Three Musketeers*. Not without cause was the story told in those days of the conductor, who, preparing a concert with a London orchestra, had been confronted at each successive rehearsal by a constantly changing personnel. In desperation, at the last rehearsal, he pointed to a venerable double-bass player. 'There, at any rate, is one gentleman who faithfully attended all the rehearsals!' 'Yes,' replied the oldster, 'but I can't come to the concert!'

The cinematograph in the gold-and-red-plush atmosphere of Covent Garden was something of an anachronism, but the splendour of the musical accompaniment cushioned the shock of it. But fine film though it proved, *The Three Musketeers* couldn't draw the London public to the inconveniently located Royal Opera House, and *Atlantide* (a superb French film for which I devised the musical setting) followed the Fairbanks picture. The public still didn't show signs of much additional interest, so *Atlantide* gave way to a super-film with the all-embracing title, *Love*, which proved to be a romantic American thriller with a sensational automobile wreck as its high spot. The events leading up to this culminating disaster in the lives of two young products of the early 'twenties were splendidly served, musically speaking, by the finale of the indispensable August Enna's *Fourth Symphony*. This was timed so well that a tremendous chord towards the end of the movement synchronized miraculously with the crashing of the automobile over a cliff into the ravine. It took three performances for me to perfect this synchronization, for a fraction too much or too little speed in playing the music caused the chord to land anywhere but where it should have done. One sleepy afternoon I recall dragging the music so badly that instead of synchronizing with the car hitting the gully, the big bang landed right on a close-up of the lovers embracing after the accident! I had to watch this at future performances. . . .

Towards the end of the second week of this lethargic season Wanger introduced an innovation which it was hoped would considerably bolster up the drawing power of the show: he engaged the redoubtable dancer Massine and a handful of assisting artists. Massine had temporarily broken with Diaghilev, and on this occasion provided a thirty-minute *divertissement*, which included the *Ragtime* of Stravinsky, but little else of interest. The small group was lost on the big stage of Covent Garden, and only succeeded in emphasizing the comparative emptiness of the theatre. The public showed no interest, and Wanger wisely decided to abandon his expensive experiment of super-orchestral-movies-plus-ballet at the Royal Opera. His effort to raise the standard of movie accompaniment in England was one more indication that the British public reacts slowly to attempts at improving its musical culture. He had also discussed with me the question of an all-American symphony concert at Queen's Hall, but prospects were none too encouraging, and after reading in the *Telegraph* the account of an interview on the subject with Richard Strauss (who was in London at the time), I persuaded Walter to drop the idea. The *Telegraph* recorded Strauss's impressions of American music with little fervour:

> He has come to London after an eminently successful tour in America, but he has found what others found before him: that America is not the best point of vantage for those who wish to know something about the Americans, and in the hurry and bustle of travelling he has had little time to get in touch with the aspiring musicians of young America. He was vaguely noncommittal on this topic. He had seen the score of a ballet by Mr. Carpenter, and a score of a composer whose name could not be remembered, and found both interesting. That was as far as he could be persuaded to commit himself, but he was evidently much impressed by the American welcome.

Another visitor to London about this time was Serge Koussevitzky, who later, as head of the Boston Symphony Orchestra, was to discover more worthwhile American music than Dr. Strauss ever dreamed of. Together with the charming Madame Koussevitzky, we lunched at his hotel in Cromwell Road, with much animated talk of the newer European music; it was a luncheon that marked the start of a lasting friendship.

Just as New York can be called the musical centre of the world to-day, so twenty years ago the influx of Continental musicians to London gave the British capital an equally enviable position. Visiting conductors and virtuosi (local ones, too) came in for a tremendous amount of social lionizing, and hardly a day passed without an invitation to the houses of the great in Mayfair and points west. Indeed, the stamina required to combat the onslaught of lunches, teas, dinners, and late suppers to which one was constantly being subjected was as considerable in its degree as was the need for a social secretary to cope with the niceties of acceptance and refusal of these gastronomic orgies. But the social whirl wasn't by any means confined to mealtimes, for Society—with a capital S—was being *actively* musical. Private concerts featuring great soloists, string quartets, and chamber orchestras were the season's high-lights, while masques and tableaux with elaborate musical settings were lavishly staged in the beautiful homes of the Hon. Mrs. McLaren,[1] Lady Colefax, Lady Mond, Lady Cunard, Lady Howard de Walden, Mrs. Morley, and many other charming hostesses. Lady Diana Manners and Olga Lynn indefatigably organized these spectacles, to which the flower of Mayfair's youth and beauty—not forgetting Tallulah Bankhead—contributed its radiance. Tirelessly too did Thomas Beecham, Anthony Bernard, and I arrange and conduct, at various times—with hand-picked orchestras— programmes as eclectic and fastidious as could be desired. And whether we were called upon for a varied orchestral programme, or—to accompany the masques—a sequence of extracts from Purcell, Rameau, or Fauré, an audience as appreciative and discerning as any in the world was sure to be on hand to relish the evening's fare. It is a far cry to those days, and from a sea of faces memory recalls but a few. Yet it seemed that no evening then would have been complete without the beautiful Leslie Jowitt, the Guinness daughters, Irene Ravensdale, Viola Tree, Elsa Maxwell, Philip Sassoon, Alan Parsons, Duff Cooper, and that coterie of literature, painting, music, and the theatre represented by the Sitwells, Maurice Baring, Seymour and Shane Leslie, Glynn Philpot, Cyril Scott, Victor Beigel, Arthur Rubinstein, and the inimitable Ernest Thesiger.

[1] Now Lady Aberconway.

CHAPTER XXXV

My wife and I were at that time sharing a large five-storey house with Grace Lovat Fraser (widow of the gifted artist and stage designer), who had found it too vast an establishment to run single-handed. To deal with an enormous amount of correspondence, we decided to engage a secretary and to share her services communally. This treasure duly appeared in the shape of a former aide of the Beecham Company, a strange, elderly, but not unintelligent woman named Miss de Thiérry. Not the least of her duties was to handle an alarming looking box-like affair called a 'private branch exchange', equipped with switches connected with no fewer than five different telephones strategically situated throughout the house, and capable of dealing with several incoming calls simultaneously; for Grace and her late husband hated climbing stairs to answer the telephone. This alarming apparatus functioned admirably but noisily when the firm hand of de Thiérry was at the controls, but without her to tackle the mysteries of its switches, calls got inextricably mixed-up, and frequently, after much jangling of bells and chattering clicks, were completely lost.

Once, on the occasion of a tea-party given by the twin hostesses of my home, de Thiérry fell ill with 'flu, depriving us temporarily of her services. For some reason, the fifty invited guests (though one could always count on double the original number turning up at a London party in those days) had all chosen that morning to telephone the house, and it fell to me, being in the adjoining study, to disentangle the calls. So just as the violinist, Paul Kochanski, was telephoning to ask whether he might bring Zoischa Kochanski, it happened that the local caterer also telephoned Grace regarding sandwiches for the party. In vain I tried to get Paul in communication with my wife, and the caterer with

Mrs. Lovat Fraser. After agonizing switching and plugging, the best I was able to do was to put Kochanski and the caterer into a seemingly unbreakable telephonic liaison concerning an order for sandwiches. The machine was giving unmistakable evidence of innumerable other calls coming in, and irascible remarks in the worst possible taste from invisible callers were being hurled at me through the earphones. I was about to rush into the street—away from that infernal horror—when my eye lighted on a sixth switch which I hadn't previously noticed. Pressing it in despair, I wrought a miracle. Both the ringing of the upstairs bells and the cascade of clamouring voices abruptly stopped. Then the quietly despairing sound of Boonie's voice, 'Hello somebody—*anybody*'! which was answered by an equally familiar and agonized voice, 'Yes, Yes—— Well, is that *you*, Boonie?'

'Why, Grace, where are you?'

'In my bedroom. Where in heavens name are you?'

'Just above you—in the attic!'

Mrs. Goossens and Mrs. Lovat Fraser enjoyed a long intra-mural conversation, and the next day we disposed of the box. In due course, its erstwhile operator wearied of the Goossens-Fraser ménage, and left us; whereupon, we discovered that one telephone sufficed for our needs. . . .

In June of this year that great producer, Basil Dean, whom I had known from the old days of the Liverpool Repertory Theatre, asked me to write some incidental music for the production of Somerset Maugham's new play, *East of Suez*, at His Majesty's Theatre in September. I agreed to do so, and went to Limehouse to see if I could find some Chinese musicians who would give me a first-hand idea of the sort of thing required by the Oriental setting of the play. At first I was unsuccessful, but one afternoon, wandering down dreary Limehouse Causeway, I came across an old Chinaman who kept a little grocery shop and sold one-string fiddles as a side line. I asked him whether he'd care to show me how to play one, or whether he could tell me where I might hear a typical Chinese orchestra. I said

I'd be willing to pay for the privilege, and pointed out how important it was to get authentic information on the subject. This impressed him, and, going to the back of his dark little shop, he beckoned me to follow. We proceeded through a door and down a flight of stairs leading to another door, opening on to a long, dark corridor, all in the best Sax Rohmer tradition. At this point I was surprised to hear a distant sound of strange music. We reached the end of the corridor, and through a third and final door walked into a brick-walled room devoid of furnishings, except for a large centre table around which eight Chinese were seated (on packing-cases), all completely absorbed in their music-making. I stood riveted by the fascinating sounds they produced. Three played one-string fiddles, another two blew reedy Chinese flutes, two others were occupied with cymbals, gongs, and wood blocks, and the last, obviously the virtuoso of the group, performed skilfully on a small cymbalum, similar to those in pre-war Hungarian bands. They paid us no attention, and only when the piece came to an end did the old grocer address the group in Chinese, explaining—so I learnt later—that I was a welcome visitor who had come to listen and not to interfere. After this, he went back to the shop, and the cymbalum player, who spoke fair English, told me something of the little band and its performance. They were mostly members of the crew of a steamer just back from China, and used the empty warehouse room for rehearsals for a celebration to be held shortly by a local Tong. The music they played, said my informant, was entirely traditional; no notation of its pentatonic meandering existed, and the musicans played solely by ear. Producing a sheet of MS. ruled paper carried for just such an emergency, I asked if I might take notes of their playing. This caused some astonishment; my friend was obviously baffled by the idea of jotting down in symbols anything remotely resembling what was being played. However, they all resumed their rehearsing, which consisted of non-stop performances of pieces which all sounded very similar. After a time I began to detect subtle differences of rhythm and tempo, and at the end of two hours had filled three sheets of MS. paper with rapid jottings of melodic and rhythmic patterns. Finally, the players, all of whom (excepting the flautists) had performed miracles of cigarette chain-smoking during their rehearsal, decided to call it a day, and we adjourned upstairs to the grocer and his shop, which by now was closed to the street. A strong aroma of tea filled the shop, and squatting on the floor, on the counter, on barrels or anything else available we accepted the hospitality of our ancient host, and drank the best Suey-Sen tea I've ever tasted. It was then that I learned the name of the cymbalum player, Mr. Chang Tim, who invited me to further rehearsals that week to take further notes. I gratefully accepted. When the published version of the *East of Suez* incidental music was later issued by J. and W. Chester the fly-leaf contained the following acknowledgement:

Many of the themes upon which the music is based are wholly or partly of Chinese origin, noted down by the composer from Mr. Chang Tim's Chinese instrumentalists. No Chinese instruments, however, are used in the orchestra, and the harmonic idiom of the incidental music is Western throughout.

The visit to Limehouse over, I began to realize that a lively amount of creative activity lay ahead during the coming summer months. Besides composing the music for *East of Suez*, I had to finish a short choral work commissioned by the Gloucester Festival authorities, both works being due for performance in early September. Ten weeks remained in which to complete them, so I devoted the first five to the choral work—a setting of a fragment from Walter de la Mare's *Silence*—and the rest to *East of Suez*. In addition, a *Sinfonietta* for performance at a London Symphony Concert, later in the year, was taking shape. I decided to put it aside temporarily and went off to the comparative quiet of Harlech (G.D., Cyril Scott, Holbrooke, Coburn, and the Morris School being already installed there), to try a combination of the Gothic abstractions of *Silence* and the Buddhist temples of *Suez*. The mixture worked according

191

to schedule, and *Silence* was duly printed and delivered in time for some rather intensive rehearsal by the cathedral choirs of Gloucester, Hereford, and Worcester, which annually combine to form the chorus for the Three Choirs Festival. The music for Maugham's *East of Suez* was dispatched to Basil Dean in London, who immediately started piano rehearsals to synchronize it with his stage production. With exquisite Meggie Albanesi and sinister Basil Rathbone in the cast, it came to its appointed première, and proved a success. Basil Dean introduced a Ford car on the stage in the Pekin street scene, and my music, as authentically Chinese as Western instruments could make it, provided a good background to the animated crowd of rickshaws, tourists and merchants in this episode. Except for some atmospheric melodrama throughout the play, the rest of my contribution, consisting of an overture and some music for *entr'actes*, might just as well not have been written, for all the attention it got from the London public.[1] *Entr'acte* music makes an appropriate background for a jabbering audience, but a composer gullible enough to suppose it holds their attention is laying in store considerable heartache. I conducted an adequate orchestra on the opening night, and handed the baton to the regular conductor at His Majesty's, Percy Fletcher—himself a good composer of theatre music—for the rest of the run.

Mr. Chang Tim came to the first night, by special invitation, and allowed that I had, in spots, produced a very tolerable imitation of his little group. But he couldn't quite understand why we hadn't engaged his musicians *en masse*, in place of the regular theatre orchestra. A few days later he informed me gravely he would return to China with his ship, saddened greatly by this thought. . . .

[1] The same thing happened later with the Delius music to *Hassan*.

CHAPTER XXXVI

Next day I went to Gloucester for the Festival and stayed at one of the oldest inns in England, the New Inn (fifteenth century). I had rehearsed *Silence* with the London Symphony Orchestra two days previously in London, and the fine choir had mastered its part quite satisfactorily at separate rehearsals under the late Dr. Brewer, organist of Gloucester Cathedral. All that remained, therefore, was to join the two forces at a final rehearsal. The chorus, unused to my chromatic idiom, was experiencing difficulty in arriving at the unison *pianissimo* B flat at the end of the piece anywhere near pitch. Brewer therefore installed a small harmonium at the back of the chorus to sound the crucial B flat as an aid to the chorus, and undertook to play it himself. He could as well have used the organ; as things transpired, it's a pity he didn't. The actual concert, with chorus and orchestra arranged picturesquely in the organ loft over the sanctuary, an impressive sight, began with a most inappropriate work for performance in a church—Scriabine's erotic *Poem of Ecstasy*. Awaiting my turn to conduct *Silence*, I sat with Elgar in the choir stalls, where, hidden from sight, we discussed the proceedings. 'To think that Gloucester Cathedral should ever echo to such music,' sighed Elgar. 'It's a wonder the gargoyles don't fall off the tower. Heaven forgive Brewer!' The *Poem of Ecstasy* drew to a noisy, disorderly close, and the groined vaultings of the Cathedral turned the blare of trumpets into a shattering infamy. I started to leave for the choir-loft. 'Write a festival Mass, Eugene, and atone for this outrage.' 'All right, Sir Edward, but Mother Church won't approve of my modernisms.' 'Never mind. I'll be in Heaven by then; I'll make it all right for you! Don't forget, plenty of percussion in the *Sanctus!*'

193

One of the most impressive things about a Three Choirs Festival is the great silence of the audience at the Cathedral concerts. The Scriabine finished in shocked silence, and I faced a silent audience to start my own *Silence*. All went well until the final unison (and perfectly in tune) *pianissimo* B flat, when, just as Brewer started to play his helping note on the harmonium, a deep rattling boom shook the awe-inspiring silence of the church and persisted till the end of the piece. One of the low pedal bourdon pipes of the organ had ciphered, and broken the very silence which was the whole point of my work. Elgar, when I returned to the choir stalls, said he thought the piece atmospheric ('and the cipher was very effective'), but too short. 'All you youngsters are in far too great a hurry nowadays.' 'If that's what you think, just wait till you hear the next piece,' I replied. This was the première of Arthur Bliss's *Colour Symphony*, which lasted forty minutes. Elgar had to admit there were exceptions, and immensely admired Bliss's vivid symphony. After the concert we ate an enormous roast-beef lunch at the New Inn, and with Arthur Bliss and Willie Reed, concert-master of the L.S.O. and close friend of Elgar, spent the afternoon walking in open country along the banks of the Severn. Elgar not only outwalked us all, but completely out-matched us in matters of local history and topography. That evening, as proof of his energy, he conducted a Festival performance of his *Second Symphony*. An amazing, lovable man. . . .

For the first time in eight years I decided to devote the autumn months exclusively to writing. Leaving the B.N. O.C. temporarily to its provincial wanderings, and installing ourselves in a so-called 'bijou' house[1] at Wetherby Gardens, Earl's Court (as an antidote to the Lovat Fraser's sprawling home), I settled down to finishing my Sinfonietta and starting a sextet for strings commissioned by Mrs. Elizabeth Sprague Coolidge for her festival of chamber music at Pittsfield, Massachusetts, the following summer. The thousand dollars I was to receive for this work seemed at

[1] Birthplace of Jane and Julia Goossens.

that time—and still remains, even at present standards—a princely incentive.

My father also received at this time a tempting invitation to make a tour of Australia. The Minister of Public Instruction in New South Wales asked him to conduct fifty orchestral concerts over a period of four months, but he declined the offer—one which, over twenty years later, I accepted! Instead, he agreed to take *The Beggar's Opera* on a provincial tour for six months. For a long time after this he was quite unable to endure listening to any of its tunes! (It is said that the five Chaplin sisters, who played in the orchestra of the London production over a period of years, towards the end of their tenure had developed an actual physical resemblance to some of the characters in the opera.)

In mid-autumn I was visited by a representative of the International Society for Contemporary Music who asked me to conduct an all-British programme in Berlin with the Berlin Philharmonic Orchestra. The Germans seemed keen to hear some English music under a British conductor, and as four years had passed since the war had ended, my visit seemed artistically and politically appropriate. I also felt flattered at being the first Englishman invited since the war to conduct Arthur Nikisch's old orchestra.[1] So in company with critic-friend Edwin Evans (who spoke fluent German) and manager Peter Taylor (who, like myself, didn't), we set out from Folkestone early on a rough December morning for the Hook of Holland. Evans, a capacious beer-drinker, fortified himself by downing three tankards of Pilsener on board the steamer before leaving English shores. This, he claimed, rendered him impervious to the worst caprices of the gale, though we noted that the dose was frequently repeated before arriving at Flushing. Young Taylor, appropriately managerial, smoked a cigar, which he soon discarded. A great lover of the sea, even in its worst moods, my own superiority must have been offensive.

Beyond noting the expensive meals on the train going

[1] Once, at London Music Club Soirée, I played in Wagner's *Siegfried Idyll* under Nikisch.

through Holland (because of that country's high rate of exchange) and their fantastic cheapness in Germany, then enduring a catastrophic inflation, the train journey to Berlin was uneventful. On our arrival at the Fürstenhof Hotel on the Potsdamer Platz, a photographer snapped us as we stood innocently enough in front of the fireplace in the hotel lobby. It was only when, a few days later, the picture appeared on the back page of the London *Times* that we noted its entire upper half consisted of a painting of Kaiser Wilhelm, with our three rather diminutive selves beneath it. In London we had some trouble explaining this.

Rehearsals with the orchestra at first proved difficult, both because of my limited knowledge of the language, and because of a latent and strangely indefinable hostility among the anti-British die-hards in the orchestra itself. On the third morning a bitter remark from a truculent contra-bassoonist brought the personnel manager—an elderly, bearded harpist—to his feet in a violent speech calling for fair play for the visitor. He then sat down—and fainted. Some said from emotion, but I really suspect it was hunger. (The musicians brought sausage-rolls to rehearsal, and a special interval was given them to eat their 'brunch'.) After this incident the attitude of the men changed for the better, and at a little ceremony after the last rehearsal the orchestra committee presented me with the baton which Nikisch used at his last concert with the orchestra, as a souvenir of my visit. (*Autres temps, autres mœurs.*) It was one of the new pear-shaped-handled sticks made in those days by Goodwin and Tabb of London; Nikisch thought them wonderful, and, I'm told, ordered dozens of them.

A critical audience of Berliners evidently enjoyed the concert, as the report from the Special Correspondent of the *Morning Post* seemed to indicate.[1]

This appreciation reflected itself also in the playing of the orchestra, which, presumably because of an overdose of the classics, was at times so stodgy and ponderous that in certain of the *Enigma* variations of Elgar I almost despaired

[1] See Appendix D.

of achieving the right effect. What the orchestra would have done at that time to something like the *Daphnis and Chloe* of Ravel one shudders to think. Yet they produced a magnificent body of sound, and the rugged tone-quality of the basses has never been approached by any orchestra since. A baffling problem was to make the whole orchestra attack a *fortissimo* unison passage *on* the beat, and not slightly *after* it. This was a trick that Nikisch alone was responsible for, he having taught the men to delay the attack by an appreciable fraction of a second after his baton had actually indicated it.[1] The stammering, irritating effect of this on a strange conductor is something that can only be fully understood by other conductors!

The Berliners, whom I had always been led to believe were a musically conservative crowd, certainly belied their reputation at the conclusion of the concert. It was as though they were determined to show that music tolerates no political boundaries; their ovation was certainly as much a musical tribute as a personal one. From the Beethoven Saal we adjourned to the home of Hofrat Hartmann, a grimly efficient German who provided a grimly efficient supper, complete with speeches. It lasted till three in the morning, the guests including many visiting artists then in Berlin. The oratory varied from a seemingly endless but fluent speech in German from 'Teddy' Evans—by that time heavily fortified with great steins of Pilsener—to a few gracious words from the beloved Kreisler. Whereupon Frau Wolff, director of the Wolff Concert Bureau, closed the proceedings with a mighty peroration in which the words *freundlich* and *zufrieden* frequently appeared. On leaving Berlin the next morning, Taylor announced that owing to the disintegration of the mark my fee for the concert now amounted to some 500,000,000 marks, and therefore might as well be forgotten. But I left Berlin the richer for an enjoyable and, I believe—at that time—a worthwhile musical experience.

[1] They still retained this mannerism when I conducted them at the 1950 Edinburgh Festival.

CHAPTER XXXVII

BACK at Covent Garden with the B.N.O.C. (and *Siegfried* to open with), the first week of 1923 ushered in what astrologers call a year 'replete with surprises'. The first of these occurred when the late Herbert Bedford, husband of Liza Lehmann (composer of *A Persian Garden*), proposed that he and I should embark on a series of contemporary chamber-music concerts at the Aeolian Hall under the title of the 'Goossens Chamber Concerts'. Herbert, a monocled and likeable man, whose twin failings were composing and playing golf with an old-fashioned driver, had developed a passion for writing what he called 'unaccompanied song'. He also composed mercifully short pieces for chamber orchestra. He undertook to go halves in the expenses of the series, provided each concert contained at least one work of his own. He presented this scheme in so breezy and plausible a manner that I immediately fell for it. In any case, I had long since decided that if I were to be associated with any further crusading in the cause of contemporary music, my efforts might as well be confined to giving smaller and less expensive concerts than those which had taken place two years previously at Queen's Hall. So we arranged to undertake forthwith a preliminary series of five concerts on Wednesday evenings at 5.25—an hour at which Londoners are not supposed to be very interested in listening to music. We began with a rather unexciting programme in order to encourage the conservatives. It consisted of Arnold Bax's quartet, John Ireland's trio, and my own piano quintet, with the superb Anne Thursfield singing contemporary songs (including only two by Herbert Bedford—one unaccompanied). The *Evening Standard* gives an accurate but laconic account of the result:

Eugene Goossens' new series of chamber concerts at the Aeolian Hall opened yesterday with great success, no seats being available long before the time. The curious hour of 5.25 arrived, and the audience was as enthusiastic in applauding as it had been in picking up the tickets, so that each item as it was performed was the subject of several recalls. . . .

This happy state of affairs lasted up to the fourth concert, in the middle of March, when for some unaccountable reason the attendance fell off. The programme for the third[1] concert was as follows:

THE GOOSSENS' CHAMBER CONCERTS AT THE AEOLIAN HALL

Programme No. 3
(Chronological)

Twelfth Century
  Pons de Capdoil. A Troubadour Song: '*Miels com no pot dir*' (with harp).
Thirteenth Century
  Nithart. A Minnesinger Song: '*Wol dir, liebe summerzît*' (with spinet).
Fourteenth Century
  John Dowland. 'I saw my lady weep' (with piano).
  Giulio Caccini. '*Deh, deh, dove son fuggiti*' (with harp).

HUBERT EISDELL

Seventeenth Century
  Henry Purcell. 'I saw that you were grown so high' (with piano).
  Anonymous. 'Have you seen but a white lily grow?' (with spinet).
Eighteenth Century
  G. F. Händel. 'O sleep, why dost thou leave me' (with piano).
  Anonymous. 'Tambourin' (with harp).

OLGA HALEY

Nineteenth Century
  Franz Schubert. 'Hark! hark! the lark! (with piano).
  Johannes Brahms. '*In Waldeseinsamkeit*' (with piano).
  Gabriel Fauré. '*Les Roses d'Ispahan*' (with piano).
  Hubert Parry. 'Whether I live' (with piano).
  Liza Lehmann. 'Dusk in the Valley' (with harp).

HUBERT EISDELL

Harp Interlude
  Hamilton Harty. *Spring Fancies*, No. 1.

SIDONIE GOOSSENS

Twentieth Century
  Herbert Bedford. 'If music be the food of love' (first time; unaccompanied song.)

[1] Details of 2nd programme are not available.

John Ireland. 'The Adoration' (with piano).
Arthur Bliss. 'This Night' (first time; with piano).
Cyril Scott. 'Tranquillity' (a song without words; with piano).
Eugene Goossens. *'Chanson de Barberine'* (with piano).
Manuel de Falla. *'El cancion del amor Dolido'* (with piano).

OLGA HALEY

Twentieth Century
Geoffrey Toye. 'To Meddowes' (first time; with piano).
Igor Stravinski. *'Un grand sommeil noir'* (first time; with piano).
Arnold Bax. 'I heard a piper piping' (with piano).
Richard Strauss. 'Freundliche Vision' (with piano).

HUBERT EISDELL

The programme of the fourth concert was chiefly conspicuous for the first performance of a suite for chamber orchestra entitled *Captions, being Five Glimpses of an Anonymous Theme.* Bedford perpetrated the theme, and the 'glimpses', in the form of variations, were as follows:

> Arthur Bliss: 'Twone, the House of Felicity'
> Herbert Bedford: 'The Lonely Dancer of Gedar'
> Eugene Goossens: 'The Strange Case of Mr. X'
> Felix White: 'Lament for a Long-Cherished Illusion'
> Gerrard Williams: 'Valsette Ignoble'

and a finale to which, I think, we all contributed anonymously. My own variation, which parodied every (up till then) known jazz device, was dedicated to Ernest Newman, who loathed jazz, and pretended to see its influence on the contemporary trend of the group. The rest, including my own, were all too, too clever, and would probably be repudiated by their composers to-day.

The fifth and last concert was played at the end of March to a medium-sized audience with the following programme:

THE GOOSSENS' CHAMBER CONCERTS AT THE AEOLIAN HALL

Programme No. 5

R. Vaughan Williams. *Phantasy Quintet* for two violins, two violas and violoncello.

FREDERICK HOLDING and CECIL BONVALOT
RAYMOND JEREMY and JAMES LOCKYER
CEDRIC SHARPE

Gustav Holst. Four songs for voice and violin.

DORA LABBETTE and ISOLDE MENGES

200

SIR THOMAS BEECHAM

ACHILLE RIVARDE

Eugene Goossens. Opus 12. *Phantasy Quartet*
FREDERICK HOLDING, RAYMOND JEREMY,
CECIL BONVALOT and CEDRIC SHARPE

Herbert Bedford. Unaccompanied Songs: (*a*) 'Evangeline passes'; (*b*) 'The hay sings'; (*c*) 'The last of the leaves on the bough.'
DORA LABBETTE

Frank Bridge. Sextet in E flat for two violins, two violas, and two 'cellos.
FREDERICK HOLDING and CECIL BONVALOT
RAYMOND JEREMY and JAMES LOCKYER
CEDRIC SHARPE and AMBROSE GAUNTLETT

On the whole, the experiment of twilight chamber concerts of new music had shown that an audience did exist for such things, but confirmed what I had already guessed: that a steady diet of novelty without a leavening of the classics was insufficient to hold a regular clientèle. I decided therefore to postpone embarking on a further series until the public showed a desire to have 'the mixture as before' repeated.

My next surprise was when I suddenly started to realize that the London critics were displaying an increasing—and therefore flattering—difference of opinion, not to mention solicitude, over the kind of music I was turning out. A rather innocuous *Sinfonietta*, composed for the second of two concerts given by the L.S.O. in January (Koussevitzky conducted the first), made this clear to me.

As with everything the London public does not immediately comprehend, its reaction to my little symphony was apathetic. My erstwhile champion, the *Daily Telegraph*, waxed piously reproachful:

From beginning to end, those qualities of spiritual form [*sic*] and imagination we associate with great works are simply not to be found. In this work the composer only drove home the conviction that his very fine talents are talents only, and have little or no relation to the divinity [*sic*] of creative genius.

The *Observer* sarcastically observed:

The exposition is duly repeated (how formal and Haydenesque our young modernists are suddenly becoming!)

And the *Morning Post* grudgingly said:

> It is one of the more attractive works that have come from the learned and striving composers who deny the place of emotion in music. Mr. G. has not cut away all emotional growth, but whenever it makes an appearance, he lops it off in the flower of its youth [and produces] a convincing little essay in decorative music.

The *Daily Mail*:

> There were murmurs last night of Schönberg and Cubism, but these easy labels are best avoided. The music is no outpouring of poetic confidences, but a curious adroit game, with coloured tones, patterned phrases, and clattering harmonies for chessmen. . . .

Fifteen years later, when Toscanini played the *Sinfonietta* on the occasion of the New York Philharmonic's visit to London, my opus elicited hosannas of praise from the same pens. Time certainly mellows first impressions . . . or is a work good only when a Toscanini sets the seal of his approval on it?

Surprise No. 3 came about when, one morning, bright and early, a Mr. George Todd of Rochester, New York, telephoned inviting me to lunch in order to discuss a matter of some importance. I arrived at the Savoy to be greeted by a silver-haired, bespectacled, monosyllabic gentleman, who, had he been made up for the occasion to resemble the average European's conception of American Big Business of the 1920s, couldn't possibly have looked the part better. After discussing the weather, Mr. Todd's diet, my domestic background, the evils of tobacco (at that time I smoked excessively), and the lack then of ice-water at the Savoy, my guest—in probably one of the longest speeches of his career—announced the purpose of our meeting. It appeared that George Eastman, of Kodak fame, who had built a big theatre in Rochester, U.S.A., had collected an orchestra of sixty for the purpose of super-movie presentations, and had decided, after a year's operation, that the orchestra should be augmented to take its place as one of America's major symphony orchestras. Mr. Eastman wished to know whether I would care to make the trip to Rochester in the coming autumn to direct the first three months of the new orchestra's season, the remaining three to be directed by my colleague, Albert Coates. Asked the purpose of this dual control, of which I did not approve, Mr. Todd was a little vague, though I gathered that Mr. Eastman had merely hesitated to commit himself to a single incumbent at the outset. Mr. Todd laconically mentioned the stipend I would receive, surprisingly lighted a cigar, and said, 'I guess that covers it. Whadd'ya say?' Unhesitatingly, in the idiom of my future homeland, I answered, 'Okay.' Whereupon Mr. Todd called for the bill, and half an hour later I was at the Cunard offices inquiring about September sailings.

CHAPTER XXXVIII

EIGHT months followed the interview with Mr. Eastman's emissary before my departure for the States—months forming a kaleidoscope of happenings which sent one newspaper (the *Evening News*) into a rhapsody. 'One day at the theatre, the next at a symphony concert, or again in chamber music, or in aesthetic debate, he enlivens the musical life of London . . . and is our arbiter of the elegancies, so far as music goes.' Two columns of this, under the title of 'London's Music Wizard', conveys the idea that England offered as great an outlet for my activities as the most ambitious musician could hope for. Actually this wasn't so, for I sought a more concentrated objective—the permanent leadership of a large orchestra, which at that time only America could offer—rather than the kind of existence which once prompted the sharp-tongued *perruquier* Willie Clarkson to observe at Covent Garden, 'My God, Goossens, you're all over the b——y place!' I even thought London too sprawling a community to be adequately serviced musically by (for many) the remote Queen's Hall and the still less accessible Albert Hall. So at the beginning of the year, I helped start a movement for decentralizing London's music by bringing it to the different suburbs through the medium of music clubs. After a preliminary drive for subscriptions, the first of these—the Chelsea Music Club—got under way, and I conducted its first concert in January at the local Town Hall. Myra Hess was soloist in a Beethoven concerto, and the orchestra was handpicked from the L.S.O. Fifteen years later, about the time Mr. Chamberlain returned from Munich to announce 'peace in our time', we celebrated the hundredth concert of the club by repeating the identical programme with the identical soloist and conductor. Other clubs sprang up, but the movement lost impetus and, like most musical experiments in Britain, eventually proved abortive.

I spent the next few weeks up north with the B.N.O.C. and the Philharmonic Society in Liverpool, and the Leeds and Bradford orchestras in Yorkshire. The first is chiefly memorable for a performance of *Götterdämmerung* I conducted about that time, which, because of a scenic mishap, took a sharp drop from the sublime to the ridiculous in the very final measures. A backcloth depicting the gods being consumed in flames and the Rhine flooding Brünnhilde's funeral pyre failed to descend at the crucial moment, leaving the brick wall of the theatre exposed to the full view of the audience. This might have been overlooked had there not also been revealed, painted on the wall in large characters, the legend, 'No smoking'. Whereupon the audience's sense of humour took command and, Wagner notwithstanding, they laughed.

A short time after this episode, Busoni came to the Liverpool Philharmonic,[1] and I thought myself fortunate to have conducted for him. He played a Mozart concerto and his own *Indian Fantasy*—a rather esoteric work. As pianist, he seemed the most towering figure I had ever known; even in Mozart he exuded an overwhelming cerebral force, and when he played, his superb head and profile were as though carved out of granite. Later, at supper in his hotel room, the tragic mask of illness he carried in those last years mellowed under quantities of black caviar and Heidsick. I asked him whether I might glance at some passages in the score of his opera, *Dr. Faustus*. Immediately he took up a MS. [piano] copy and, asking his wife to excuse us, sat down at the piano, and began a long verbal explanation of the character of Faust. This was interesting, but I was more concerned about the music. Eventually he played about the first twenty pages, grunting the voice parts stertorously. Finally, throwing up his hands, he exclaimed. '*Ach!* What's the good. This thing needs the orchestra. More champagne!' So we had more champagne, and then he said, 'Now you play something.' I squirmed and said, rightly, that I knew

[1] Siloti was my other soloist that season.

nothing by heart. 'Easily remedied, my friend,' he replied, disappearing into an adjoining room, and emerging again, brandishing a copy of my *Nature Poems*. 'Chester sent this yesterday—so play!' There was nothing for it, and when I'd stumbled through the piece I was told: 'For a conductor you're a very good pianist!' Then he made me play the 'Bacchanal' a second time, and without comment went to bed. At that moment he seemed less the inscrutable colossus than a very weary old lion. . . .

At the end of March I landed in Antwerp as a guest of the Société des Nouveaux Concerts, to conduct the local orchestra. The Committee having previously given me to understand that I was being invited both as pioneer of modern music and Belgian (*sic*) conductor-composer, stipulated that the programme should contain one ultra-contemporary piece, and one work of my own. I therefore brought with me the *Five Orchestral Pieces* of Schönberg—still the most debatable of modern works, despite its age—and my own *Four Conceits*, the rest of the programme consisting of Brahms, Berlioz, and Ravel (*Spanish Rhapsody*). The orchestra wrestled manfully with the Schönberg, but as nothing remotely resembling it had ever come within their previous experience, my patience at rehearsals was sorely tried. The audience frankly expressed a very audible and contemptuous disapproval of the novelty, and it took all the blandishments of Brahms' No. 1 to restore their equanimity. Antwerp's foremost critic was moved to write:

As for the famous Schönberg, opinions were sharply divided. Some found this music atrocious, others idiotic, so any success the piece enjoyed was at best controversial. Loud hissing mitigated the final applause, intended for orchestra and conductor. It was, in my opinion, an experience not to be repeated.

The criticism concluded with the following estimate of my conducting, which I reproduce as a remarkable piece of hyperbole:

The excellent conductor combined the British qualities of calm deliberation, sure mastery, and measured distinction with the coloured fire, warmth, and vibrant tonality which gives to Flemish art its abundant savour and communicative zest. Imagine the clear, precise vision of an English diplomat, subjected to a solid and energetic temperament, whipped up and exalted magnificently by the contemplation of beauty. So seemed to us the young general who led his orchestral troops to victory with a sure hand and a fervent but serene spirit.

Block that metaphor, as the *New Yorker* would say!

Back in London, I conducted an annual Good Friday *Messiah* at the Albert Hall, with a thousand-strong Royal Choral Society—a performance which, tonally at least, always puts any other I've heard completely in the shade. It is a deeply moving, solemn affair, with a sombre-hued audience and far-flung masses of choristers observing what by now almost amounts to a ritual.

Then to jovial Dan Godfrey's orchestra at Bournemouth, and, the following week, to the Dome at Brighton, to direct festival performances of some of my pieces. These South Coast towns had fine, workmanlike orchestras which would give you a well-disciplined performance of music in a minimum of rehearsal time. (The indefatigable Sir Dan did almost as pioneer a job for British music in Bournemouth as did Henry Wood at Queen's Hall.) From the Regency stucco of Brighton on to Bath to adjudicate at the Somerset festival: dozens and dozens of pianists and violinists all playing the same piece, a torment to the flesh and little else to the spirit! Frederick Austin had asked me to direct the first performance of *Polly*—sequel to *The Beggar's Opera*—at the Kingsway in London, which I did early in May. He arranged the lovely old tunes as felicitously as he did those of the long-lived *Beggar*, but in spite of a stunning production and a fine performance of MacHeath by a singer picturesquely named Pitt Chatham, the public refused to journey to High Holborn, though before, it had made the Hammersmith pilgrimage without hesitation. So *Polly* was withdrawn after a short run. Meantime, the B.N.O.C. season at Covent Garden opened with the English composer Holst's opera, *The Perfect Fool*, a work of which the splendid ballet music alone survives. I enjoyed directing this vigorous one-act piece, but it was too full of a certain mystical whimsy to please the British public. The millionaire Barry Jackson spent a fortune at a neighbouring theatre before he succeeded in inducing this same British public to patronize an equally whimsical effort by Rutland Boughton called *The Immortal Hour*. This finally rode to success on a single three-minute song, 'How beautiful they are, the lordly ones.'

In June, Lionel Tertis, history's greatest viola-player, and Beatrice Harrison, who taught nightingales to warble to the sound of her 'cello, gave recitals with orchestra, at which I conducted for them performances of the Bloch viola suite and the Elgar 'cello concerto. After this, and a surfeit of music, I beat a retreat to George Davidson's home at Antibes for a scorching August holiday. G.D. had forsaken the rainy summer of Harlech for the warmth of Southern France: needless to say, the ubiquitous Margaret Morris dancers and Fergusson followed in his wake. They immediately invaded the Grand Hotel du Cap, to the delight of the proprietor and the faint amusement of his clients. The school also had a visitor in the person of Picasso (a near neighbour), much to Fergusson's delight; they hadn't met since the old days in Paris. One day Meg Morris, Picasso, Fergusson, and I were at Eden-Roc, and a small octopus half crawled out of the sea on to a nearby rock and posed for us. This delighted Picasso, but he didn't draw it. I got sunstroke on the way back to the hotel, and Picasso insisted on my wearing his black felt hat, with a wet handkerchief tucked into it.

CHAPTER XXXIX

ON arrival in London at the beginning of September, and full of my coming trip to America, I had a message from Basil Dean asking me to conduct his production of James Elroy Flecker's *Hassan* at His Majesty's. Delius had written the incidental music, which called for a fairly large-sized theatre orchestra and sensitive handling. So I promised to do the opening night—two days before sailing date—and hurried off to Delius to get the score, and his ideas on it. I was shocked to find him in quite decrepit physical condition. His sight was failing, and he showed evidence of the illness which was soon to cripple him totally. He talked animatedly enough of his music for the play, and was emphatic about its being meticulously rehearsed—which it was; and the first night at His Majesty's Theatre was memorable. A fine cast, indescribably beautiful scenery, and the Delius music, combined to give Flecker's poetic masterpiece a presentation it probably will never get again.

Delius had been peevish at rehearsals, especially about tempi and dynamics. He need not have troubled, for, as usual, during the *entr'acte* music the public insisted on keeping up a subdued but painfully audible gabble. The most effective numbers were the 'Serenade' and the 'Procession of Protracted Death'—a grisly march which accompanied the lovers to their torture and death. These pieces, occurring during the course of the play, were at least uninterrupted. The finale, 'The Golden Road to Samarkand', though atmospheric and wistful, was not enhanced by the merchants of Baghdad singing off pitch, back-stage. At rehearsal this infuriated Delius; he shouted, 'We must have a larger orchestra; they can't hear the orchestra.' To which Basil answered, 'You can't have a larger orchestra, Mr. Delius. This production is costing enough as it is!' Dean, never a niggardly producer, had certainly spared no expense to make this a lavish one, and the orchestra alone numbered about thirty men—a large group for a medium-sized play-house. The London Press hailed *Hassan* as a spectacular and atmospheric triumph—one of the few occasions on which Dean got his just deserts as England's gifted and most enterprising man of the theatre. Delius, while admitting that the music was played completely to his taste, left the theatre after the performance acutely depressed by what he called that 'stupid first-night audience of scatterbrains'. I accompanied him and his wife to their hotel, hoping to enliven him with some champagne. But he insisted on retiring, pleading an early departure for Paris next morning. 'When you return from America in the spring, come over to Grez,'[1] he said. 'We'll go walking by the river.' Alas! I never did, for his condition grew rapidly worse. With Mrs. Delius and the faithful Eric Fenby, who, when blindness overtook the great man, took down his last works from dicta-tion, he lived out his final years in the solitude of the French countryside, a lonely figure. A Delius festival organized by the untiring Beecham, to which the composer painfully journeyed shortly before his death, was London's act of homage to a great Englishman that must have brought an unimaginably joyful light into the shadow of his last months.

Two days after the *Hassan* production, we stood on the boat-deck of the *Aquitania* watching the gap between shore and ship widen irrevocably as tugs swung the vessel away from the dock-side. With the roar of the whistle—a soul-stirring sound—the shouting and farewells, the fluttering handkerchiefs down on the pier receding in the distance, and the strains of 'Land of Hope and Glory' played by the ship's band, a lump rose in my throat as I realized that even though this venture into the unknown was for a short preliminary span of months, it would inevitably result in permanent exile. The landscape of England never seemed softer and greener than when, that day, the *Aquitania* headed down the Solent and out to the open sea for Cherbourg and the U.S.A.

To the traveller making his first Atlantic crossing, the daily routine of shipboard, with its rituals of deck-chair occupancy, morning broth, afternoon tea, shuffleboard,

[1] Grez-sur-Loing, his French home.

exercise ('five times round the deck equals one mile'), black tie for dinner, smoke-room pools, and so on, is a fearsome and wonderful thing. I managed to add a few of my own: identifying passing ships with Zeiss binoculars (I was rather good at this), visits to the engine-room and the third class movies (more fun than first class), dodging swimming-pool parties and the ship's concert, and taking on the ship's bore at chess when my wife was incapacitated by sea-sickness. The *Aquitania*, a notorious 'pitcher', put on a terrific exhibition during a heavy three-day blow. This effectively reduced a racehorse on board called Papyrus to such a state of exhaustion that after landing in New York it was quite unable to beat an American contestant named Zev, and was later returned ignominiously in the same padded cabin to its country of origin. William Somerset Maugham kept to his cabin for most of the trip, but emerged in the end with a completed short story.

The skyline of New York produced the same effect on me as on every new visitor to America. I thought it breathtakingly beautiful. Reporters and photographers boarded the ship at Quarantine. Here, I thought, was my chance for some sensational, world-shattering publicity. I would answer their questions with craft and sang-froid, and possibly make headlines in the morning Press. After a, to me, strangely unaccountable delay, and just as we were docking, a man with a slouch hat came up to me—furtively, I thought. (Possibly he wanted to beat his fellow reporters to a scoop!) I straightened my tie and looked him squarely in the eye as he handed me his card. I glanced at it and read:

GUISEPPE,
500 E. 62nd Street,
New York.
[Knock twice and ask for Joe.]

A nearby passenger had a New York paper, and I caught sight of a headline: 'Sensational raid on East Side speakeasy.' I passed down the gangway, sadder and wiser. . . .

As a result of the gales, we docked several hours late, which was a pity, for I had promised to stop off at Mrs.

Coolidge's chamber-music festival at Pittsfield in the Berkshires to hear the première of my recently commissioned string sextet. Partly because of my own ignorance of local geography, and that of a colleague who should have known better, I found myself that night exploring the intricacies of an upper berth to Boston, and next morning enduring the clammy stupor of a six-hour day-train ride to Pittsfield. On my arrival I missed the actual performance of the sextet, but was in time to acknowledge the applause; and it didn't lessen my chagrin to learn that we could have taken a night train to Albany and eventually got to Pittsfield in ample time to hear the entire afternoon concert.

From all accounts, my work had pleased the radicals in the audience, but baffled the old guard, who were present in force in that picturesque music-shed on South Mountain. I had expected this, but was in a state of too pleasant bewilderment to care much. Only twenty-four hours had elapsed since landing in this beautiful new country, and here we were conversing on a pleasant hillside with American and British composers and performers, all guests of a unique patroness of chamber-music, Mrs. Elizabeth Sprague Coolidge. Small wonder that when the English contingent greeted us (Myra Hess, May Mukle, Rebecca Clarke, Frank Bridge, Arthur Bliss, and the members of the London String Quartet), we found it hard to believe this really was America, and that over a week had elapsed since we had left home to come to its hospitable shores. The vexations of the train journey to Pittsfield were quickly forgotten in the warmth of our reception, and arrival at New York next day seemed an almost too abrupt transition by comparison. Fortunately, the colourful Bill Murray, at that time artists' representative of the Baldwin Piano Company, was on hand to reveal the wonders of Manhattan to two of the most guileless 'rubbernecks' he had ever had to cope with. After three days' sightseeing, lunches, dinner, theatres, and the hospitality New Yorkers love to heap on their overseas guests, we descended early one morning to the caverns of Grand Central Station and boarded the Empire State express for Rochester, N.Y.

CHAPTER XL

THE bustle and excitement one always associates with the departure of a European train were so conspicuously lacking in the Grand Central catacombs that I was aware of a vague depression as the silent train of Pullmans, drawn by an electric engine, glided away. It left from an interminable platform, made all the more sombre by contrast with the animated scene in the concourse upstairs. The feeling of adventure that I always experienced in the daylight of a big London terminus, with its crowded platforms, shouting newsboys, perspiring porters, and vitalizing, breathless excitement of steam locomotives, was dismally lacking in the lower depths of the funereal New York terminal. Even the thronged concourse upstairs had a strangely muted character. It was only later when we emerged on to the elevated trestles of Park Avenue that I realized the extent of the engineering feat that had contrived this neat, inconspicuous burrowing of a great railroad under a great city. And when later we sped along the sunlit Hudson, and a familiar sound came from the 'head-end', I realized we had shed the smokeless nonentity that had brought us out of Manhattan, and taken on a steam-engine —without which, for me, a railway isn't a railway. Contemplating from the window the splendour of mountains and water, my spirits rose. . . .

Arrived at Rochester, the genial Harper Sibley and his attractive wife whisked us to a suite in the Sagamore Hotel which seemed to contain everything except a bedroom. My preoccupation over this apparent oversight on the part of the architect was removed when an 'in-a-door' bed was revealed, hidden behind a glass door in the sitting-room. This struck me as nearly as exposed as the communal sleeping-behind-curtains in a Pullman; but since the entire hotel was similarly equipped, my sensitiveness seemed out of place. A great babel of voices came from a neighbouring room. An emissary sent by the party-giver—Vladimir Shavitch, conductor at the Eastman Theatre—requested that we adjourn there: so Harper Sibley took us in tow, and effected introductions. It seemed that the affair was a farewell tea for the departing Director of the Eastman School of Music, a Mr. Alf. Klingenberg, and his wife. The twenty-four year old Howard Hanson, his successor, struck me as extraordinarily young to take over such a responsible post, but Eastman was obviously a firm believer in youth. Opinions concerning the Kodak King and his 'arbitrary' methods were expressed, with astonishing frankness, and I began to wonder what manner of narrow-minded tyrant had brought me out on the long journey to Rochester. This series of uninhibited opinions by musicians present gave me a compact picture of the petty musical factions prevalent at the time in the city. I judged that this situation needed diplomatic handling both by the new Director of the school and myself, and that the sooner we got to work on it the better. Such a revelation of local politics, while something of an eye-opener, stood me in good stead when the time came to estimate at first hand the qualities of my new employer and his entourage.

I did not have to wait long for this opportunity; some flowers and a note of welcome from G.E., inviting me to breakfast at 7.30 the following morning, awaited me in my room. I had been warned not to be late, so at 7.28 next day I arrived at 900 East Avenue, and was admitted by a smiling Negro butler. George Eastman emerged from an adjoining room and in friendly fashion greeted me, and we adjourned to the breakfast table in the rear part of the hall. Punctually at 7.30 we sat down, while Harold Gleason, the organist, began playing a piece by Palmgren on a large Aeolian organ hidden behind a bank of chrysanthemums. This synchronized beautifully with the chiming of three clocks and the entrance of the butler, bearing grapefruit. Against a subdued musical background ranging from Bach to

Karg-Elert, and after a few polite enquiries concerning my journey, my host began—in the manner, I recalled, of his henchman, Mr. Todd—a virtually monosyllabic exposition of his ideals and ambitions regarding the orchestra in its relation to the city, and his conception of my functions in connection with it. These I listened to politely, rather in the style of a production manager (which in G.E.'s eyes I surely was) taking orders from the chairman of the board (which he most certainly was). His monologue, clipped and to the point and in many respects wide of the mark musically, gave me an insight into the mental processes which govern the functioning of the business mind when it toys with things musical. Yet his enthusiasms were so infectious and his concern over the community's musical future so real that, by comparison, it seemed—and actually was—a small matter to adjust certain impracticabilities and misconceptions he had built up and nourished about his pet scheme. In this sense he was, contrary to general opinion, amenable to suggestion, and let it be known that he relied implicitly on the opinion of the experts he hired. Like all other ruthless business heads, too, he judged them finally and implacably by results.

Breakfast came to an end, and with it Harold's organ recital, and G.E. announced curtly that he was heading for his office, and would I like a 'lift'. My astonishment at the idea of a plutocrat like my host bothering to go to an office at 8.30 a.m. merely reflected a British insularity of thought which imagines business magnates driving up to their offices in state about 11.30 to sign a few letters, and departing again for a heavy lunch. A few months in America soon disillusioned me about this.

I visited the superb Eastman Theatre and Eastman School of Music that morning, and marvelled at the luxurious furnishings of both, and thought how fortunate a community was Rochester to possess a wealthy patron who could suddenly sky-rocket it to the position of a major orchestral city by a few strokes of the pen. I also thought of the years it had taken to build up the musical foundations of European cities which had no George Eastman to endow them with the cultural wealth that, like all sudden overdoses of any rich food, sometimes induces acute indigestion in its victims. Be it said to the credit of Rochester that she easily assimilated those early symphonic doses. She was likewise subjected to a welcome diet of more intimate music. Every Sunday afternoon during the winter season a specially invited audience gathered at G.E.'s home to listen to a recital of chamber-music and organ given by the Kilbourn Quartet—Eastman's private group—and Harold Gleason. Two classic string or piano quartets, a sonata, and a group of organ pieces were the fare, plus a supper which also rarely varied between a classic oyster stew and a species of what is known in England as 'shepherd's pie'. The hundred or more guests each Sunday were chosen from Rochester's social and intellectual groups, and rotated alphabetically, so that an invitation was usually forthcoming about once a month, unless you happened to be a regular *habitué*, like the heads of the Music School and Orchestra, for whom attendance was *de rigeur*. Acceptance of an invitation to one of G.E.'s Sunday evenings was likewise virtually compulsory for the other guests, and only illness or a prior engagement were considered valid excuses, unless you wanted to be permanently in the boss's bad books. The host himself, though completely ignorant of music, doted on these concerts. I have known him summon the quartet to play specially after a small dinner-party on week-days, when the guests were treated to one of the later Beethoven quartets and whatever else the players selected. At such times G.E. would sit fascinated by the complexities of the first Rasoumovsky or the 'big' B flat quartet as though he had known them all his life.

The duties of my new post were in no way onerous; indeed, I would have welcomed a far more rigorous schedule. The fact that the nucleus of the Rochester Philharmonic Orchestra was the sixty players of the Eastman Theatre ensemble, a group which twice a day provided a strenuous musical accompaniment to the silent films shown in the

WILLIAM MURDOCH (PIANIST)
ALBERT SAMMONS (VIOLINIST)
CEDRIC SHARPE (CELLIST)
AND THE AUTHOR

A GOLFING FOURSOME AT WIMBLEDON PARK, 1916

SIR DAN GODFREY AND THE AUTHOR AT
BOURNEMOUTH FESTIVAL, ABOUT 1920

theatre, prohibited too frequent symphony concerts. Moreover, G.E. was determined that these should be run on a sound economic basis, though he could easily have shouldered enormous deficits had he chosen. But the concerts were to be no rich man's plaything, and consequently the management ended by adopting almost too frugal a policy in the matter of the number of concerts offered the public. It also remained to be seen whether Rochesterians would flock to the Eastman Theatre in sufficient numbers to justify the innovation of a symphony season. A hall with a seating capacity of nearly four thousand for a small city of two hundred thousand calls for an enthusiastic public to fill it adequately. The opening concert showed that confidence in the musical taste of the city wasn't misplaced.

CHAPTER XLI

JUDGED by symphonic standards of twenty years ago—
with the orchestras of Boston and Philadelphia as bright
particular ornaments of that time—the début of the
new Rochester Philharmonic was rather remarkable.
Preliminary rehearsals had revealed some outstanding first-
desk material among its ninety players, and the rank and file
of the string body produced a much better than average
resonance of tone for a comparatively inexperienced group.
The first concert, on 17 October 1923, showed an ensemble
full of virtuoso promise—sufficient, anyway, to propel it
immediately into the upper middle class of its sister orchestras. The audience which packed the Eastman Theatre made
as brilliant a showing as the orchestra: never before in its
history had East Avenue been jammed with such a collection
of automobilia as converged on the theatre that evening,
nor had the pride and fashion of Monroe County mustered
in such pomp and circumstance as at these preliminary
exercises of the new orchestra. The programme consisted
of the following:

1. Overture, *Tannhäuser* — Wagner
2. *L'Après Midi d'un Faune* — Debussy
3. (*a*) *Dubinushka* — Rimsky-Korsakov
   (*b*) *Londonderry Air* — Grainger
   (*c*) *Shepherd's Hey* — Grainger
4. *'Cello Concerto* (soloist, Press) — Dvorak
5. *Symphony No. 2 in D* — Brahms

It aroused plenty of favourable out-of-town and local critical
comments, with scribes from the nearby communities of
Buffalo and Syracuse biting their nails at the idea of Rochester stealing a march on them in the symphonic field. At the
end of the concert there were long ovations, elaborate floral
offerings—embarrassing to a European who associated

flowers with courtship, funerals, and table decorations exclusively—and an overwhelming number of after-concert invitations which crystallized, as they usually did, into buffet supper at the Cunningham's studio (Kathleen painted, and Frank built *de luxe* motor cars) with the Allens, Warners, Beardsleys, Taylors, Wards, Sterns, and Rogers constantly in attendance.

G.E. beamed with joy at the safe launching of his pet musical project. Rochester at last now had a major orchestra all to itself: would the public support it? The public did. All concerts up to the close of the year were played to capacity houses, and a community of two hundred thousand showed it considered a symphony orchestra indispensable to its cultural make-up. My schedule in those early days was by no means rigorous; a mere three months of a divided six months' season—Coates being due in January—made my incumbency seem too ephemeral to warrant an arbitrary routine. Apart from the actual concerts, and the administrative work connected with their programmes and personnel, besides lectures and recitals given for the students at the School of Music, there was ample leisure time to get the 'feeling' of my new environment. I was tremendously impressed by the autumnal beauty of western New York State. The richness of the Genesee Valley country, colourful Watkins Glen and its nearby 'finger lakes'—I had seen nothing quite like Canandaigua and Cayuga even in the Lake District of England—still induce in me a real nostalgia. And like a good tourist, I motored to Buffalo over the 'Million Dollar Highway' to gaze open-mouthed at Niagara, which looks so much more impressive when you cross over to the Canadian border.

The hospitable people of the new country in which I found myself frightened me a little by the disarming warmth of their welcome. So utterly unlike was it to anything I had known, so foreign to the insular reserve to which I was accustomed, that for a long time my shyness seemed intensified, and hampered early friendships which should have spontaneously generated, but which at first did not. However, you soon thaw under the warmth of a people who stop at nothing to let you know that their anxiety is for your comfort and well-being, that their houses are open to you and yours, and that the talents (if any) you bring to their midst are desirable and to be admired. In those far-off and leisurely days America seemed to the artist—and indeed was—the heaven-sent country of opportunity, a fertile soil in which to sow the seed of endeavour and reap an often bountiful harvest of achievement.

When the time came for my return departure for London, I realized with a pang that in spite of an invitation to return to Rochester the following season my prospects of permanent association with the U.S.A. under the temporary arrangement existing seemed fitful. The last concert had been followed next day by a banquet in our honour given by George Eastman. He seemed determined to stage as lavish a function as money could command, and his obvious approval of my short incumbency warrant. Miniature fountains welled from the floral pieces on the tables, just as the oratory of mutual appreciation welled from both the host and his guests of honour in speeches which breathed fervent and confident hopes for the orchestral future of Rochester. The city's 'four hundred' were invited *en masse*, and came in elaborate confections which added to the brilliance of what a local writer graphically described as Rochester's 'all time high in social *éclat*'.

Next day we left for New York, where the Algonquin Hotel furnished atmospheric headquarters. The Sixth Avenue 'El' rattled past our windows, and I slept not at all; but Frank Case, the Algonquin's host, saw to it that we lacked for nothing in the matters of good company and good fare. An evening spent there with the Knights of the Round Table—Alex. Woolcott, George Kaufman, Marc Connolly, and attendant lesser literati—is a convivial and stimulating memory. Woolcott had brought some purportedly genuine Scotch (a rare commodity in that era of bath-tub gin), which we drank under the guise of ginger ale.

This fooled no one, but added point to Woolcott's paradox that life in those days centred exclusively round surreptitious drinking, and ways and means to avoid a painful death caused by alcoholic poisoning. This latter I nearly achieved the evening before boarding the *Majestic*, after consuming 'imported claret' from a tea-cup at a local speakeasy. As a result, my memory of leaving New York was less an impression of the Statue of Liberty and the skyscrapers vanishing in the mist than of an ice-bag weighing heavily and coldly on throbbing temples and nauseating aches racking my whole being—that is, until we passed Ambrose Light, whereupon the cold breezes of the boat-deck revived me, and I escaped with nothing worse than a chill.

Back in London I made straight for the old studios of 2 L.O. at Savoy Hill—predecessor of today's B.B.C.—to conduct a symphony concert. The announcer said, 'We welcome the return of Eugene Goossens, who has been conducting the Rochester Orchestra with great success.' Next day the Mayor of Rochester, Kent, wrote telling 2 L.O. that his town had never boasted a symphony orchestra, and asked the radio officials to correct the false impression created by this announcement.

CHAPTER XLII

IT took me some time to adjust myself to the old familiar routine of the English scene, and I did so a little reluctantly because of what I had absorbed from my short stay in America. By contrast, the London of early 1924 seemed a rather grim place from which I was anxious to escape permanently. That glimpse of new horizons and artistic expansion across the Atlantic had planted a restlessness which made the intervening months before my next departure for Rochester seem unconscionably long in passing. But the old round had already started; the *Messiah* at the Albert Hall with the Royal Choral Society (a thousand strong), an opening *Mastersingers* with the B.N.O.C. at Covent Garden, the newly organized Chappell Popular Concerts with the Queen's Hall Orchestra on Saturday afternoon at the Queen's Hall, a London Symphony concert at the same place, and a performance of *Siegfried* which lasted till well after midnight because of a recalcitrant dragon whose steam-breathing apparatus developed engine failure just before Act II. All this, which I conducted up to the end of January, was supplemented by the inauguration of a further series of Goossens Chamber Concerts at the Aeolian Hall, which began inauspiciously with a half-empty house. Stravinsky's *Histoire du Soldat* and Milhaud's *Catalogue de Fleurs*—literal settings for voice and orchestra of a seedsman's catalogue describing violets, begonias, and hyacinths in the prosaic language of the B.B.C.'s gardening expert, the late Mr. Middleton, rather baffled the audience.

My brother Leon, and Fransella, the flautist, produced Holst's fugal concerto for flute and oboe at a Philharmonic Concert under my direction early in February, and the following day I departed for Zürich for the jury meeting of the first International Society for Contemporary Music Festival to be held later that year at Prague. My fellow jurors were the composers Bartok and Casella, with Ansermet, conductor of the Geneva Orchestra and one of the foremost interpreters of contemporary work, giving us invaluable help. We stayed with Dr. Volkmar Andreae, head of the Zürich Orchestra, and waded through some two hundred and fifty orchestral scores during our three days' stay there. Casella, Ansermet, and I disposed of half this number in the first day, largely by eliminating at first glance the inferior or second-rate works. Bartok, however, having picked out a couple of MS. scores which seemed at first glance to appeal to him most, wandered away to another part of the house, and spent the entire morning digesting them there. In vain we pointed out to him that unless he speeded up his methods of score-inspection we would never get through our job in under a month. He refused to be hustled, and in the end we finished by ignoring him entirely, and selected the half-dozen best works at the end of the specified three days without his aid. Bartok admitted to having scrupulously read through only five manuscripts in that time, and we departed for home leaving him in Zürich browsing among the remainder to his heart's content! During our incarceration at Dr. Andreae's house, it rained interminably. Ansermet and Casella smoked endless packages of cigarettes, and I contracted influenza.

Returning to London, I called on Arnold Bennett and broached the subject of writing an opera with him. We discussed several plots, and finally I persuaded him to convert his three-act play, *Judith*, into a one-act libretto, which he promised to do. Some weeks later he got around to it, and produced a compact book which I found ideal for my purpose. I worked fitfully on it, but many months elapsed before the finished product was ready for consumption. Frankly I was in little mood for creative work, being too preoccupied with my concert ventures, of which I was now bearing the full brunt because of my partner's withdrawal. The last of the Goossens Chamber Concerts took place in May and was something of a family affair, Sidonie and Leon being among the artists taking part in it with me.

The attendance was sparse; it seemed as though the public was definitely showing either its indifference or aversion to contemporary music. The programme bristled with stimulating novelties; yet perhaps, had I announced nothing but the works of Beethoven, Bach, and Brahms, the perverse Londoners might have patronized them. So I counted my losses, which (added to those incurred in the previous Queen's Hall orchestral series), were not inconsiderable.

In view of this, I had no qualms in turning a hand to professional activities which I would not ordinarily have undertaken. One of these was the writing of a series of articles on musical topics for the *Daily Express*, done at the request of Lord Beaverbrook. They had a mixed reception. Journalism wasn't exactly my forte, and I found it difficult to write untechnical articles for the average reader. At that time it was considered *infra dig* for a musician of any repute to write newspaper articles, and this didn't endear me to my professional brethren. Then I developed a complex about being able to meet the 'deadline' and finally gave up, after having turned out over a dozen forced specimens, none of which warrants exhuming at this time. Beaverbrook, when I told him I'd had enough, seemed visibly relieved, and offered as a parting shot something concerning the shoemaker sticking to his last. . . . So I orchestrated some scenes from the original *Boris Goudonov* in the manner of Moussorgsky, at Chester's request, just to convince myself that my *métier* lay in writing as an expert musician rather than a bungling journalist.

A producer named Fairbairn conceived the idea about this time of producing a dramatized version of the Coleridge-Taylor three-part cantata *Hiawatha* in the arena of the Albert Hall, and asked me to conduct it for a run of two or three weeks. The thousand choristers of the Royal Choral Society were enlisted for this effort, and, dressed in Indian garb, complete with such anachronisms as eye-glasses and wrist-watches, made a brave showing as they performed mass evolutions during the big choral and solo scenes of this fine work. The New Symphony Orchestra was placed at the north end of the hall, leaving the concert platform and central arena free for dramatic purposes. One scene, which I conducted with an illuminated baton, took place in complete darkness, and was rather frightening, especially when at one performance the house lights refused for a long time to rise to the occasion. Under Sir Malcolm Sargent's subsequent direction, the venture remained a great attraction until 1940, when it ceased to be an annual feature of the spring music season.

Not to be outdone by the International Grand Opera season at Covent Garden, the gallant B.N.O.C. opened up activities early in June at His Majesty's Theatre with a performance of *Figaro*, which I conducted. The smaller theatre proved ideally suitable for Mozart, just as it was for a new production on the following night of Debussy's *Pelléas and Mélisande*, which I also took charge of. It was memorable for two things: the singing of Maggie Teyte (the composer's favourite Mélisande) and an English translation by Edwin Evans. *Pelléas* had up to that time been considered untranslatable, but Evans disproved this, and his English version is a fine example of the difficult process of converting the elusive Maeterlinck-Debussy French into poetic but comprehensible English. Other features of the season were a scale-model *Parsifal* (as effective as in a larger theatre) and the production of Vaughan Williams' *Hugh the Drover*, marking the operatic *début* of an English conductor, Malcolm Sargent, who showed his mettle valiantly. So did a good new tenor, Tudor Davis, who blacked his opponent's eye in good earnest during the fight scene which is the work's chief claim to fame.

CHAPTER XLIII

S OME tiresome and unpleasant litigation arising out of the losses incurred by my different concert schemes of the past two or three years attracted considerable publicity about this time. Its generally unfavourable nature—since I rather quixotically refrained from blaming certain others for my plight, which I could justifiably have done—found a pleasant and unsolicited exception in the London *Musical News* editorial published just before my departure for a second American season. Since the Editorial's small solitary voice carried none too far at the time, the inclusion of part of it in the appendix[1] of this book may, perhaps, be excused. It dealt with the indifferent public support and financial failure of the concerts, and its conclusions heartened me greatly. A perhaps excessive zeal for the cause of new music had resulted in this situation, and the chances of being able to repair the damage in full would have seemed very remote without the roseate prospects of a profitable American career ahead. While I counted on this—and I was not to be disappointed—temporary crumbs of comfort such as the editorial were nevertheless comforting, especially just prior to departure.

On the *Majestic* were Basil Dean, anxious about the final rehearsals for his New York *Hassan* production, and Noel Coward, tense about the production of *The Vortex* (which established his name on Broadway). Thanks to them, I over-ate and over-laughed at meals and so arrived at New York with chronic indigestion.

The pattern of my half-season at Rochester, again shared with Albert Coates, resembled pretty much that of the previous year, with the addition of some opera. The Russian tenor, Vladimir Rosing, an intelligent and progressive man with unconventional ideas of opera production, had per-

1 See p. 313.

suaded George Eastman to allow him to undertake an experiment at the Music School. Rosing maintained that, given four years in which to train a picked group of young American singers, he could organize an opera company which by the end of that time could give performances of great expertness. This idea won G.E.'s sympathies immediately, and an opera department was duly created, with Rosing as producing director and myself as musical head.[1]

Rosing infused all concerned with such enthusiasm and sense of urgency that a trial performance of *Boris Goudonov*, in English, was staged within three months of the start, and showed of what potentially excellent material the department was composed. In later years the American Opera Company (the department's ultimate development) created mild operatic history in its New York presentations of *Figaro*, *Faust*, and *Butterfly*.

All this seemed at the time, and virtually *was*, very much worth while; to-day, the Eastman School of Music, forging ahead always under the guidance of energetic Howard Hanson, and coupled with the activities of the Philharmonic and Civic Orchestras, is leaving its stamp indelibly, not only on the musical life of Rochester, but on all America.[2] Towards the end of that season of 1924, when I had completed my Rochester concerts, I embarked on a short lecture tour which took me (and a travelling companion, Jack Warner, critic of the Rochester *Times Star*) to Chicago, Detroit, Omaha, Denver, and Minneapolis. The talks on 'Modern Music' delivered for the 'Pro Musica' Society are, I believe, still remembered on occasions as very lively events. In those days the subject was not a popular one. There existed more general ignorance and hostility towards it (particularly in the Middle West).than towards any other branch of contemporary art.

[1] Reuben Mamoulian, the film director and play producer, and Martha Graham, the dancer, both started their careers in the Rochester Opera Department as teachers of dramatic action and ballet respectively. Later, too, Paul Horgan, the novelist, came to it; and Otto Luening and Ernst Bacon, composers.

[2] Hanson's work on behalf of the American composer is already epic.

Before returning to England for Christmas on the French liner *Paris* (the worst crossing I've ever experienced, during which a bronze statue of Venus and an Erard grand piano tore from their moorings in the saloon and met under a large potted palm), I conducted one of the Sunday night Composers' Guild Concerts in New York. A fantasy for nine wind instruments, which I had written on my lecture tour, met with strong disapproval from the New York Press, and works by Varese, Salzedo, and Ruggles received equally strong castigation. But one never could please those New York critics. . . .

The fantasy for wind instruments was responsible for some excitement at the concert of the Chelsea Music Club which I conducted in London early in 1925. I had left the orchestral parts in New York, and a cabled request had failed to produce them right up to the morning of the concert. The postman brought them two hours before the concert was due to begin, and I decided to ask my wind-players when I reached the hall whether they would care to prove their expertness by taking something of a risk. They consented, and after explaining the circumstances to the audience and asking their indulgence for the delay, I prolonged the interval before the second half of the programme[1] to half an hour and rehearsed the work in the artist's room. The nine players, with music propped up on violin-cases and chairs, read the piece once through like a flash, and further painstaking, concentrated rehearsal enabled us to present it in performance at the appointed time as though nothing had ever been amiss. The audience's applause was as much a tribute to this superb feat of musicianship as to any merits of the fantasy itself, and left me personally speechless with admiration for the London players' *tour de force*. The *Telegraph* critic next morning thought the same, adding, rather disparagingly, that the

[1] The remainder of the programme consisted of Gretry's overture to *L'Epreuve Villageoise*, a Glazounov serenade, a *Little Symphony* by Milhaud, Bartok's *Roumanian Folk-dances*, the Ravel *Tzigane* and one of the Italian overtures of Schubert.

work left him with 'the impression of having listened to a clever conversation on a frivolous theme'. This same writer must have had the same thought in mind when, the following week, after my giving the first English performance at a Royal Philharmonic concert of Honegger's *Pacific 231*, he wrote:

What a hit for the Southern Railway. It is difficult to label this music at all, but Goossens swept his train along in such fine style that I would suggest that *Pacific 231* is repeated for the benefit of the directors of the Southern Railway, who, headed by Sir Herbert Walker, might be led along to Queen's Hall to listen to it. For one thing, *it started punctually!*

The next three months passed fairly uneventfully. There was a Royal Choral Society concert; and a British National Opera Company season at the Golders Green Hippodrome, during which Gustav Holst's opera, *At the Boar's Head*, had its first production. This praiseworthy attempt to set Shakespeare to folk-song may be set down from the public's point of view as a plucky failure. Musically, its skilfulness is undeniable but unconvincing, and still leaves us with *Savitri* as Holst's only really successful operatic essay. The Golders Green season proved again that Londoners won't accept surburban operatic fare as a substitute for West End performances. London ballet fans are an exception to this, and, whether it is Sadler's Wells, Croydon, or the Coliseum, they'll flock to whatever is offered, irrespective of location. Serge Diaghilev, however, had little choice in this matter when he accepted an offer at the latter theatre to present a series of isolated ballets in early summer, after a preliminary season in Barcelona. His fortunes had vacillated considerably since the company had last appeared in London, and even though the ballets at the Coliseum were to be sandwiched in between vaudeville turns, he was in no position to turn down the offer. I agreed to conduct both in Spain and London for him ('*parceque, mon cher, Barcélone est vraiment séduisante à cette époque*'), and arrived by the middle of May in the Catalonian city. There were two days' preliminary rehearsals with Casals' orchestra at the Liceo Theatre—one of the best opera houses in Europe—and we embarked on a fifteen-day engagement, during which I conducted thirteen different ballets. This entailed a daily rehearsal with the ballet in the morning, the orchestra after lunch, and an evening performance (including Sundays) consisting of four ballets—starting at 10 p.m. and ending at 1.30 a.m. This schedule proved so exhausting that I hired a motor boat every afternoon, and told the captain to cruise around the harbour while I slept.

I liked Barcelona, particularly the shady Calle de los Ramblas, which was Diaghilev's customary walk—that is, when he felt like walking to his favourite café, with the inseparable Boris Kochno and Lifar. One night we all went to 'Villa Rosa' where, for the price of a glass of wine, we saw some of the best *gitana* and *flamenco* dancing in Spain. I saw Carmen Amaya dance there, a gipsy child of five with precocious talent; and many others who didn't achieve her fame.

CHAPTER XLIV

'AFTER the dinner, flower-like ladies of the Russian Ballet—the blonde Sokolova, the exquisite Nemtchinova, the lovely Tchernicheva—all, alas! somewhat more prosaic in their pretty frocks than behind the footlights, fox-trotted with the nonchalance of quite ordinary people. . . . "Heaven alone knows what I am doing here with the Russian Ballet," groaned Jim Thomas.[1] "If it gets known outside, all the morning posters will be shouting, 'J. H. Thomas with the Bolsheviks again!' But I've given away no political secrets to-night, anyway!" ' So wrote the *Daily Sketch* about the dinner at the Hotel Cecil given by the members of the Coliseum Orchestra in my honour at the conclusion of the season.

Two weeks later I returned to America, where the Rochester Orchestra had adopted a new régime. G.E. had decided that the system of dual control over the orchestra was unworkable, and handed me a contract as its sole musical director. This entailed a full season's activities and also enabled me to accept offers further afield as guest conductor. The first of these came as an invitation from Walter Damrosch to conduct two weeks' concerts in New York with the New York Symphony Orchestra early in January 1926. (Otto Klemperer also made his New York début that season with this orchestra.) The programme for the first pair of concerts included the Brahms *Second Symphony*, the Haydn 'cello concerto with Casals as soloist, and the *Sacre du Printemps* of Stravinsky, which the President of the orchestra, the great Mr. Flagler, characterized after the concert as 'obscene music'. Most of the elderly lady subscribers, incidentally, agreed with him, for we finished the afternoon

---

[1] J. H. Thomas, M.P. and General Secretary of the National Union of Railwaymen.

Carnegie Hall concert to rows of empty seats, after a mass exodus of indignant patrons. The enthusiasm of the Press for our performance proved some compensation, the *New York Times* stating vigorously that a new prophet of Stravinsky had arrived in the city. Frieda Hempel and Gieseking were soloists at the three concerts of the second week, and I remember at Mecca Auditorium Gieseking's performance of the Hindemith concerto as an astonishing *tour de force*. The orchestra was a fine, sonorous body of players, with perhaps less virtuosity than its rival, the New York Philharmonic, but with some outstanding virtuosi, notably the French woodwind quartet, Barrère, Mathieu, Duquès, and Letellier—flute, oboe, clarinet, and bassoon players extraordinary. . . . Georges Barrère was surely the greatest flute player of all time. He played two duets of mine for flute and oboe with my brother Leon. Pan and the shepherd together surely never evoked sweeter sounds.

No sooner had the New York Philharmonic been disposed of than I was on my way to conduct four concerts with the Boston Symphony Orchestra, an invitation I had received from Koussevitzky some weeks previously. The first concert took place at Infantry Hall in Providence, and the remainder at Symphony Hall in Boston. The programme for the latter included three works new to Boston, the Delius *On Hearing the First Cuckoo in Spring*, Debussy's *Iberia*, and my own *Sinfonietta*. The Boston Symphony Orchestra was (and still is) so superior in subtle quality to any other of the major orchestras that directing it proved an emotional experience far beyond anything I had known. Not such good readers as the Philadelphia Orchestra or the best London orchestras, the players of the B.S.O. produced nevertheless such a mellowness of tone and well-balanced sonority that it seemed as if no greater perfection of instrumental blend could possibly be achieved. Here again the principal wind players were French; Laurent and Gillet, on the flute and oboe, being outstanding. I had thought the Damrosch Orchestra a fine group. The Boston players transcended them out of all knowledge.

Philip Hale of the *Globe* and Parker of the *Transcript* wrote long and laudatory articles about the concerts. The length of the Parker critiques in particular (a column and a half of close type and erudite thinking) astonished me after the laconic effusions of the London and New York critics. After the final Boston concert, I left for New York to conduct a Sunday-night Composers' Guild, the programme of which was typical of the spicy musical fare available to the enterprising listener in those days. It contained works by Respighi, Casella, Germaine Tailleferre, Salzedo, and myself. All the composers, being in America at that time, were present. A later concert featured Florence Mills, the Negro singer from the Plantation Revue, in a group of beautiful songs by William Grant Still and a group of traditional spirituals. All of these she rehearsed with me and a small orchestra in the record time of half an hour, a tribute to her superb musicianship. At the concert Toscanini sat entranced, and, for a wonder, came back-stage to congratulate her. We survived, incidentally, a grim piece for strings by Carl Ruggles, the New England modernist who, like his fellow countryman, Ives, wrote next to unplayable music.

The season in Rochester ended unexcitingly in March, and we returned to London in April just in time to experience the worst rigours of the General Strike. All forms of transportation having come to a halt, one found oneself walking fantastic distances, and as a protest I recall volunteering to drive an underground train. This offer, fortunately for passengers, was turned down, and I decided to await the end of the strike, which, as it comes to all strikes, duly arrived. In June, Diaghilev asked me to conduct a long season of Russian ballet at His Majesty's Theatre, to include the production of eight newly commissioned ballets. He also decided to make a feature of 'symphonic interludes' between the ballets, all consisting of new or unfamiliar music. Diaghilev himself chose them—proof of his eclectic taste and knowledge of orchestral music. A list of these 'interludes' makes interesting reading:

Auric. *Malbrouk s'en va t'en guerre*
Auric. *Five Bagatelles*
Lord Berners. *Fugue*
Borodine. *Scherzo*
Bizet. *Jeux d'Enfant*
Chabrier. *Fête Polonaise*
Chabrier. Suite, *Pastorale*
Delibes. Overture, *Le Serpent à Plumes*
Dukelsky. Overture, *Gondla*
Darjomisky. *Fantaisie Finnoise*
Darjomisky. *Baba-Yaga*
Goossens. *Nonet*
Gounod. Little symphony for wind instruments and overture; *Le Médicin malgré lui*, overture
Glinka. 'Lesginska' from *Russlan and Ludmilla*
Honegger. *Pacific 231*
Maxim Jacob. Overture
Mozart. *Eine Musikalische Spass*
Moussorgsky. *Intermezzo in Modo Classico*
Poulenc. Overture (orchestrated by Milhaud)
Rieti. Concerto for wind quintet and orchestra
Ravel. *Alborado del Gracioso*
Rimsky-Korsakov. *The Battle of Kershenitz*
Satie. *La Belle Eccentrique. Les Grimaces*
Sauget. Nautical dance and nocturne
Tailleferre. *Le jeune matelot*
Walton. Overture, *Portsmouth Point*

Many of these were first performances, and the only trouble we experienced was to persuade the audience to listen to them. Eventually they caught the idea, but rather resentfully, as anyone knows who has tried to get the average ballet audience out of the foyer and back to their seats for the next ballet! Karsavina rejoined the ballet that year, and Lifar and Balanchine were newcomers. The programme for the opening night consisted of *Carnaval*, Stravinsky's *Les Noces* (first performance in London), and *Matelots*, by Auric. The front page of the programme had the following. 'Serge Diaghilev Season of Russian Ballet', and '*Le Ballet Russe de Monte Carlo, sous le haut patronage de S.A.S. La Princesse Héréditaire de Monaco*'. *Les Noces*, for which Nijinsky's sister devised the choreography, created a sensation with the public, but not such a great one with the Press, with the result that H. G. Wells, who was present at the first performance, wrote the following letter to *The Times:*

I have been very much astonished at the reception of *Les Noces* by several of the leading London critics. There seems to be some undercurrent of artistic politics in the business. I find in several of the criticisms to which I object, sneers at the élite, and in one of them a puff for some competing show. Writing as an old-fashioned popular writer, not at all of the high-brow set, I feel bound to bear my witness on the other side. I do not know of any other ballet so interesting, so amusing, so fresh, or nearly so exciting as *Les Noces*. I want to see it again and again, and because I want to do so, I protest against this conspiracy of wilful stupidity that may succeed in driving it out of the programme. How wilful the stupidity is, the efforts of one of our professional guides of taste to consider the four grand pianos on the stage as part of the scene will bear witness. Another of these guardians of culture treats the amusing plainness of its backcloth, with its single window to indicate one house, and its two windows for the other, as imaginative poverty—even he could have thought of a stove and a table; and they all cling to the suggestion that Stravinsky has tried to make marriage 'attractive', and failed in the attempt. Of course, they make jokes about the mothers-in-law—that was unavoidable. It will be an extraordinary loss to the London public if this deliberate dullness of its advisers robs it of *Les Noces*. This ballet is a rendering in sound and vision of the peasants' soul, in its gravity, in its deliberate and simple-minded intricacy, in its subtly varied rhythms, in its deep under-currents of excitement, that will astonish and delight every intelligent man or woman who goes to see it. The silly, pretty-pretty tradition of Watteau and Fragonard is flung aside. Instead of fancy-dress peasants, we have peasants in plain black and white, and the smirking flirtatiousness of Daphnis and Chloe gives place to a richly humorous solemnity. It was an amazing experience to come out from this delightful display, with the warp and woof of music and vision still running and interweaving in one's mind, and find a little group of critics flushed with resentment and ransacking the stores of their minds for cheap, trite depreciation of the precious and strongest thing they had had a chance to praise for a long time.

The pianists in this production were the four composers, Auric, Poulenc, Rieti, and Dukelsky. Nevertheless, I had more trouble securing an ensemble from them than I did from the fine Russian chorus (imported from Paris) and my English percussion players combined, who were all crowded into the orchestra pit, with the four pianists placed both sides of the stage in view of the audience.

Other interesting novelties, such as Stravinsky's *Pulcinella* and Rieti's *Barabau*, followed during this season. Auric's *Pastorale* and Dukelsky's *Zephyr and Flora* were stimu-lating, while the revival of *Thamar*, featuring Karsavina in her original role, was of outstanding interest. It is still the perfect ballet. A little ballet called *Jack-in-the-Box*, based on dances to unpublished music by Eric Satie and scored by Milhaud, proved interesting. Edwin Evans wrote in the programme:

The music of *Jack-in-the-Box* consists chiefly of piano pieces which were composed about a quarter of a century ago as incidental music to a scenario by Jules de Paquit. The composer always believed that he had left the MS. in a cab, but he was in the habit of accumulating his discarded suits, of which a large number were found at his death, and in the pocket of an old jacket were discovered the long-lost dances which have since been orchestrated by Darius Milhaud.

During the last week of the ballet, the orchestra gave me a complimentary dinner at Pagani's restaurant: it was they who really deserved the dinner, for they had had a strenuous time with a minimum amount of rehearsal. The ballet ended on 23 July, and on Saturday the 24th I sailed from Southampton on the *Carmania*. During the voyage, which took nine days, I wrote all the music for Margaret Kennedy's play *The Constant Nymph*, consisting of the song, 'When Thou art Dead', the Charade and the sung recitatives. Two days before my departure Basil Dean had asked me whether I could undertake it; strangely enough, up to that time he seemed to have overlooked the important matter of incidental music for the play. He asked me to get the music to him within three weeks, as the production couldn't be held up. I therefore devoted myself exclusively to the job during the trip across the Atlantic, and daily, and often nightly, occupied a corner of the smoke-room, set aside religiously by the steward for this purpose. By the time New York appeared, I had finished the work without the help of a piano. On going ashore, I mailed the music to Dean, and it arrived in London a week later by the *Aquitania*. Noel Coward and Edna Best played the principal parts; and Edna sang 'When Thou art Dead' (which was soon hummed all over London) very appealingly. Noel hadn't time to learn the accompaniments adequately, so these were valiantly shouldered by the lady who played the servant-girl—in private life a good pianist!

CHAPTER XLV

Back in America for a fourth season,[1] I went to Hollywood to conduct four concerts at the Hollywood Bowl —a new experience, and the first of many visits there. In those days the audiences for concerts in the beautiful hillside open-air Bowl, with its perfect acoustics, rarely fell below 10,000 or 15,000. In 1929 I conducted there once to a crowd of nearly 30,000 people. To-day, with the landscaped alterations and changed artistic attractions of the Bowl, such throngs are rarely seen. It requires the presence of film stars or an Easter morning service to conjure up a crowd exceeding four figures.

As usual, I included plenty of new music in these programmes. Novelties on the Pacific Coast in the 'twenties were virtually non-existent; the two incumbents of Los Angeles and San Francisco cared for little else but the standard classics, and so even Saint-Saëns was looked upon as a modernist. To these starved audiences the adventure of any novelty was exhilarating, for neither the radio or the phonograph at that time commanded the following they do now. So when the Lion's Club—a business-men's fraternity —decided on an outing to the Hollywood Bowl during Henry Wood's week of concerts,[2] Elgar's *Symphony No.* 1 played on that programme probably counted little more to them than, at best, 'Land of Hope and Glory'. At the end of the performance of this long work, during a lukewarm spatter of applause, the limelight was suddenly switched from the bowing figure of Sir Henry mid-stage to a large papier-mâché lion, complete with wagging tail, on an adjoining hillside. This coincided with the explosion of several

[1] 1926.
[2] Alfred Hertz, then the genial bearded *maestro* of the San Francisco Orchestra, Oberhoffer, van Hoogstraten, and myself were the other conductors engaged for that season.

237

rockets back-stage—all contrived by a well-meaning but thoughtless club committee to celebrate the Lions' presence at the concert—and the discomfited Sir Henry withdrew from his darkened stage to seek refuge in the artists' room, from which he later emerged, rightly indignant, with Lady Wood, to return to his hotel without conducting the second part of the programme. This was taken over by the concert-master, and Wood returned to England; nor did he ever go back to the Bowl. This regrettable incident didn't in any way affect my reception the following week, and nothing occurred to mar the four concerts, splendidly played by the Los Angeles Philharmonic. The orchestra included three former colleagues from the Queen's Hall Orchestra: Henri de Busscher, oboist, Alfred Brain, horn-player, and Alf. Kastner, harpist; three virtuosi of first rank whose westerly migration proved highly profitable for all three of them. For fine players, Los Angeles was—and still is—a financial Mecca. The revenues from playing in the movie studios, plus symphonic engagements and teaching, formed a lucrative combination—when they did not impose too great a strain on the player's health. My own health benefited much, about this time, from frequent deep-sea fishing expeditions on the Pacific with Arthur Alexander, who handled a rod as expertly as he teaches singing. Setting out at dawn from Catalina Island in a diesel fishing-boat is as good a form of escapism as any I know. If you are subsequently fortunate enough to hook a three-hundred-pound marlin, so much the better. If not, there are always the long Pacific swells and the tang of salt air to give an exhilarating sense of well-being as compensation for other deficiencies.

There was also the composer, Henry Eicheim, with whom I stayed in his lovely house at Santa Barbara. Henry had been to Bali, China, and Java, and brought home many native instruments which he had skilfully incorporated into a series of picturesque tone-poems, *Bali*, *Java*, etc. But unless you borrowed the actual instruments—mainly percussion—you couldn't play his music: a distinct handicap for such a gifted and imaginative writer as he was. One room of his at Santa Barbara was filled entirely with different-sized Burmese gongs. You could strike these gongs successively and start up a prodigious clanging and booming, and return half an hour later to catch the faint hum of them still lingering in the stillness.

Finally, in Hollywood itself there would be endless rounds of after-concert suppers and parties, with Mary Pickford, Gloria Swanson, Marion Davies, Pola Negri, Chaplin, Novarro, and others playing hosts and hostesses. They made you feel that the movie colony was not the pleasure-loving congregation of numbskulls they are usually painted, but a group of intelligent people of culture who could discuss music as well as the best. Their comings and goings to the Bowl remained usually unnoticed by the audience, to whom they were everyday figures. How different to-day, with the bobby-sox type of gawking lunatics who gloat at the slightest rumour of the presence of a 'name'! . . .

Back in Rochester, we embarked on the 1926–7 season with the usual round of symphony concerts and performances by the Opera Department, which had made great strides towards its professional goal of an opera company. Mary Garden happened to be in Rochester at one of the performances of *Figaro*, and was so astonished and delighted by what she saw that in a moment of enthusiasm at the end of the evening she exclaimed, 'What a superb, professional-like show. Why, I almost felt like taking part in it myself!' I said, greatly daring, 'Miss Garden, we're putting on *Carmen* in February. Won't you come and sing *Carmen* with us?' 'Well,' said she, 'I might *think* about it!' Nothing further was said, but I immediately went to George Eastman and told him of her reaction. 'She may have only been joking, G.E.,' I said, 'but no harm would come if you were to tell her how honoured we'd feel if she would really consent.' 'I'll try,' he said.

And try he did, for later he telephoned me and said with a chuckle, 'She'll do it!' So it came about that in February, after a mere couple of orchestral rehearsals, Mary Garden sang, with all her old fire and still quite a lot of her former vocal artistry, the role of Carmen with the members of the Eastman School of Music Opera Department. The event took place in the Kilbourn Hall of the School, and my small orchestra of thirty-six never at any time overpowered the singers in the beautiful hall, though the *diva* overpowered *us* by her electrical vitality and the fire of her performance. All the intensity and vigour at her command were thrown into that characterization, as though she were determined to show that she had lost none of her cunning. The fact that she sang in French, while the rest of the opera took place with the English translation, passed comparatively unnoticed. Hedley, the Don José, was completely shaken by the whole thing, and related that in the last act he felt as though Carmen might conceivably put the knife into *his* heart rather than he into hers!

After the opera George Eastman dispensed sandwiches and champagne to his distinguished guest and her fellow performers. I have never seen that crusty old bachelor so openly fascinated by anyone as he was by the alluring Mary that night. Some indeed whispered that he had, for the first time in his life, fallen in love! . . .

Across the seas, in England, the operatic year had started with a B.N.O.C. season in London, with my father conducting *Manon*[1] on the opening night, thus celebrating the sixtieth year of a lifetime given over to the cause of opera in English. Later in the year I saw him conduct *Gianni Schicchi* with this company, and marvelled still at his precise, quiet, and unassuming manner at the conductor's stand. He always had an unfailing catholicity of style, which accounted for his ability to tackle a really enormous repertory without seeming to experience any difficulty in switching from one idiom to the other. Wagner, Mozart, Gounod, Puccini, all came alike to him, so that I never heard him referred to

[1] A few weeks later he conducted the same opera in Liverpool, in connection with which the following appeared in the Liverpool *Mercury*: 'Mr. Goossens conducted the opera a few hundred yards away from the theatre in which, over forty years ago, his father [my grandfather] conducted the first performance of the work in England. . . .'

as a fine conductor of such-and-such a work, but rather invariably as the expert conductor of 'repertory opera'. An enviable reputation, difficult to emulate.

Another member of the family, my brother Leon, was active in the European scene this year, when he appeared with the Venetian String Quartet at the International Music Festival in Venice. He played the Bliss and Bax oboe quintets, dedicated to him, with the quartet. I started sketching an oboe concerto for him, so that he would have a short but transcendentally difficult work to play on his projected American tour. There was literally nothing in the range of technical complexities he couldn't cope with.

My sisters Marie and Sidonie were now respectively harpists of the London Symphony and British Broadcasting Company Orchestras. For them too I devised a tentative concerto, but scrapped it as being impracticable, and rescued merely enough material for *Two Ballads*, which harpists usually distort because of the time signature (7/8).

Back in New York, my *Three Greek Dances* for small orchestra were played at one of my Sunday-night Composers' Guild concerts. The critics, to a man, detested them, but none took the trouble to say why. I have discussed this strange reluctance on their part with my brethren. Ernest Bloch ascribes it to badly functioning livers, Stravinsky to complete technical ignorance, and Cyril Scott used to quote Richter's famous dictum about their resemblance to the keepers of harems, familiar with their master's prowess, but incapable of emulating it! My own experience is that most scribes find themselves incapable of formulating and sustaining a verdict in a strictly limited period of time. Their often flimsy technical equipment collapses under pressure, and whatever impressions were gathered during the actual concert have defied any precise mental formulation between the concert-hall and the office. But give men like Newman, Downes, Thomson, Cardus, Evans, Yeiser, Frankenstein, and a few others of that calibre a bare half-hour at their desks, and the threat of an imminent deadline calls into play not a panicky floundering of mental processes, but a tautening of critical ones, backed by judgment and knowledge. Composers with something to say, not to mention most conductors of integrity, have always been exposed to the ineptitudes of inferiorly equipped reviewers: the pity of it is that editors can't be persuaded or frightened into keeping such people off their staffs. So long as music criticism is considered of no more importance than social reporting, so long will it be handed to the tender mercies of the sports reviewer, the movie critic, and, worst of all, the *soi-disant* critic with a veneer of smug education but no more than a nodding acquaintance with the skin and bones of creative and interpretative musical art.

CHAPTER XLVI

Two other happenings in New York during that spring season of 1927 made some stir. The Opera Department of the Eastman School of Music finally blossomed in full flower as the American Opera Company at the Guild Theatre in New York, and a few days later I conducted George Antheil's *Ballet Mécanique* at a concert of his works at Carnegie Hall. Both events aroused the excited comment of the New York critics, who lavished hallelujahs on the one and lambasted the other. At the Guild we opened with a sparkling performance of *Figaro* in English which, I think, for perfection of style, *mise-en-scène*, and ensemble, can rarely have been surpassed. This was not a student performance, but a thought-provoking and entertaining exhibit by finished artists. The credit goes largely to Rosing, whose production was original and novel in a subtly detailed way. It certainly vindicated his theory that young American artists could adequately present small-scale productions of opera on original lines as opposed to the conventional ones featured elsewhere.[1] The singers were of first order, and exceptionally competent in their roles. My picked orchestra would have done credit to Glyndebourne at its most polished, and the scenery of Norman Edwards was stylized without being precious. *Butterfly* was presented the second night, with Cecile Sherman effective in the title-role, and a second act with a quite novel ending. Until then the harbour of Nagasaki had always appeared on the back-cloth, with the watching Butterfly silhouetted against the paper screens, as the curtain fell. Rosing reversed the procedure, with Nagasaki in the audience, and the silhouettes behind semi-transparent

[1] The Rochester venture undoubtedly paved the way for companies like the New York City Centre Opera.

shoshi drawn across the proscenium arch. This departure from tradition seemed fully justified for a theatre with a small proscenium. A refreshing feature, too, was the elimination of much of the conventional and rather silly business with the relatives in Act I. I also found that a reduced string section in the orchestra improved the tone-quality in the love duet. Other operas were later added to the season, but I did not conduct them.

Antheil's *Ballet Mécanique* required for its execution twelve grand pianos (with an equal number of grand pianists, all playing independent parts), one pianola (played by the composer), six xylophones, one sheet of steel and riveter, half a dozen different-sounding electric pushbells also played by the composer, two aeroplane propellers revolved manually against ratchets, and one conductor (static and self-possessed). The difficulties of the fifty-minute work were formidable, and at least eight or ten rehearsals were required before the pianists, a picked group, had accustomed themselves to the intricacies of constant time-changes and passage-work. The final effect achieved by my dozen devoted artists, playing this wickedly inhuman music by themselves, was uncanny. Their marvels of rhythmic valour had to be heard to be believed. But the moment the percussion instruments were added, much of the detailed team-work was lost, and when the aeroplane propellers joined the fray, near-pandemonium ensued. I tried to temper this at the final rehearsal, but accomplished only a tolerable balance.

The huge audience gathered for the concert was a strangely mixed one. Along with a sprinkling of musical intelligentsia was a large coloured contingent from Harlem, who came to hear Duke Ellington's band, which played one of Antheil's jazz experiments in the first half of the programme. Carnegie Hall was jammed to the rafters; the boxes bulged with Ellington fans. We started the *Ballet Mécanique* in the second half of the programme, and there were snickers and thinly veiled guffaws after the first few measures. I knew then that this audience, whetted by reports of the *scandale* which followed the première of the work in Paris, had, in the main, come to scoff. As the piece proceeded, the hubbub grew worse, till finally the audience kept up a steady chorus of jeers, catcalls, and whistles which lasted throughout the whole piece. Missiles began to fall on the stage, but never once did we flinch! One man in the stalls stood on his seats and waved a handkerchief tied to an umbrella, shouting, *'Kamerad!'* Others paraded down the aisles. This lasted until we had finished the work, though just before the end the audience seemed to relapse into a shame-faced half-muttering. Then came the final chords, and a great outburst of booing, hissing, cheering, and stamping broke from an audience the contemptibility of which had never been seen or heard at any concert in the United States. The performers had throughout the work preserved a seriousness worthy of a happier cause, and certainly no composer was ever served better by his interpreters. I had to direct every measure imperturbably; any signs of indignation or hesitation on my part might easily have let loose a riot in the hall.

Next morning the New York papers came out with front-page columns reporting the scenes of the previous evening. There was little attempt to estimate the worth of the piece, since much of it was barely audible to those serious critics who came and stayed. Newspapers all over the world devoted editorials to the concert. The sound sentiments of an English daily may here be quoted:

Possibly, then, the American composition may be an original masterpiece, not yet grasped into the consciousness of musical New York. The fact that aeroplane propellers were employed in its performance was certainly not in itself sufficient reason to condemn it or, for that matter, to praise it. Everything depends on how the propellers were used. After all, people accustomed to hearing taut, stretched skin banged with sticks, brass blown into or hit, and animal guts scraped, have, on the face of it, nothing to complain of if the propellers are whizzed in addition. The new is not good because it is unusual, but because it is unusual it is not therefore bad. Perhaps the deeper truth is that in art the merely sensational, whether acceptable or not, can never last.

The concert thus remained a nine-day wonder. But only just, for a repeat concert announced the next day for a fortnight ahead was cancelled for lack of interest. The *Ballet Mécanique* was a noisy product of its time, an abortive attempt to emulate the success of the *Sacre du Printemps*, but resulting only in a rather Dada-esque fiasco. Fortunately its composer, after some fifteen years of musical obscurity, has lately shown in his *Fourth Symphony* the fruition of talents which the best pages of the *Ballet Mécanique* undeniably revealed.

Shortly after this excitement, I received a cable from Diaghilev asking me to get to Barcelona by the beginning of May for another three-week season there. So a few days later I found myself again at 'Villa Rosa', drinking the wine of the country with Diaghilev, Kochno, Lifar, and Wolheim. The season was strenuous; four ballets a night (beginning at ten o'clock) and orchestral rehearsals each morning. But the change of scene was welcome. Pablo Casal's orchestra was in good form at the Liceo Theatre, and my old friend Lamote de Grignon still performed his miraculous transcriptions of Albeniz with the Banda Municipal. Diaghilev had several new ballets in preparation, but, fortunately for my health, he decided to produce these in London; the season was sufficiently strenuous. So we adhered to the repertoire ballets, and at the end of the season I returned with the company to London. Only a fortnight elapsed before recommencing activities, this time at the Prince's Theatre, where the orchestra pit was uncomfortably small, necessitating an overflow of brass players into the audience. The novelties I conducted were Prokofiev's *Le Pas d'Acier*, Sauget's *La Chatte*, Milhaud's *Train Bleu*, and Berners's *Triumph of Neptune*, in addition to the regular repertoire, including revivals of *Matelots*, *Facheux*, *Les Biches*, *Pastorale*, and Constant Lambert's charming *Romeo and Juliet*. The first, an exciting affair in Prokofiev's best manner, with a scenario of machines and workers, threatened at first to create a *scandale*. That is, anyway, as Diaghilev would have wished. Rumours had circulated that, as the ballet was Bolshevist propaganda and London was extremely anti-Bolshevist, the audience would certainly put up a hostile demonstration on the first night. I entered the orchestra for the première, receiving the usual applause from the audience—unusually cordial, I thought, under the circumstances—followed by Diaghilev, who took a seat next to the first flautist. He had previously told me of his intention to do this. 'I'm carrying my revolver,' he said, 'and at the first signs of any demonstration I shall fire it in the air.' What he hoped to accomplish by this I never discovered, but my theory is that a well-timed pistol shot would have really brought about the disturbance Diaghilev was secretly hoping for. Needless to add, no interruption whatsoever marred the exciting performance, and as the curtain fell the audience burst into a stupendous ovation. Diaghilev made his way out of the orchestra, more than ever perplexed by the unpredictable British public.

Sauget, founder of the young group of composers styling themselves 'L'Ecole d'Arceuil' (in contra-distinction to 'Les Six') was unknown to British audiences. His music for *La Chatte* proved almost Gounod-like in its deliberate self-conscious sophistication, and blended strangely with Miro's metallic *décor*. The ballet marked the London début of Serge Lifar, a fine dancer. *Train Bleu* was rather commonplace Milhaud, with Dolin in blue bathing trunks heading a group of equally undressed holiday-makers at some fashionable plage. Lord Berner's work was an adroit period piece with a score of more real ingenuity and charm than many a more pretentious ballet. Six weeks of nightly performances proved a heavy physical and nervous strain, and I found myself unable to contemplate the prospect of any further seasons with the Ballet, especially in view of increasing musical activities in America. Diaghilev heard my decision with some emotion. A real friendship had grown up between us during those six London years together, and I admired him, with all his faults, for the great man and impeccable connoisseur he was, just as his regard for me rose from a full confidence in my handling of ballets which he himself knew backwards, and, I am convinced, could at a pinch have conducted without a qualm. So on the closing day of the season we ate a final lunch at the Carlton grill, with the ever-present Kochno and Lifar, and that night, to my great surprise, Diaghilev, who rarely took a bow, appeared on the stage while I was taking a call. With no attempt at a speech, he smilingly handed me a small package, and walked quickly off again without waiting to acknowledge the outburst which greeted him. The package contained an engraved gold fountain-pen which I contrived to keep for the record period (for me) of ten years, and with which, in due course, I wrote two operas. The day it finally fell out of my pocket in the Strand, every London newspaper copied the Scotland Yard announcement of its loss.

CHAPTER XLVII

AFTER a few weeks' rest, I left Southampton for the Hollywood Bowl. Instead of staying at the usual hotel, I accepted the hospitality of some Hollywood friends[1] who lived in a remarkable Frank Lloyd Wright house. Its central feature was a rectangular swimming-pool, around which stood the house, leaving an open end backed by a hillside, with the large studio living-room at the opposite end, and eight bedrooms on both remaining sides. After three pleasant weeks' stay, my hosts suggested inviting the members of the Los Angeles Orchestra to a party in their honour after my final concert. After much pressure, I accepted their offer on behalf of the orchestra, though warning both parties of the possible consequences of too convivial an entertainment. As I feared, on the night in question, three performers had to be fished out of the pool; one, a member of the orchestra's percussion section, having to undergo emergency treatment before showing signs of animation. This hilarious evening, coming in the middle of the Bowl season, produced, I was told later, a quite deleterious effect on the orchestra's morale and ensemble for at least the three following concerts.

Some weeks later, on arriving in Rochester for the beginning of the 1927–8 season, I found some interesting particulars from my father concerning the tour of the British National Opera Company in England, to which group he had returned as conductor. Thomas Beecham had taken the company over, and planned a National League of Opera, which would, if it came into existence, firmly establish the fortunes of the company for good and all. A clipping from the *Yorkshire Post*, reporting Beecham's speech on the subject to the people of Leeds, is worth

[1] Mr. and Mrs. John Sowden.

reproducing here because of its forcefulness, characteristic grim humour and relevance:

Beecham said the scheme he would submit was so humble in its economic appeal, so businesslike in its practical application, that no excuse could be offered for not accepting it at once. Putting aside the delusion that help was to be expected from the Government or municipalities, or that opera could be permanently sustained by a few rich people, he said there was in England a substantial, resolute minority of music-lovers. Taking London and nine or ten other cities of the country, he calculated that the number of people would not be fewer than 200,000. They went regularly to whatever operatic performances were available to them, good or bad, and it was upon the support of this faithful element that his scheme was founded. The details of it were to be made known on Monday. To be on the safe side, he proposed to deduct 25 per cent. from the 200,000, leaving 150,000, and he would say to these people—not ghosts nor spooks, but real people—'I will give you the finest opera in the world, and I will do it at a price that is no more than a glass of ale. I will give opera as good as Vienna, and a little better, I think. I will give you opera as good as you can hear in New York, where there are eighteen millionaires. It will cost me £60,000 a year—not a shilling less. £60,000 divided among 150,000 people—what does it mean? It means just eight shillings a year each—tuppence a week—the price of half a glass of ale, a bun or a slab of Yorkshire pudding!' (*Laughter*.) He would say further to the musical salt of this English earth: 'Do you want the finest opera in the world for tuppence a week, or don't you—because if you don't want it, for the love of heaven say so, and I will take the scheme somewhere else? If you do want it, you will get opera as good as any in the world. You will have a permanent orchestra; there is not one in England to-day. You will have the choice of seats in the house, but you will not pay any more for them than you are paying for them to-day, and you will pay less than the despised entity known as "the general public".' It was not ill-will, he added, that was the matter with this country; it was inertia. (*Hear! Hear!*) When he asked opera-lovers of this country for ten shillings a year for five years, as he proposed to do, he wanted it to be understood that the response must be immediate and complete, and if it was not forthcoming, there would be no opera. All his experience proved that the basis of opera must be democratic, and upon that healthy basis one institution would beget another into it. The nucleus of 150,000, would, in five years' time, grow into 200,000, and so on until we had a musical public of a million people. (*Applause*.) Opera would not then be at the mercy or caprice of a few rich people who did not go to it (*laughter*), but who liked to read of it on the Riviera in the columns of the *Yorskhire Post*. In present circumstances the British National Opera Company was living from hand to mouth—a company of vagrants inhabiting spiritual lodging-houses (*laughter*), and he was waiting for the time, which he believed was not far distant, when they would come to him saying, 'The game is not worth the candle.' This, he insisted, was his last attempt to draw attention to the seriousness of the situation, and if this particular scheme of his did not succeed, or one like it, they might take it that in two years' time there would be no opera in this country. They could see the red light now, in the baleful influence of that Minotaur in music, the British Broadcasting Company (*laughter*), and he predicted that in five years' time the whole musical civilization of the country would be the culture of robots—not living people.

It seems incredible that the logical and very practical scheme outlined in the above terms by its originator was, like all Utopian schemes on behalf of opera in England, doomed to failure. The response of the public was half-hearted and apathetic. The artists of the struggling B.N.O.C. looked to the projected League to place opera in England—and themselves—on a thoroughly permanent economic basis, so their disappointment at the eventual outcome may be imagined.

My own opera, the one-act *Judith*, with Arnold Bennett's libretto, was virtually completed; I had put the finishing touches to the vocal score earlier in the year in Barcelona. Chester in London had undertaken to print it, a fact which greatly pleased Bennett. Before sending the vocal score to Chester, on returning to Rochester, I decided to suggest one or two textual alterations to the librettist, and mentioned my proposal to add a preliminary chorus and ballet. The letter also contained some reference to the business side of our collaboration. A few weeks later Bennett wrote:

13 *October*, 1927.
My dear Eugene,—Many thanks for your letter. I am like you; I leave the questions of terms in the hands of my agents. I am informed that Chester says that if you and I cannot come to an agreement about the division of spoils, they will not print the score at all. This seems to be a very odd attitude—in fact, I do not understand it in the least. How can our division of the royalties affect Chester?

I note what you say about your suggested alterations. They seem to me to be quite all right, but no doubt I shall have a proof to-day.

I quite agree in principle to the suggestion about the preliminary chorus and the ballet.[1]

Ever your,
A. B.

Back in the States the sudden death of Verbrugghen, conductor of the St. Louis Orchestra, had left that orchestra without a head. The directors therefore divided the season

[1] The matter in the first paragraph was duly settled, and I finally added a ballet, but not the preliminary chorus.

between three 'guests'—Arbos, Oberhoffer, and myself, and I managed to rearrange the Rochester schedule to fit in with that of St. Louis. The Spaniard, Arbos, conductor of the Madrid Philharmonic, I had not seen since those pre-war days at Muriel Draper's studio in London. He had not changed, and was the same witty *raconteur* as ever, telling inimitable stories which have become established classics in the profession. His unaffected style of conducting produced extraordinarily effective results; this is more than could ever be said for his violin-playing, which was nervous and uncertain. I always enjoyed concerts at the old Odeon, which, in spite of shabbiness and rats, had gratifying acoustics—better, in my opinion, than the new hall with which St. Louis is at present blessed.

My brother Leon arrived early in 1928 for a long-projected oboe recital in New York at the Guild Theatre, and made the New York public and critics rub their eyes at his incontestable artistry. The Marianne Kneisel (daughter of the famous violinist) Quartet assisted at the recital, and so did I, in the capacity of accompanist. The programme consisted of the Mozart and Arthur Bliss oboe quartets—transcendentally difficult works for any oboist—a new sonata for oboe and piano by David Stanley Smith (then music professor at Harvard), and a group of solos. It seemed as if all the wind-players in New York were at the concert; and Mr. Smith was present, much to my discomfiture, to hear his somewhat gloomy work. The concerto I had designed for Leon's visit turned out not to my liking, and I decided to postpone its production till the following season, when he was to return to America.

The first four months of the year offered a pleasantly varied prospect of guest conducting; Baltimore, New York, St. Louis, and Pittsburg, in addition to my own group in Rochester, were all on the schedule. The Baltimore Orchestra in those days could not begin to compare with the present organization. Consequently, except for a reunion with genial Fred Huber, the city's Director of Music, and a trip to a roundhouse of the Baltimore and Ohio R.R. (to see those historical locomotives brought together by my friend Ed. Hungerford for the B. and O.'s 'Fair of the Iron Horse'), my visit was not memorable. The concert at the Lyric Theatre was scratchy, and the orchestra plodding and unreliable.

A different matter was the New York Philharmonic's benefit concert at Carnegie Hall, held in March in aid of the American Academy in Rome and the National Music League. Five conductors—Toscanini, Bodanzky, Arbos, Damrosch, and myself—lent an appropriately international flavour to the event, and each conducted a piece by a fellow countryman. My own choice was *Brigg Fair*, by Delius, which the orchestra played accurately but stodgily. We had only a single rehearsal of two and a half hours—my share being thirty minutes—in which to prepare the whole concert. A pretty question of protocol might have arisen, on whether Toscanini or Damrosch should have first say as to when and how long he would rehearse. That same day, however, was announced the amalgamation of the Philharmonic (Toscanini) and the N.Y. Symphony (Damrosch) into the New York Philharmonic Symphony. Anyway, the *maestro* played an Italian work, which he was currently performing that same week with the Philharmonic, so he didn't choose to rehearse at all! This solved the problem.

After the concert I took a train to St. Louis for a final concert with the local orchestra. The Italian Molinari and the German Schuricht had meantime been added to the roster of visiting conductors for that orchestra; St. Louis was certainly getting its diversified fill of guests. Molinari, the most ridiculously hot-tempered of all *maestri*, was giving the orchestra the 'works' with a vengeance. Stories of his stick-breaking, desk-biting, and watch-smashing exploits at rehearsal have long since passed into the realm of legend. At that time they were new to the country, and the St. Louis Orchestra was taking to them none too kindly. In this respect he made his countrymen, Mugnone and Toscanini (neither of them exactly kindhearted at rehearsal), look like people of mild disposition! I found the St. Louisians writhing under the smart, but all nevertheless full of respect for Molinari's musicianship. But they played no better than usual, which confirmed again my theory that the velvet glove over the iron hand is as effective a way as any for getting results from an orchestra.

In April, before returning to England for the summer, I went to Pittsburgh to conduct the first of the concerts of the reconditioned Pittsburgh Symphony Orchestra. Elias Breeskin, the concert-master, had trained the refurbished orchestra, the concerts of which had long been isolated and sporadic events until the decision was taken to start afresh a new series of concerts, with guest conductors and under new management. A certain Mrs. Hall had been the prime mover in this revival, and considerable excitement was created by her announcement that the first concert would be given on a Sunday night. This was directly in contravention of the 'blue' laws of Pennsylvania, which forbade any kind of entertainment on the Sabbath. I arrived for this first concert to find the city agog with anticipation of trouble, and the city fathers hurling threats of what was likely to happen if we went through with the concert. Mrs. Hall, in order to gild the pill and appease the wrath of the Lord and the city fathers, had taken due steps. Consequently, when I arrived for the concert, I found an Episcopalian minister ready to precede me on to the stage, and deliver an invocation and a blessing. This crafty subterfuge deceived no one, for at the end of the concert, warrants were issued for the arrest of six members of the committee and 'one musician'. The latter presumably referred to me, but at the time the arrests were executed (the following morning) I had already boarded the *Mauretania* in New York on my way to England, and so escaped the fine or imprisonment meted out to the others. Syria Mosque was packed for the concert, and the orchestra, no doubt inspired by the occasion, played well. Harvey Gaul, the spirited critic of the *Post Gazette*, was in good form. I cannot forbear quoting him:

Beau Sabreur of the conductorial business, this Merlin from Rochester, came down here, waved his stick, told the men a few things about crescendos, and the result was the best concert we have ever had with this organization, *etc.*

I frequently went back as guest conductor to Pittsburgh on subsequent seasons, until such time as Antonio Modarelli was made permanent conductor. Finally, Fritz Reiner was appointed the distinguished head of the orchestra, and under him it became a fine ensemble.

The Grand Season at Covent Garden was just about to get under way when I arrived in London. It presented the usual galaxy of international stars, taking part in very often unrehearsed, improvised performances with a sprinkling of British singers and a British chorus for good measure. I was roped into one such performance in the middle of June. The opera was, as on a previous similar occasion, *Faust*; the night before this particular performance, Colonel Blois, Harry Higgins' successor as 'intendant' of Covent Garden, telephoned, asking me whether I would conduct the performance because of the illness of the regular French conductor. I suggested he ask Percy Pitt, the regular Musical Director at Covent Garden, but Percy was either unable or unwilling to play substitute. So next morning I had a short piano rehearsal with Chaliapin, who had just arrived from Paris, and discovered that the great man was, as usual, very shaky in the matter of both words and music. He covered up his inaccuracies in both respects by pleading fatigue, but I recalled that some time before, when we had made gramophone recordings[1] together, his French was found to be sketchy. In note-values he was notoriously inaccurate, and always led conductors at the opera a merry dance in this respect. I remembered that only a month previously the papers had contained details of serious altercations between him and Koussevitzky in Paris, and Emile Cooper in Moscow. It seemed that history might again repeat itself that night. All went fairly well at the performance (though Chaliapin faltered badly twice in the

[1] Later that year I conducted his recordings of the *Death of Boris*, for H.M.V., which necessitated much rehearsal.

255

opening scene), up till the second scene of Act I—the *Kermesse*—when, during the waltz, he missed a lead, and, forgetting the words, started extemporizing with some impromptu 'la la's'. His floundering was obvious to the audience, especially when, to cover it up, he came downstage and started conducting the orchestra, trying to give the impression that I was not playing the music to his liking. I kept on serenely, with undeviating tempo, and paid no attention to him, till he was shortly engulfed by the *corps de ballet*. The curtain fell, and Chaliapin appeared to take a call with John Charles Thomas, who was making his London début as Valentine, and who, after his aria in the *Kermesse* scene, had received a thunderous ovation. The audience immediately renewed its *bravos*, obviously *not* directed at Chaliapin. This predilection had undoubtedly discomfited him, and contributed something towards his demoralization in the Waltz music. No further incident marred the evening save that the tumultuous reception for Thomas's singing of '*Dio possente*' in the third act again unmistakably eclipsed Mephistopheles' star. And through-out the performance the Devil's musicianship and French diction were consistently wanting.

Next morning I was awakened by a six o'clock call from a news agency asking me to comment on a front-page story in the *Daily Express*, which, I was informed, gave a highly coloured, exaggerated, and rather one-sided version of the previous evening's 'violent altercation' between singer and conductor. The article, obviously written with an eye to the sensational, told how Chaliapin, in his exasperation, was compelled to go down-stage to indicate the correct tempo of the music, and more such rubbish. I told the reporter my version of the affair, and stressed that Chaliapin and I had always enjoyed the most friendly relationship. In the other morning papers the incident was mostly minimized.

The Times said:

In the first act, it seemed that there was going to be a struggle between the conductor and the conducted. We are glad to see that the conductor intended to retain command. . . . One felt that there was a live wire at the conductor's desk and a high explosive on the stage most of the time.

The *Daily Mail*:

No one will forget this unique Mephistopheles—least of all Mr. Eugene Goossens, who conducted the performance with exquisite skill, and who must have had the most exciting five minutes of his life during the Katerina serenade.

Ernest Newman in the *Sunday Times* wrote:

. . . It was clear that Mr. Goossens had made up his mind that in any opera there can be only one conductor, and he rightly stuck to his convictions. ·

The whole affair was summed up two days later by an editorial in the *Daily Mail*, which was headed 'Chaliapiniana'. It said:

Greek meets Greek when an operatic singer of the first eminence crosses the path of a distinguished conductor. The production the other night at Covent Garden of a hackneyed opera which would ordinarily have stirred only a languid interest took on a dramatic tension. This was not only through the vivid art of a Mephistopheles who made the mortals around him seem mere puppets, but also through that personage's challenges to the authority of one to whom even the archfiend usually has to bow—namely, the orchestral conductor. Mr. Goossens is far too able to look after himself for any condolences to be in place. The Great Man's caprices did indeed lead him in a dance—a dance that would have turned into a cropper with a conductor of less exquisite skill. The suggestion has been made that the almighty Chaliapin, his head at length a little turned by so many years of adulation in the hemispheres, was deliberately not playing the game; but that strikes us as ungenerous. Rather we prefer to believe that he had acquired such a confidence in the brilliant young Englishman's almost uncanny alertness and flexibility that he felt it safe to give the reins, for once, to his wildest fantasy, and Mr. Goossens, so far from having to be condoled with, probably enjoyed giving this exhibition of jugglery with the baton. It was certainly the most entertaining *Faust* seen at Covent Garden for a generation. All the same, the Great Man may be reminded of the dangers (if there is a Russian equivalent of our idiom) of 'swelled head'.

CHAPTER XLVIII

I LEFT for Paris that morning, but not before giving an interview to the *Evening Standard*, minimizing the whole incident. I said that the singer and I were the best of friends, and that we did not customarily indulge in public displays of temperament. Side by side with this appeared a similar one from Chaliapin, containing further assurances and protesting that we had never had a misunderstanding in our lives. How much of this the public swallowed I do not know, but the incident was closed from that time. In Paris I saw Rouché, the sapient Director of the Paris Opéra, who had asked to hear my ballet, '*L'Ecole en Crino-line*'. Diaghilev, who I had hoped would produce it, had not cared much for the subject, based on an early Victorian scenario. He probably found it excessively stylized, though he never actually said so. Finally Rouché, who was on the look-out for a novelty for his *corps de ballet*, arranged an audition in his room at the Opéra, and I fumbled through my piece feeling something like a pupil at the Conservatoire playing for the Director. '*C'est épatant, Monsieur! Mais c'est pour Diaghilev, pas pour moi!*' And so I was back where I started and took my leave of Rouché, a man of considerable charm and culture. You could comb Hollywood and not find a more perfect type for the role of Director of the Paris Opéra. His musical tastes were limited, and my little work obviously exceeded the bounds. So, later, did my operas, but that is a different story. . . .

I went to Baden-Baden, the delightful town in South Germany, for the dual purpose of taking a cure and listening to the musical festival, transferred from Donau-Eschingen. I do not know which was the dullest—the all-meat diet of Dr. Dengler's Sanatorium or young modern German music. Long early morning walks through the pine-woods of the

Schwarzwald helped to dissipate the after-effects of both, but I remember being inexpressibly bored by the monotony of meat and music. German music had then reached its nadir of stodgy abstraction, and an atmosphere of artificial *Kultur* exuded from those owlish young men who later became ornaments of the Hitler régime.

So I wasn't sorry to find myself, ten days later, *en route* to Amsterdam and the Concertgebouw Orchestra. Mengelberg, with whom I was then on cordial terms, had invited me to do a concert with his orchestra, with the pianist Elly Ney as assisting artist, playing the first Brahms concerto. An embarrassing episode at this concert comes to mind. The conductor enters the stage at the Concertgebouw from the top of the orchestra risers, and descends the steps in full view of the audience until he reaches the front of the stage. That afternoon the attendant escorting me from the artists' room opened the door to the stage, and stepped on my loose shoelace. I moved forward, and to the consternation and doubtless the amusement of the audience fell heavily on the top step, narrowly missing one of the double-bass players and a precipitous fall down the remainder of the steps. It was small consolation to learn afterwards that others more myopic than I had survived a similar fall. With what grace was left me, I recovered myself, proceeded unscathed to the rostrum, and embarked on a stimulating concert. At that time, the Concertgebouw was considered as fine an orchestra as any in Europe, but I found it heavy-handed, with the same irritating trick of attacking a fraction *after* the beat that I had found with the Berlin Philharmonic. The string volume and rich brass tone were superb, but in quick movements the orchestra seemed surprisingly cumbersome.

After a final day in Amsterdam, spent mainly at the Rijksmuseum, I left for a third visit to Hollywood, where the town seemed sharply divided over the programmes announced for my concerts. Many were of the opinion, including the old conservative subscribers of the Los Angeles Symphony, that they featured too much modern music; especially as the *Sacre de Printemps* was to close the series. The preponderance of symphony 'fans' was, however, all for a little gingering up of the programmes, and one group, signing itself the 'Goossens group', wrote to the Bowl office saying that it would not attend a concert which did not contain at least one contemporary novelty. Some letters on the subject had appeared in the local Press before my arrival and, the day of the first concert, the *Express* carried an editorial which reflected the peculiarly superficial kind of aura surrounding the Hollywood concerts, an aura through which one's artistic integrity penetrated with increasing difficulty season by season:

To-night Eugene Goossens will take the stand at the Hollywood Bowl. Such a statement, quiet enough sounding in itself, is full of potentialities. Incident to the occasion, there are a lot of things to be recalled. One of them is Goossens' first appearance at the Bowl in 1926, when almost with the first lift of his baton, a new and enthusiastic group of persons came into being. It was the 'Goossens group', hundreds of men and women who love Bowl concerts, but who feel that the Bowl has not really achieved a season until Goossens comes back. To-night he comes back for the third successive season, having travelled twenty thousand miles by steamship and rail since he came here last August. It means that there are more after-concert supper parties than the remainder of the summer season, all told, has produced. It means that hundreds of new gowns are on display, that Mr. Goossens' two weeks of concerts here, besides proferring the most gratifying two weeks of programmes ever scheduled, will be crowded from morning to night with beach parties, lunches, teas, garden fêtes, dinners (but not on concert nights, if you please!), and after-concert suppers. To many, the advent of Goossens to the Bowl is the peak of the season, etc. [*ad nauseam*].

A big audience came to hear the first performance on the West Coast of the Stravinsky opus. To quote the *Times*:

Out of the tremendous audience—about 25,000—a few hundred expressed their opinion by taking their departure. About 20,000 remained to listen with the keenest appreciation. [The mind boggles at the thought of the *Times* reviewer clocking the exodus of sceptics in the obscurity of the Bowl.]

At the end there was a great demonstration; the audience remaining to debate the work so long that over half an hour elapsed before the last stragglers had departed. I don't suppose the *Sacre* has ever sounded so dynamic and full-throated as on the occasion of that open-air performance.

Technically, the performance was amazing, especially as rehearsals had been none too plentiful; the fact remains that I recall no other concert performances I ever conducted of this work, whether the first in London, or later in New York or Rochester or Cincinnati or Sydney, Australia—all fine playings—that had as authentic a sound about them as the one under the stars in the Bowl valley that night.

Before leaving for Rochester, I made some open-air recordings with the orchestra of familiar numbers in the Bowl repertory—later issued under the title of *A Hollywood Bowl Album* by the Victor Company. These, I believe, were the first open-air recordings ever made by a symphony orchestra, and turned out amazingly well. The faint sound of a high-flying aeroplane may be discerned by experts in the slow section of Dvorak's *Carnaval Overture*; this novel effect, though detected by the sound engineers during the orchestral recording, I did not consider too much of an anachronistic blemish to warrant condemning the record; nor indeed, is it really audible.

The reader will have remarked that the process of plunging into a winter season in those active years of the 'twenties was, so far as I am concerned, rather like a dip in a 'lucky bag'. You never knew what you might draw out, but it was invariably interesting. It was fortunate for me that the spacing of events in Rochester was such as to permit excursions further afield without interfering too much with my regular duties. Thus I was able to pay several visits to Pittsburgh for more Sunday concerts, over which a legal battle was still raging between the city fathers and the orchestra. My first concert there again opened with prayer. The irreverent Harvey Gaul wrote next morning:

The Rev. H. Boyd Edwards, Rector of the Church of the Ascension, gave the Invocation. He's a strategist, that man, and knows exactly what to say. . . .

Ossip Gabrilowitsch, whom I had frequently heard both as a pianist and a conductor, but knew very slightly, wired before Christmas asking whether I'd take his place at

Detroit for a pair of symphony concerts and a Sunday afternoon one. I had heard that the orchestra was very fine, but was hardly prepared for as polished a virtuoso group as I found on arrival. All the first-desk men were excellent artists: Scholnik, the concert-master, led a brilliant string group and John Wummers, now flautist of the New York Philharmonic, headed a fine wind section; I was delighted to find too that the discipline of the orchestra was irreproachable—something often lacking nowadays, especially in some of the first-rank 'name' orchestras. But the orchestra played comparatively little modern music (in spite of assistant conductor Victor Kolar's attempts to remedy this deficiency); its Director was fundamentally a classicist, and often failed to realize that his orchestra needed some contemporary galvanizing to display its best qualities. Nevertheless, the players gave me a memorable first concert.

I spent a delightful time in the company of Gabrilowitsch and his wife, Clara Clemens (the daughter of Mark Twain), for, like their parent, they possessed a keen sense of humour and caustic observation. G.'s idiosyncrasies of dress—especially an abnormally high collar and a severe frock-coat—set off a definitely *fin-de-siècle* personality. He was even dubbed a *poseur* by those who failed to see in him almost the last survivor of the grand manner of piano-playing.

I returned again to Detroit for further concerts on New Year's Day, 1929—a repetition of my previous experience—and a week later my brother Leon arrived from England. Together we gave several New York concerts, ending up with a programme of my own works at Jordan Hall in Boston. The programme for the latter, at which, together with Leon, I was assisted by the Burgin Quartet, consisted of my piano quintet, the sketches for string quartet, the string sextet (in which I played third violin), a group of piano pieces, some songs sung by Gertrude Ehrhart, and the new oboe concerto, which the Bostonians liked far more than did the New Yorkers. Leon, for whom I had written a tremendous display piece, complained that the cadenza was not showy enough. I therefore added some coruscations, which he negotiated brilliantly, but which seem to have placed the work permanently out of the range of all but two or three great oboe virtuosi. It is nowadays used chiefly as a *morceau de concours* by conservatories, and perhaps deserves its fate, though I lavished much thought on its construction and ideas.

If it is thus only periodically exhumed, the same, happily, cannot be said for another work written about that time, the *Concertino for String Octet*, nowadays played chiefly by string orchestras under the title *Concertino for Double String Orchestra*. It had a first performance that February in London by the combined Mangeot and Poltronieri quartets —the latter a fine group from Milan. The critics could not reconcile the rather neo-classic style of the piece with my usual idiom, and produced all sorts of silly arguments to prove that a composer cannot write in classic mould without producing a *pastiche*. Discounting the host of suites 'in the olden style' copied almost note for note from Vivaldi *et al*, there still remain such works as Stravinsky's *Pulcinella*, Bloch's *Concerto Grosso*, Ravel's *Tombeau de Couperin*, and many others which are as characteristically original and representative of their composers as anything they ever wrote. But they definitely are not *pastiches*; nor, for that matter, is my concertino.

CHAPTER XLIX

At the end of January, Toscanini, having developed a painful neuritis in the right arm, was unable to conduct his regular pair of New York Philharmonic concerts. Accordingly, Fritz Reiner of the Cincinnati Symphony was dispatched to take his place, and my manager, Arthur Judson, asked me to fill the gap at Cincinnati. At the time I had no inkling of my future association with that city, so I undertook the visit with no presentiment other than the usual pleasurable anticipation. I found a fine orchestra, much too big (a hundred and five players) for the rather small hall and stage which accommodated it, and a warm greeting from Herbert French, then President of both the Proctor and Gamble soap-works and the Institute of Fine Arts, which controlled the orchestra. The founders of the Institute were the late Mr. and Mrs. Charles Phelps Taft; its main object being to carry on the orchestra and concerts. To finance the latter, the Tafts offered the Institute a million dollars provided an additional two and a half were raised for an endowment fund by public subscription. This remarkable feat was duly accomplished and was being celebrated about the time of my visit. I called on Mrs. Taft at her beautiful colonial house (now a museum); she was very courteous, but took no special interest in me until I began to admire her Corots and other *objets d'art* scattered throughout the house. She died the following year, and the orchestra lost a great benefactress in her passing. I found the Cincinnati players responsive, but not too inspiring. I think the fact of their being packed like sardines on the stage of Emery Auditorium had not a little to do with this. They produced a torrential sound with great technical accuracy, but string phrasing which lacked sweep and spaciousness. Again, it was largely a matter of faulty acoustics and cramped stage.

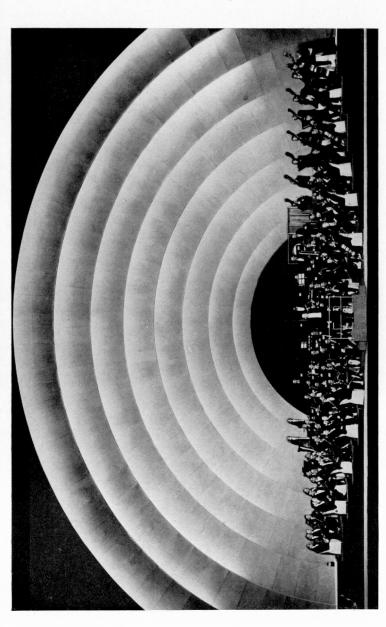

EUGENE GOOSSENS III CONDUCTING THE LOS ANGELES ORCHESTRA
AT THE HOLLYWOOD BOWL, 1931

Up to February 1929 I had conducted most of the major orchestras of America, but three or four were still to come. Of these, I relished most the thought of first-hand contact with what I considered then the most opulent of all orchestras—the Philadelphia. Thomas Beecham, so often the cause of exciting last-minute experiences for me in former English years, now provided the occasion for this. Engaged by Stokowski as a 'guest' at Philadelphia, he became indisposed before the rehearsal for his final pair of concerts, with the result that I found myself, two days later, making a Philadelphia début. The reaction of the public on this occasion was politely cordial. But I revelled in the sumptuous sound of the orchestra, inconceivably lush and vibrant. This tonal splendour emanated from a group, each player of which was a virtuoso in his own right. Stokowski thus had gone the logical way about providing himself and the community with the best orchestra art and money could produce. But it is a tribute to his qualities as leader—whatever reservations one may make about his interpretative idiosyncrasies—that he succeeded in moulding what might have proved an unmalleable group of stars into a homogeneously balanced entity. In all, during the course of a few days, I conducted seven of its concerts. Besides the pair mentioned above, there were two more concerts in Baltimore and Washington, two more again in Philadelphia, and finally one at Carnegie Hall in New York. During this tour we played four different programmes, of which those in Baltimore and Washington created the least impression. The 'stuffiness' of the audience in these cities was in direct ratio to their musical perceptiveness. Washington, where the audience seemed to be made up of deputations from the different embassies, yawned its way steadily through the concert. The New York public, on the other hand, gave all evidence of complete satisfaction with their programme and the way it was played; it included the Brahms *Fourth* and a new suite from Lord Berners's ballet, *The Triumph of Neptune*. Not so the critics, who gave an astounding exhibition of critical ineptitude. The morning papers—Downes, Henderson, and Liebling—praised the concert to the skies. Sanborn, Chotzinoff, Oscar Thompson, and Stokes (all of the evening papers except Chotzinoff, who wrote for the now defunct *World*) disapproved thoroughly. So great was the difference of opinion concerning my version of the Brahms (I think an extremely conservative one) that one of the music papers reprinted all the criticisms side by side, under the heading, 'How should Brahms be Played?' and added rightly:

No one who was not present at the concert could have any idea of what Goossens actually did by reading the Press reports. . . .

Then, as now, to most of the New York critics the guest conductor was fair game. It did not matter *what* you did, or how well or indifferently you did it, two-thirds were out to 'get' you, purely as a matter of principle. They are wise in their generation who have overcome the delusion that taking an orchestra from the hinterland to New York or even appearing there with the three big Eastern ones is anything but openly courting what can be the most humiliating critical contumely. New music on your programme, however good, counts for little if the verdict has gone against you in the classics. Berners's *Triumph of Neptune*, a worthwhile contemporary novelty, was dismissed on this occasion (by the same four writers who derided the Brahms) as an insignificant piece of amateurishness, which it certainly is not.

I left the Philadelphia Orchestra in New York with considerable regret. I had come to know and like many of the players, particularly Hilsberg, the concert-master, Liffschey, the principal viola, and those fine artists, the principal flute, oboe, and trumpet-players, Kincaid, Tabuteau, and Caston. It seemed inconceivable that one could ever rest satisfied elsewhere with any standard and quality of performance lower than that of this orchestra. Still, I found nine concerts with the St. Louis Orchestra the following two weeks a pleasant experience. (A trip on a 3,000-ton liner can be just as enjoyable as a week on the *Queen Elizabeth*!)

I liked this orchestra for its geniality. It played music good-humouredly, as though it enjoyed doing so—and it did. The audience was a kindly, intimate one; and, particularly in the old Odeon of that time, one realized the importance of contact between players and listeners. This atmosphere of intimacy made music-making an especially pleasurable business in St. Louis. Only once did the audience ever show signs of discomfort at the proximity of any of the performers. This was when, at one of my concerts, Gieseking played Falla's *Nights in the Gardens of Spain*, a performance spoilt by the artist's habit at that time of snorting and grunting in passages of either great emotion or ferocity. He played the Strauss *Burlesque* at the same concert, one of the most astonishingly dexterous feats I have ever heard. Such was the tremendous physical impact of his hands on the keyboard in *fortissimo* attacks that a piano string snapped under it. Yet when Gieseking played the quietest Debussy, his *pianissimi* were almost inaudible. Georges Enesco, the Rumanian violinist and composer, played there the week following Gieseking. During our rehearsal of the Mozart violin concerto a rat jumped up into one of the front orchestra seats, and crouched spellbound till a well-aimed bit of violin resin dislodged him. He did not appear again, but Enesco was a shaken man.

A Mr. Baldwin, then President of the Missouri Pacific Railroad, was also President of the orchestra; through him I was frequently able to indulge my hobby of riding loco-motives. Once I acted as assistant fireman on the oil-burning locomotive, No. 5336, pulling the 'Texan' (all one had to do was to inject the oil-fuel when the steam pressure fell, and also watch the gradients) and almost forgot a dinner that evening at the 'Coronado' in my honour. But I remembered it in time to board a returning train from Bismark in the Ozarks, and created something of a sensation by appearing in oil-spattered overalls just as dinner had started, to explain to my hostess that I would return after a ten minutes' interval for changing my clothes. Which I did, and was forgiven.

I left for England on the *Homeric*, impatient to discover what progress, if any, had been made on the preparations for the production of *Judith* at Covent Garden in June. After long-drawn-out negotiations, Colonel Blois, new Chairman of the Royal Opera Syndicate (which had ignored the native product for more years than I care to name), decided with some courage that a couple of performances of the Goossens-Bennett opera could not possibly hurt the season too greatly, either financially or from the point of view of prestige, and so had boldly inserted one hour's all-British operatic fare bang in the middle of the sacrosanct Grand Season. It was with some (possibly mistaken) sense of my own importance in the operatic cosmos that I hastened to the theatre one day about seven weeks before the production, to ascertain exactly how much progress had been made in the matter of rehearsals and production. But no rehearsals were listed on the call-sheet; I could find none of the musical staff or scenic department on duty in the theatre, and the few singers I met seemed to be completely unaware of the impending great event. I enquired of old Austin, the stage-door-keeper, Harold, the call-boy, and Jones, the fireman, whether they had heard anything which might point to my opera being in preparation. No; they knew nothing. It was obvious that I would have to make enquiries elsewhere, and on my way out of the theatre for that purpose ran into Moore, producer and stage-manager of the Syndicate. Yes, he could tell me something; the cast had been chosen, but hadn't started musical rehearsals. There was a model of the scene upstairs in the paint-room, if I cared to see it. Costumes? Oh well, there was plenty of stuff in the wardrobe that could be adjusted to the period. So, apprehensively, I went to see the model of the scene. Two palm trees, complete with coco-nuts, and a striped awning—Holoferne's tent—against a blue backcloth comprised the specially designed *décor!* I enquired concerning the cast. Admirable, with one important exception! The title role had been allotted to a *Swede*—Göta Ljungberg. This was discomfiting news. An English opera should be sung by English singers: I knew

Continental singers and their ideas about English pronunciation. Bennett's text was important and had to be
understood by the audience. But perhaps Ljungberg was an
exception and sang understandable English; I asked Moore
when I could hear her. He regretted much that I couldn't;
she was at the Charlottenburg Opera in Berlin and wouldn't
be in London for some time. In a flash I sized up the whole
situation—that Nemesis of opera in English, procrastination, was about to wreck the production, and it was necessary
to act quickly to avert a catastrophe. Moore disclaimed
responsibility and Blois was away for the week-end. I rang
up my friend, Frank St. Leger (chief *répétiteur* at Covent
Garden and later Edward Johnson's assistant at the Metropolitan Opera), asking him as a personal favour to me to
begin immediately coaching the four other principal singers
in their roles (which they hadn't even started), and to give
Judith priority over everything else. He immediately
agreed, adding significantly that it was a great pity I hadn't
returned from America a few weeks sooner. I then went to
Cook's, bought a ticket for Berlin, and wired Mme Ljungberg to expect me in twenty-four hours. On arrival I found
she exceeded my worst expectations. She hadn't even begun
to study her formidable role, and the little she read at sight
convinced me that her fine voice wasn't even suitable
for the part. Moreover, worst of all, her pronunciation of
English—of which she hardly knew a word—was with
a thick Swedish accent.

I arranged to stay in Berlin for two weeks to teach her the
role, note by note and word by word. To her credit be
it said, she abandoned everything else to concentrate on
mastering it, though frequently I felt justified in wiring
Blois to cancel her engagement. Only the thought of jeop-
ardizing the production made me always reconsider the
consequences of doing this. Eventually, in the last week of
June, that somewhat (to me) melancholy event duly took
place under my direction. The dress rehearsal the day before
the performance was, of its kind, farcical. The orchestra
played its part admirably, but the stage was not ready. The

scenery, while an improvement on the original model, was incomplete (as were some of the costumes—Bagoas, the eunuch, wearing 'plus fours'), although one extra palm tree had been added, and the tent conveyed less the idea of a catering job. The lighting plot was non-existent, and the rehearsal was punctuated with such shouts as 'Dim number two, Alf', 'Bring up yer —— foots, Bill', 'Gawd's truth! Where's George?' and similar effusions as assistant George King and machinist Ballard tried to carry out their very sketchy instructions. The amateurishness and apathy displayed by everyone in the theatre in connection with my new piece (except at the actual performance) would have been impossible even in a fourth-rate Italian opera house; it could only have happened in England.

To make matters worse, four or five of the leading critics had either made their way or been invited surreptitiously to the rehearsal, and at least two of them wrote their notices —mainly hostile—on the strength of it, without troubling to hear the actual performance. Their reactions to the *contretemps* at this rehearsal may well be imagined and deplored. During the scene where Judith pretends to seduce Holofernes, she gradually removes her tunic. To everyone's consternation, on arriving at this particular moment, instead of revealing a greater degree of epidermis, Ljungberg was seen to be wearing a sort of sequined bust bodice. This threatened not only to arouse derision, but to undermine the whole dramatic *raison d'être* of the opera. I stopped the orchestra and with some heat conjured Ljungberg to remove the offending garment. (Some of my more lurid remarks on this occasion have gone down in the annals of Covent Garden.) The performance was incomparably better than the dress rehearsal. By some miracle, the stage forces had transformed the bits and pieces from stock operas, which constituted the scenery, into something rather more exotic than the previous set, and most of the lighting cues synchronized roughly with the libretto. The public took to it, and at the end there was genuinely prolonged enthusiasm. I spotted Bennett in a box, but nothing would induce him to come on stage; his shyness got the better of him, a fact that he himself admits in the entry in his journal dated 25 June 1929:

Another oath broken. After some fantastic experiences at my own first nights, I had sworn never to attend another. But when I told the authorities of Covent Garden that I should not be present at the first performance of the Goossens-Me opera, *Judith,* there was such horrified, outraged protest that I accepted a box on the spot. And there I sat on the first night, hiding behind a curtain and surveying the crowded house. My highly nervous state was mitigated by the realization of the unquestionable fact that I was not Eugene Goossens, exposed defenceless to the public and conducting the orchestra. I kept carefully in the box, but well-intentioned friends and quidnuncs would insist on visiting me both before and after the performance. I had not the courage to tell them that, with the important exception of loud and prolonged applause, all an author wants on a first night is to be left alone. I paid what I was afraid would be a state visit to the *prima donna.* But it was not in the least stately. After I had kissed her hand, we forgot ceremony and were realistic with one another about all manner of things, and laughed like girl and boy.

Critics, with two notable exceptions, were luke-warm about the opera. The *Daily Express* headed its notice with the words: 'Opera without a Tune', and said that an opera from which you couldn't whistle anything was hardly worth noticing, or words to that effect. Most of them seemed unable to comment intelligently about the music, and confined themselves to vapid remarks regarding the similarity, in places, of the score to Strauss' *Salome*, which it doesn't resemble at all. The one thing all of them seized upon was the Eunuch's make-up, for the producer, Moore, had given him a slight beard. Even Ernest Newman couldn't resist this, and said at the end of his article:

May I ask for information from experts on a little point of stage realism? Mr. Widdop, as Bagoas, wore a moustache and beard. This is physiologically incorrect.

He then quoted a passage from a book called *Eunuchs through the Ages*, which further derided the unfortunate Bagoas; but he atoned by referring to the music as 'a marvel of subtlety', which pleased me immensely.

Many of the reviewers criticized Bennett's libretto and

its rather staccato style, forgetting entirely that this was precisely the type of libretto needed to fit my music. The opera was broadcast by 2LO (then the B.B.C.), and the voice of Achior, heard at the beginning of the opera, with the curtain down, was projected through an amplifier placed in the ceiling of Covent Garden. This alarmed a great many people (especially old ladies and late-comers) but proved extremely effective and ominous. The Russian ballet shared this programme (*Judith* only lasted an hour) with performances of *Sylphides* and *Petroushka* to wind up the evening. They had also danced the ballet in *Judith*, but the alternately langorous and frenetic atmosphere in my music was not realized in the dances, which, like everything else connected with the production on the stage, bore the definite stamp of improvisation.

CHAPTER L

Two days before the production of the opera I gave a mighty afternoon concert at Queen's Hall. This had been hurriedly planned with the agents Ibbs and Tillett, on my return from Berlin, as an experiment to help bridge the orchestral gap in London between the end of the winter season and the start of the summer promenade concerts. I had collected a hundred and ten of London's best players—virtually the same used in my series of modern concerts seven years previously—and decided on a trip to Paris to persuade Stravinsky to take part in the concert as soloist. I found him in his little studio at the new Salle Pleyel, practising the piano vigorously with the aid of some iron dumb-bells which, from time to time, he would lift over his head and then slowly deposit again on the floor.

'What are you using them for?' I asked him.

'For the development of the forearm,' he replied, and added:

'I find this additional muscular strength very helpful in playing my music.'

I then asked him to play his piano concerto at my London concert in a month's time, to which he agreed, after some little discussion about terms.

The programme consisted of the *Fourth Symphony* of Brahms (I wanted to see whether the London critics would disagree about it as did their New York brethren), the Stravinsky piano concerto, and Respighi's *Roman Festivals*, both the latter being first performances in London. The hall was sold out and the enthusiasm overwhelming.

The critics are worth quoting here on the subject of the Stravinsky concerto, with Capell of the *Mail* providing by far the most picturesque (but questionable) opinion:

273

Stravinsky played the solo in his concerto for piano, wind instruments, and double basses. The audience of *cognoscenti* showed a distinct liking for this curious work—a parody, and rather a grim one, but interesting in its way. The programme drew analogies between this Parisian freak and eighteenth-century concertos and sixteenth-century masters—analogies which no plain man need bother his head with. There is the same relation between Stephen Leacock and Milton. What we heard, whatever Stravinsky may have meant, was a parody. Stravinsky, good musician that he is, writes what the age wants. There is enough serious music to go on with, but such a work as the new concerto of Stravinsky provides the compiler of orchestral programmes with something odd, rather perverse and rather learned—a piece of clever, academic frivolity, as a relief from the severe music of the standard repertory. This music, unimportant but rather stimulating, ugly but not odiously ugly, is what the best of the jazz-mongers of the day would like to do if they only had enough intelligence and technique. To try another description of the concerto, it is probably rather like Bach as Bach seems to wireless listeners who hate the name Bach and want nothing but coon songs.

Evening News:

To the initiates, or propagandists, it is no doubt a miracle of beauty, better than the *Matthew Passion*. The plain man would call it a hoax.

Sunday Times (Newman):

The pleasure of seeing the composer of Petroushka again was equalled only by the pain of hearing the composer of the piano concerto. It was sad to think that the one-time man of genius had degenerated into the manufacturer of this ugly and feeble commonplace.

New Age:

Of the incredibly, lamentably feeble and dreary display made by M. Igor Stravinsky and his piano concerto, it is difficult to write adequately.

Re-reading these effusions to-day, the adjectives 'feeble' and 'dreary' seem far more applicable to these 'criticisms' than to the work of a serious composer, who, whatever the ultimate worth of his concerto, can at no period of his development ever have merited the adjective 'feeble'!

The verdict on the Respighi was mostly adverse, *The Times* making the extraordinary assertion that it seemed 'to have been constructed in order to satisfy the craving of the Americans for mere size'. The same critic, however, concluded his review with: 'If for nothing else, Goossens deserves our gratitude for demonstrating that we have in London an orchestra, permanent or not, which invites comparison with any in the world.' But the perfectionist Newman, differing with all his colleagues, began with: 'Mr. Goossens had only a moderately efficient and obviously tired [certainly not with excess of work] orchestra under him at his concert on Thursday afternoon. It was a long time before he could get out of it either the tone or the feeling desired in Brahms' No. 4.' This being the only querulous note in the entire Press concerning the Brahms, it seems unnecessary to add that New York history did not repeat itself.

By now the years had taken on a geographical monotony of pattern in which a summer visit to the Hollywood Bowl seemed inevitable. It differed in this particular year in two respects, being prefaced by two concerts with the San Francisco Orchestra, and being of twice the duration of any previous visits to the Bowl. San Francisco, after a rough crossing on the *Aquitania* and a scorching trip from New York was, by contrast, a refreshing experience. Two concerts were scheduled: one at the Woodland Bowl, Hillsborough, a miniature Hollywood Bowl near San Mateo, and the other at the Civic Auditorium, in San Francisco itself. Neither was particularly noteworthy from an artistic standpoint; Alfred Hertz's orchestra was responsive, but lacked the qualities of precision and virtuosity that Pierre Monteux was to bring to it later in such a marked degree. So I wallowed through pleasant enough concerts in the sylvan glades of Woodland and the great expanses of the Auditorium—jammed with a crowd of 7,000 enthusiasts— and thought how different the city and its people were to any other city and people in the world, and how little the Easterners really knew of its character and sophistication. After this I travelled south, and knew I was back in Hollywood again when, the morning after my first concert there, I read this effusion:

Hailed like a visiting delegate, a round-the-world-flyer and a heavyweight champion rolled into one, Eugene Goossens last night entered upon his series of sixteen concerts at the Bowl. Los Angeles showed what it thought of him by turning out in numbers that approximated twenty-three thousand.

These four weeks, filled with quantities of music entirely new to the West Coast, were characterized by something unique in the annals of orchestral concerts. Arriving one night at the Bowl for the opening concert of the third week, I found a conference proceeding between Mrs. Irish, acting President of the Bowl concerts, Mr. Toberman, President of the Bowl Association, Raymond Brite, Manager, and the President of the local musicians' union. The orchestra was already seated on stage, ready to begin the concert. I was told that the Union of Stage Employees of Los Angeles was objecting to one of the local gardeners (a non-union employee) switching the Bowl Lights on and off before and after the concerts. The musicians—belonging to a sister union—would immediately be called out in sympathy unless a union employee replaced the gardener that very evening. At 8.30, starting-time for the concert, both sides were deadlocked, the Bowl authorities stubbornly—and mistakenly—refusing to give way. Brite, the Manager, refused my request that he go out on stage and ask the indulgence of the audience, which, as time went on, naturally started demonstrating and blaming me for the delay. At five minutes to nine, just as I had determined to take matters in my own hands and explain my non-appearance to the audience, which had now become noisily demonstrative, Mrs. Irish went on stage and informed them that as the Stage Employees' Union had forbidden the musicians to play, the management had no alternative but to cancel the concert. Those who wished could have their money refunded; as for the others, their tickets would be valid at a future date. Whereupon an audience of 20,000 emitted a collective groan, picked up its coats and blankets and made for the exits. The programme had included a Sibelius symphony and Strauss's tone poem, *Zarathustra*. Next morning the reporter of the *Times* wrote:

The voice of Zarathustra spoke from the score of Strauss as it lay on the darkened desk of the director: 'Thou tremendous planet, when would be thy happiness, if thou hadst not those to whom thou givest sight!'

An apt commentary on the whole affair. The strike cancelled three concerts that week, and it was only the following Saturday that a telephone call to my hotel announced that they would be resumed that night. The orchestra was reassembled and we played, without rehearsal, the programme we were to have played the night of the strike. The public turned up, but one sensed their resentment at the unwarranted upset of their beloved concerts—an upset which need not have occurred had the Bowl authorities acceded to the quite legitimate request of the union in the first place. They had to give in eventually, so it was all the more regrettable that the hostility of the Bowl President to unionism at that time caused the loss of three concerts.

An innovation at these orchestral concerts was a lecture-recital[1] on contemporary music, at which I delivered a running commentary on each number before playing it. Among the composers featured were Prokofiev and Bartok —unknown quantities on the Pacific coast—and I scandalized the audience by concluding the concert with a performance of Schönberg's *Five Orchestral Pieces*, which promptly emptied the Bowl to the accompaniment of cheers and hisses! Another episode was the performance of a work by the French composer, Charles Koechlin, which won the Bowl prize awarded for the best specially-written modern work. As I was not one of the judges, I took no credit for the choice; but it proved too esoteric for Bowl audiences.

The autumn season of 1929 in Rochester had barely got under way when the stock market crashed, and with it countless private fortunes, endowments, and nest-eggs, great and small, crumbled into nothingness. On the actual morning of the crash I cancelled a rehearsal in order that 60 per cent. of my players could spend their time at their brokers, throwing good money after bad! When a trombone-player announced that he had lost a fortune representing close on $100,000, I decided to take Mendelssohn's *Calm Sea and Prosperous Voyage* overture out of

[1] Only the natural 'acoustic' of the Bowl made this possible.

the current programme and substitute something more appropriate.

Alexander Smallens and I conducted a concert of the League of Composers in New York a few weeks later (the old Composers' Guild having merged into the newer society) at which Anton von Webern's *Symphony for Chamber Orchestra* and my *Concertino for Double String Orchestra* had their New York premières. Neither created much stir, though von Webern's shorthand squeaks elicited reciprocal ones from the audience, while my own particular brand of neo-classicism flopped dismally. (It has since vindicated itself.) Shortly after this I went to Philadelphia for the American première of *Judith*—almost a repetition of the Covent Garden fiasco so far as its 'production' by the Philadelphia Grand Opera Company was concerned. The redeeming presence of the Philadelphia Orchestra in the pit, plus Bianca Saroya's performance in the title role, were the bright features of an otherwise distressing evening. A coconut falling heavily from a property tree narrowly missed braining the Russian Holofernes (something I had longed to do during the Christmas Eve dress rehearsal). The opera had a remarkable public success, strangely enough, which still encourages me to believe that if it ever found a competent producer, it might remain in the repertory of serviceable one-act operas. Presumably because of the head episode, the Philadelphia critics echoed their London brethren by comparisons with *Salome*, though the music can hardly be called Straussian. Emil Mylnarski conducted *Cavalleria Rusticana* for the rest of the evening, and fared little better with his singers than I did.

Back in Rochester, Gustave Tinlot, our concert-master, played my *Lyric Poem* with orchestra, thus sharing with Ruth Posselt the dubious distinction of having played what is seemingly the world's most ungrateful violin piece.

The following season there was little opportunity for inflicting too much modern music on the Rochester audiences, for frequent engagements with other orchestras seemed to presage my departure for another and more permanent post. The amount of guest conducting I had undertaken to date could only have been accomplished at the expense of continued absences from my regular post, and although the Rochester concert schedule was comparatively light, thus considerably facilitating my free-lancing operations elsewhere, the sense of impermanence of relationship with my own orchestra was æsthetically unsound and disturbing. What proved the logical outcome of the above must not be anticipated, since this is a chronological narrative. Twelve months elapsed before I relinquished my post.

Meantime Koussevitzky again invited me to do some Boston and Providence concerts with his orchestra early in the year. Among the works I scheduled was the first Boston performance of Respighi's *Roman Festival*, the quasi-vulgarity of which scandalized the Boston Press, but delighted its audience. I have rarely seen a Symphony Hall afternoon audience behave in so uninhibited a manner as at the end of this work; the elderly ladies were quite transported. I began the concert with Wagner's *Faust* overture, which prompted H. T. Parker of the *Transcript* to observe: 'With this work he restores long neglected music to Symphony Hall.' But when I ventured to play Schumann's *Spring Symphony*, it seems I committed the unforgivable sin. H.T.P. gravely ended his notice: 'Hereabouts Dr. Koussevitzky, and no other, is Schumann's prophet.'

The St. Louis Orchestra, in the absence of a permanent conductor, had divided its current season between its 'guests', Arbos, Szell, and myself, and I therefore went straight from Boston to the Middle West. Out of my ten symphony concerts, none was very memorable, for the orchestra was never at any time more than second-rate. (The last score of years have produced in this respect a vast change for the better, thanks to the alert and sensitive Vladimir Golschmann.) One concert, devoted to the *Faust* subject, proved an exception, and prompted the usually acid Thomas Sherman to remark the following morning: 'It is not likely that the orchestra as it is constituted now will ever play better.' The programme—

Overture: *Ein Faust*	Wagner
Excerpts from *The Damnation of Faust*	Berlioz
Faust Symphony	Liszt

did, in fact, galvanize the orchestra into some splendid playing, but subsequent concerts, even with artists such as Elman and Bailly (the superb Flonzaley viola-player), fell below this standard.

During my St. Louis stay Toscanini played my *Sinfonietta* in New York with the Philharmonic, and incidentally discovered a couple of misprints in the printed score which I had overlooked. Those dim eyes certainly missed nothing when they searched the printed page, and my piece didn't escape. The performance, which I heard on a later visit of this orchestra to London, was apparently a glowing one, which didn't prevent old Henderson writing in the *Sun*:

It struck this hearer as a remarkably fine piece of exceedingly tiresome music. . . . One felt in listening to it that there was no use in trying to argue with the composer, as he was bound to have the better of the debate.

One could say this of anything, I felt.

THE AUTHOR AND SIR HENRY WOOD, 1932
AT SIR HENRY'S COUNTRY HOME, APPLETREE FARM HOUSE,
CHORLEY WOOD, BUCKS

CHAPTER LI

I was anxious to do another opera with Arnold Bennett, and when I got back to London we decided after some discussion that his four-act privately printed play, *Don Juan de Manara*, would make an extremely suitable and dramatic subject for collaboration. Arnold promised to start work immediately, and did so. He went to Cornwall, and I never saw him again; he died late in the year, but not before completing—among other things—the libretto he had promised me. For part of the summer I went to Devonshire, and in our adjoining counties we kept up an almost daily correspondence on the subject of the new libretto. Every other morning the postman would bring me a fresh instalment, which I would acknowledge on alternate mornings with suggestions for alterations when necessary. Bennett had a tremendous flair for the short, precise sentences I needed to fit my musical idiom, a fact which makes *Don Juan de Manara* one of the most vividly dramatic libretti of its kind. But it didn't go easily; excerpts from the three characteristic letters written to me later that year in America show how typical of the methodical Bennett they are!

I now enclose the final form of Act One. There has been some delay, but I have been much put about, especially by dental troubles.

I fully understand that in the libretto of an opera a certain amount of literary elegance and subtlety must be sacrificed to musical elegance and interest, so that is quite all right. I have embodied practically all your suggestions.

During the next two days I shall finish Act Two and send it to you at once, and within a week or so after that I will send my draft of Act Three. You will thus have plenty of material.

I do not expect to see Blois, but it is possible I may see Szarvasy or Cunliffe-Owen (whose wife, I believe, interests herself considerably in Covent Garden). It is much better that an opera should be a bit short than too long.

All our love,

Ever yours,

A. B.

One dated 24 September:

I now enclose the final version of Act Two. You will see that I think the serenade ought to be vocal—I have left the question of the number of voices. If you prefer only one, Don Juan, that will be all right. I have begun Act Three.

Our love,

Ever yours,

A. B.

Another one dated 26 September:

75 Cadogan Square, London.

30 *September* 1930.

My dear Eugene,—I was very sorry that you had to cable me about my delay in feeding you. I really could not help it. I have been in the hands of the dentist, and also have been obliged to take a little time off. Nevertheless, I owe you an apology, which please receive and accept.

Acts One and Two, all finished, have already been sent to you. I now enclose the draft of Act Three, together with the original version of Act Three of the play. It is certainly the most dramatic of all the acts, and the movement is so quick it is very difficult to get into it speeches of any length. I am beginning the draft of Act Four to-day.

Our love,

Ever yours,

A. B.

Blois and Szarvasy were at that time the powers at Covent Garden, and I had suggested to Bennett that he should try to secure a revival of our *Judith*, and also get some promise of a definite production of the new opera when it was completed. Alas! he obtained neither, for *Don Juan* waited till the Coronation season of 1937 for its production.

Early summer in London was a period of many activities. Among them was the Annual Dinner of the Musicians' Benevolent Fund at the Savoy Hotel, an interesting feature of which was some specially composed fanfares by Ethel Smyth, Walford Davies, Bantock, Bax, Bliss, Quilter, and myself, played by trumpeters of the Royal Military School of Music, Kneller Hall. (Thematic subjects of the fanfares were varied and unmilitary; 'A Frog He would a-wooing go' and 'Hot Potatoes' were two of them. My own was 'A Fanfare for the Regiment'.) Enough that when the twelve trumpeters came to an end of their strenuous blowing, both diners and performers took on an apoplectic hue.

Shortly after this I was chairman at a luncheon of the Anglo-French Music Club given to Gabriel Pierné, the composer, who was also conductor of the Colonne Orchestra of Paris. Wood, Ronald, Boult, Cameron, and several other British conductors were present; it fell to me to propose the health of the guest of honour. That morning General Weygand, French Chief of Staff, had unveiled a statue of Marshal Foch in Grosvenor Gardens. I only learnt just before lunch that the little General and Madame Foch were to be present as our guests, together with half the French Legation, and that I was expected to extend greetings to them also, preferably in French. This called for some quick thinking, as I did not trust my extempore powers to the extent of a delicate political address in French. I ruined the soup and beef courses by trying to collect my thoughts sufficiently to scribble some appropriate sentences in a foreign tongue, and had almost given up in despair when I suddenly caught sight of my old friend, Mangeot, to whom I explained my predicament. He valiantly sacrificed the rest of his lunch to turn out on the back of a menu a high-sounding and completely appropriate oration in French which I was unblushingly able to read as a supplement to my main improvised speech of welcome to Pierné. The day was saved! Later, in the columns of the *Sussex Daily News*, I read with some smugness the following:

Goossens was also complimented by the French speakers [General Weygand and others had replied eloquently] on the excellent French in which he delivered the second part of his speech.

Thanks to André Mangeot for supplying its substance. Some concerts in London at the time must be mentioned here. The first was an attempt on my part to repeat the successful summer concert I had given the previous season at Queen's Hall with Stravinsky. Either the lack of a supporting artist or an unsensational programme resulted in an extremely poor audience and, in spite of the usual large hand-picked orchestra of previous years, the baffling London public again ran true to form. I had hoped that the first performance in London of Arnold Bax's *Second Symphony* might have proved a drawing card—the composer was enjoying great vogue at the time—but even this, with the addition of some Brahms, d'Indy, and de Falla pieces, couldn't compete against a fine Saturday afternoon. The programme and the playing came in for some warm praise from the Press, and the public was duly castigated for its failure to rally to the cause. It had previously been called to account that season for its apathetic response to visits of the Berlin, Vienna, Amsterdam, and Paris orchestras; Furtwängler, who conducted both the Berlin and Vienna groups, told me of his disappointment at the cool reception of his programmes which, if I remember rightly, had contained both some Bruckner and Mahler. . . .

Only when Toscanini arrived, shortly after my concert, with the New York Philharmonic-Symphony Orchestra for his two concerts at Queen's Hall and another two at the Albert Hall, did London music-lovers throng both buildings in their thousands, a fact, I suppose, that speaks for itself. The *maestro* again included my *Sinfonietta* in one of his programmes and played it miraculously. I went round to thank him after the concert, but this being his first experience of the Albert Hall and its then appalling acoustics, the great man was inconsolable and near to tears at what he considered fine performances ruined by the triple echo of the hall. I tried to explain that many seats in the hall were immune to this echo, but he refused to be comforted and repeated: '*Non, non, non; orribile, brutto, spaventevole, acusticamente ridicolo,*' and further choice expletives. At Queen's Hall he was happier, but complained, '*Molto risonante, ma troppo piccola per un gran' orchestra.*' Toscanini and the superb orchestra swept London like a fire, and furnished for some years a standard of performance which, alas! judging by present-day English playing, is but a vague memory of the past. After a Devonshire holiday at Strete, where from the cliffs you can follow liners halfway across the Channel to and from Le Havre, we boarded one of them and found ourselves in Philadelphia for more opera.

I had promised to conduct Massenet's *Le Jongleur de Notre Dame* for the Philadelphia Grand Opera Company, and did so, with the ever youthful Mary Garden in the title role. She played the role better than she sang it; as a piece of histrionics of the subdued kind, it was the most masterly and impressive thing I had ever seen. Her boyish costume and make-up put to shame the *prime donne* who permit themselves to 'go to seed' in their physical appearance so early in their careers. Even the Philadelphia audience seemed greatly moved by this performance, though the following from a Philadelphia paper is caustic comment on their manners:

E.G. displayed vitality and vexation—vitality in his reading of the score and vexation with those members of the audience whose premature applause made almost inaudible the orchestral ending of the second act. Mr. Goossens glared reprovingly over his shoulder, and stamped his foot. It was his only cue all evening that wasn't obeyed.

Later that year with the same company I conducted a performance of *Tosca*, in which the eminent Richard Crooks made an impressive operatic début as Cavaradossi. Though in no sense a vain man—very much the contrary, in fact—Crooks must have felt a little deflated by the laconic morning tribute which characterized him as 'a very *respectable* tenor who has achieved an excellent reputation in serious concert work'. It referred to his voice as 'effective, if not over-whelming, and good if not glamorous; he sings with sin-cerity if not with splendour'. A masterpiece, it struck me, of verbal procrastination. In the same performance Scarpia was sung by a full-blooded Indian, Chief Caupolican, whose antics with Bianca Saroya in the seduction scene fully accounted for Tosca's handling of the table knife. The next night John Charles Thomas sang Athanael, with the young Helen Jepson and Rose Bampton cooing as prettily as doves in a performance of *Thaïs*. The performance will also be remembered for the handsome Thaïs (a Miss Gonitch), plus a fusing of the light on my desk, which rendered both me and the score invisible for the last ten minutes of the second act. Miraculously, the ensemble and my memory remained intact.

Back in Rochester I discovered that rumours of my impending departure for another place had begun to seep through the community. At the end of 1930 negotiations proceeded quietly to a head between the Director of the Cincinnati May Festival Association, the management of the Cincinnati Orchestra, and myself, by which I was to succeed Frederich Stock and Fritz Reiner to the conductorship of those respective organizations. In consequence, the President of the Rochester Civic Music Association announced before Christmas my forthcoming transfer from western New York to southern Ohio in the coming spring. George Eastman followed this up with a generously worded tribute.[1] My letter of resignation reflected very genuinely the regret I felt at leaving the friendly people who had made my sojourn in Rochester a thing of great pleasure:

> The friendship and associations of the past seven years will remain indelible memories, and the splendid work accomplished by the orchestra will always be to me a source of intense pride. There is every indication that this present season [the eighth and last] will be a brilliant one, and I shall spare no effort to make it outstanding. I am grateful for the co-operation and sympathy which has always been shown to me in the past, and I want to assure you of my enduring loyalty to the ideals which have helped to establish the cause of orchestral music in Rochester.

The local Press paid its share of sincere tribute,[2] but it was left to the London *Evening News* to add a really pungent note to its acclaim:

> Cincinnati, America's most German and perhaps for that reason, most musical city, has engaged Mr. Goossens, the young London composer, as conductor of its celebrated Symphony Orchestra. This is a triumph for British music, of which, in a day when a Labour Government thinks fit to devote British taxpayers' money to subsidizing foreign opera, the public should take due note.

The *Boston Transcript* took a shot in the dark:

> The appointment will also have repercussions in Boston, for whenever there is casual talk of the successor, at some distant time, to Dr. Koussevitzky

[1] See Appendix C.   [2] See Appendix C.

at Symphony Hall, it often wavers between Bruno Walter and Eugene Goossens. Now, some are sure to say that at Cincinnati he is running a trial heat.

I often recall my good friend Serge Koussevitzky saying, '*N'oubliez pas*, I keep this orchestra warm for you!' That was over twenty years ago at the present time of writing. Fortunately for Boston, he 'kept it warm' all that time; and who, contemplating the long subsequent course of events, would have had it otherwise, nor wished for a finer successor than the present incumbent?[1]

[1] Charles Münch.

CHAPTER LII

So at the end of February I conducted my final Rochester concert, an event characterized by presentations from orchestra, faculty, and management of the gold watch and chain, dress studs etc., which seem always to accompany the closing of a pleasant association with pleasant people. Somewhat anticlimactically, we gave an additional concert the following week in the big neighbouring city of Buffalo, which in those days depended on our visits for its symphonic nourishment, but to-day boasts its own orchestra. The concert took place in an acoustically vile ballroom of the Statler Hotel, but nowadays there is a fine Concert Hall which is Buffalo's pride.

Only two further orchestral concerts remained before my forthcoming début with the Cincinnati May Festival Association. One of these was the final concert of the Pittsburgh Orchestra's season—the orchestra which (the reader will remember) made a Sunday début in the face of, and in spite of, the Pennsylvania 'blue' laws. Gladys Swarthout sang, and 4,200 people jammed in the Syria Mosque for the event. The *Pittsburgh Press* next morning indulged in a little pardonable propaganda:

Five years ago last night, the orchestra gave its first concert. Since then it has made vast strides in the face of adverse circumstances and opposition. The organization has proved its metal in surviving, and is pointed to great accomplishments provided it receives proper support. [Under the brilliant Fritz Reiner it later fulfilled this prophecy]. Eugene Goossens, who conducted its first concert there five years ago, and who has been an ardent friend and adviser to the Pittsburgh Orchestra, was at the baton and helm last night. . . . His personality and musicianship imbued the men with an unanimity of spirit that was productive of fine playing.

At the conclusion of the programme I made an appeal for funds to enable the orchestra to carry on—a sad commentary on the cultural apathy of wealthy Pittsburgh.

The other of my two guest appearances with orchestras

288

at that time was in Minneapolis, where my old friend, Henri Verbrugghen,[1] was conductor of the local symphony orchestra prior to Eugene Ormandy's appointment. It was not the expert group then that it is to-day, but gave a fine local first performance of the Moussorgsky-Ravel *Pictures from an Exhibition* in the then newly constructed Northrup Auditorium.

Immediately afterwards I left for Philadelphia, where the management of the Grand Opera Company, with that bland confidence in future events which characterized many of their decisions, now suddenly informed me that (for some unknown reason) they lacked a conductor for their production of Ravel's *L'Heure Espagnole*, which was scheduled in a double bill with *Cavalleria Rusticana*. They also announced that precarious finances only permitted one and a half orchestral rehearsals for both operas. It is a tribute to the marvellous sight-reading of the great Philadelphia Orchestra, which was, as usual, engaged to play for this season, that it contrived to perform this feat without a blemish. When the intricacies of Ravel's score are recalled, it seems almost incredible that any orchestra could reproduce them, even passably, at first sight. I can testify that the Philadelphians did more than this very thing. For myself, it was one of the most stimulating events in which I ever participated, especially as the supporting cast of singers was a good one. *L'Heure Espagnole* is almost a symphonic poem with vocal commentary—witty and *risqué*; these qualities the singers fully emphasized, in spite of their prim audience. I remained in the Quaker City to conduct a production of *Tannhäuser*, given by the same company. John Charles Thomas sang Wolfram, and Cyrena van Gordon, also a fine singer (with welcome pulchritude), was the Venus. The first of the four pages was the glamorous Helen Jepson. (The equally glamorous Rose Bampton had sung an unprepossessing-looking Mother Lucia in *Cavalleria* the previous evening!)

[1] Henri Verbrugghen was the first of my predecessors at the Sydney Conservatorium in Australia. The Conservatorium owes its existence to his labours.

The name of the artist who sang Tannhäuser escapes me, but I recall that the vocal hazards he encountered before finally reaching Rome gave me some bad quarters of an hour. A Philadelphia paper emerged next morning bearing the heading 'Lengthy and Cumbersome Wagnerian Composition for Philadelphia Farewell'—pithy, but biased!

And when next day the Ohio State Express stopped at Rochester *en route* for Cincinnati, a little group had gathered on the platform to bid a second farewell. There were Reuben Mamoulian and Paul Horgan of the School of Music Drama Department, the one soon to find fame as stage director and the other as novelist;[1] Martha Graham of the Dance School, now the Sunday night idol of New York; the ever-faithful Rosing, fine singer and partner of many opera productions; Guy Fraser Harrison, my gifted associate; managers Arthur See and Eric Clark, loyal seconders of my projects; and, finally, Jack Warner, critic of the *Times-Union*, sensitive connoisseur and friend. Theirs was an expressive valedictory, and seemed to presage the melancholy stretch of years during which I never returned to evoke from the Rochester players memories of their old prowess.

[1] *Porgy* and *The Fault of Angels* are two of their enduring creations, the latter a witty picture of early Rochester days.

CHAPTER LIII

I NOW went to Cincinnati to take the final rehearsals for the May Festival. A week's strenuous music-making calls for considerable final polishing-up and co-ordination of one's choral and orchestral forces. This, as always with the May Festival, was accomplished with a maximum of co-operation from all concerned, though the final layout of joint rehearsals presented some pretty problems of synchronization, especially as some of the soloists participating came from England and the Continent, besides the usual quota of American artists. The programmes were as follows:

Tuesday: Brahms' *Requiem* and Mendelssohn's *Hymn of Praise*.
Wednesday: *Phoebus and Pan* (Bach); Mahler, *Symphony No.* 8.
Thursday afternoon: Mozart excerpts, followed by Act I, *Tannhäuser*.
Friday: *Childrens' Crusade* (Pierné).
Saturday afternoon: Mixed orchestral programme, including Scriabine's *Prometheus*.
Saturday evening: *Sea Drift* (Delius) and *King David* (Honnegger).

The Festival is, or was at that time, a biennial event. For two seasons a fine choir of some 500 or 600 singers, drawn from all walks of life, rehearsed in preparation for what Cincinnati still regards as its outstanding social and musical event; to the natives at large it is America's best choral festival. Its successful organization has always been in the hands of the remarkable J. Herman Thuman, who combines a fine managerial sense with one of the most encyclopaedic musical minds I have ever encountered. No question baffles him; he will tell you the orchestration of a Mendelssohn oratorio or a Bach cantata as readily as he will hum you any Handel aria or Beethoven second subject. The compilation of programmes with such a knowledgeable colleague proved therefore a task of pleasure.

Unquestionably the Festival's highlight was a performance of Mahler's *Symphony of a Thousand*, which, with a mixed chorus of 600, a children's chorus of 250, orchestra of 130, and 10 soloists, fulfilled its title quite literally. I think it can be said that no performance of the work elsewhere ever approached that one for fidelity to the composer's intentions. Music Hall rocked with stunning climaxes, and the mystic quiet of the opening of the second part of the work was very impressive. At no time before or since have I ever known forces more ideally suited to their task, so that the remaining events of the Festival paled by comparison. I think of it always as the nearest approach to a conductor's dream performance I ever heard.

Petite Lily Pons made her very first concert début on the following day, so scared by her unfamiliar surroundings that one forgave her false entry in the second 'Queen of the Night' aria from the *Magic Flute*. I have yet to hear better singing than she gave us on that occasion. For range and virtuosity, her voice remains peerless.

Among other features of the Festival was an indifferent performance of Kaminsky's thoughtful *Magnificat*, marred by the poor singing of Edith Fleischer of the Metropolitan Company, who was indisposed, and a presentation of Pierné's *Children's Crusade* with some 600 children and a small adult choir, which still remains the most moving thing I ever heard in a concert hall. Honnegger's *King David* received its American première as the closing feature of the Festival; a work which by its incisiveness and craft still reduces all other contemporary 'cantatas' to the consistency of thin gruel. Of the ten Festivals I conducted up to the time of my departure from the Queen City of the Ohio (1947), the 1931 event stands out as the most brilliant and well-rounded.

From the Cincinnati May Festival to a quiet house near London's Kensington Gardens for work on my new opera provided a logical and much-needed contrast; but the seclusion was short-lived. Beecham had opened a season of opera and ballet with an all-Russian company at the Lyceum. Rimsky-Korsakov's *Sadko* was announced for performance, among other works, but history once again repeated itself when T.B. telephoned me the morning before the production asking that I take it over (for some reason I've forgotten). As usual, I said, 'Yes.' This meant only a piano rehearsal with the principals, and none at all with orchestra and chorus. I had never heard *Sadko*, but the adventure was too alluring to resist, and by performance time I had most of the full score 'under control'. To someone lacking my past history of countless emergency opera and concert performances—at twenty-four hours', or less, notice—the ordeal of taking over a virtually unknown work the day before production date would be understandably nerve-breaking and an unconscionable risk. I looked at it in another light, so when the curtain rose on Act I, that whiff of scenery and 'back-stage' was like the smell of sawdust to the trapeze artist, for whom mistakes and hesitation spell only disaster. There is thrill in such a challenge, so I was more than usually alert when the tenor Pozemkowsky and his Russian chorus launched into their drinking song, establishing a keynote of accuracy which characterized the whole performance. Orchestra and principals, too, knew their work well, and I found additional stimulus in following a language totally unfamiliar to me. The ovation which followed the opera counted less in my ears than the sweeter music of thanks from the singers for a completely—to them—routine and uneventful evening. A few nights later I conducted the ballets, *L'Amour Brujo*, by de Falla, *Chout*, by Prokofiev, and revivals of *Petroushka* and *Pulcinella*—all danced by a completely unfamiliar (to me) group of dancers. Only when Chaliapin appeared still later in an act of Massenet's *Don Quixote*—almost his best and most moving role—did I recognize a familiar friend.

The Ninth Festival of the International Society for Contemporary Music took place at Oxford about this time, and I went there to hear Sammons and Murdoch repeat their performance of my second violin sonata, a work into which only Heifetz now seems able to infuse the lyrical intensity realized by Sammons on that occasion. The acoustics of the old Ashmolean Museum at Oxford, however, were quite disastrous to my harmonic subtleties, and therefore the performance was, on the whole, unsatisfactory. The sight of the trio I encountered that morning, gesticulating wildly in High Street, cheered me somewhat. Portly Edwin Evans, gaunt Alfredo Casella, and undersized Maurice Ravel, all wearing precisely the same sombreros and dark coats, looked like the three Musketeers, and they argued violently with appropriate gestures about something I could only guess at. A clue to it, as I greeted them, was in Casella's triumphant remark: '*Mais la musique italienne, c'est moi!*' There were many such gatherings; every composer in Europe seemed to have gone to the old city to hear his music.

Because of the lack of a suitable hall in Oxford, the orchestral concerts of the Festival took place in London's Queen's Hall, with the B.B.C. Orchestra, and Adrian Boult as chief conductor. This orchestra had by then achieved a virtuosity of playing and sight-reading which placed it head and shoulders above many foreign orchestras with a much bigger reputation. That it no longer commands the pick of London's virtuosi may account in part for its failure nowadays to maintain its old standards. I conducted it just before the festival in the old Big Tree Wharf studio across the river through a miraculous hour of beautiful playing, in a programme including several difficult novelties. The mellow brass, liquid wood-wind, and a string section of unsurpassed calibre established an orchestral standard London has not known since. Leon again played my oboe concerto, and returned to his seat in the orchestra for the rest of the concert.

After the Oxford Festival I went back to Devonshire and tried to finish Act II of *Don Juan de Manara*. It didn't go fluently; Bennett had given me a compact libretto which a too luxuriant flow of musical ideas might easily distort. So that just as I was getting back into my stride, the holidays had ended; and there was Southampton, with the *Leviathan* waiting for my return to hospitable America and the first season of a long incumbency at Cincinnati. And that will be for another volume.

CHAPTER LIV

So far only the outlines of about twenty years of professional life have filled these pages. A further score of years remain still to be chronicled, so it seems timely to call a halt, and reserve for a future volume events since 1931. Covering nearly a century's span of family history, as this book does, the narration involved has probably imposed something of a strain on the reader's power of absorption. And if my reason for this factual recital is chiefly the recording of worthwhile musical history in which I have sometimes played no greater role than witness, so, because of this, any ill-remembered conversations with many people whose friendship I enjoyed (and still enjoy) have been scrupulously avoided in these pages. Perhaps my excessive observance of such a practice has deprived certain events of the vivid glamour which often characterized them, or with which other writers might have invested them. However, I can in part remedy this; I can still atone by 'naming names'.

Life in London, immediately before and after the First World War (notably from 1920 onwards, when musical art showed an unparalleled resurgence) was more truly bohemian than at any time since *Yellow Book* days. The procession of faces and memories which it evokes is, strangely enough, closely identified with the actual topography of London. In fact, a circular bus ride from the Strand to Chelsea, via Bloomsbury, Hampstead, St. John's Wood, Campden Hill, and Hammersmith conjures up for me a whole phantasmagoria of the aesthetic London years of 1918–26. For a mere musician who, in a manner of speaking, lived both inside this charmed circle, yet, because of constant professional duties, ever on the fringe of it (becoming eventually an inextricable part of it, and welcomed to it as someone other than a narrow specialist), the evocation induces a real nostalgia.

So my bus ride would start from the Strand, where nearby Adelphi Terrace housed both the Savage Club and George Bernard Shaw. As a 'Savage', I spent more time in the Club's quiet writing-room on the top floor, with its familiar Thames-side panorama stretching from Westminster to Tower Bridge, than I did in the adjoining card-room, with *its* equally familiar occupants, Mark Hambourg, Moisei-witsch, Max Mossel, and Douglas Furber—fine artists and fine sportsmen. But the intimate atmosphere of the old club has never been recaptured in its present newer, and colder, Georgian premises at Carlton House Terrace, where the shades of versatile artist Aubrey Hammond of the stentorian voice, and skinny ninety-year-old Odell (of the whinnying squeak) seem to hover in reminiscent protest. Not being of the stuff of which 'good clubmen' are made, I am only equal to noting, after long periods of absence, that the 'Savage' spirit of warm-hearted, tolerant, generous bohemianism thrives in its present premises as warmly as ever it did in the old terrace on Thames-side.

A short bus ride from Adelphi to Bloomsbury landed you at the end of Percy Street, where Rudolf Stulik presided over his Eiffel Tower Restaurant and ministered to the epicurian taste of a motley group of customers. A small, select, un-elaborate place this, where only those Stulik liked and knew were really welcome, and where his generous impulses (tem-pered by a practical wife) found full expression. Painters and writers were the staple attraction which brought May-fair shoulder to shoulder with Chelsea and Bloomsbury; it would be a rare night, especially during the opera and ballet season in the 'twenties, if you didn't find Augustus John, 'Tommy' Earp, Michael Arlen, Curtiss Moffat, Alan Parsons, Viola Tree, Nancy Cunard, Ansermet, Poldowski, Maynard Keynes, and a *mélange* of art and intellect feasting off Stulik's *spécialité de la maison*. And if at times there were among us those whose *gourmandises* exceeded the state of their finances, the proprietor could always be counted on for a system of credit, extended, it seemed, in direct ratio to some least likely to prove in the long run equal to their obligations! The chronicles of Stulik remain still an unexplored and vivid subject for some contemporary eye-witness's fertile pen.

In nearby studios the painters Roger Fry and Sickert coloured the Bloomsbury landscape with their personalities and influence. I remember a gathering at Curtiss Moffat's rooms in Bloomsbury Square, when the spectacle of Fry debating with Clive Bell the essentials of painting, and surrounded by a host of listeners, formed a group of sombre colour such as Manet himself might have painted with zest. With more vivacity and less portentousness this scene duplicated itself at the St. John Hutchinsons' Hammersmith house after a *Beggar's Opera* performance. The guests, including the jovial host and his *chic* wife, were a typically fastidious and varied group: Lytton Strachey, Middleton Murry, Aldous Huxley, the Sitwells, Clive Bell, the painters Gertler and Nash, Desmond McCarthy, the Leslie brothers, Nigel Playfair, and a couple of visiting musicians, Malipiero and myself. Of such were 'parties', so called, made up in those days. And if at the end of them champagne slightly fuddled the coruscations of wit and spirit into a jumbled medley, the memory of them transcended other more ephemeral joys.

CHAPTER LV

From Bloomsbury to Hampstead and St. John's Wood was a short step, and here lived many of the musicians. Elgar, Harty, Wood, Bax, all seemed to find this higher ground of London both conducive to creative effort and convenient to Queen's Hall. On one of my visits to Elgar, shortly after Lady Elgar's death, I noticed the newly finished MS. of the orchestration of Bach's *C Minor Fugue* lying on his desk. After he had told me what it was, he added: 'Now that my poor wife has gone, I can't be original, and so I depend on people like John Sebastian for a source of inspiration. Anyway, it probably won't be played. . . .' I begged him to let me have it for the opening of the third of my Queen's Hall concerts, in a month's time. He said: 'Take it. I'll be at the first rehearsal.' And he was.

A wealthy widow named Dalliba gave studio parties for musicians in her St. John's Wood home, on the lines of those formerly made famous by her sister-American Muriel Draper. But those of Mrs. Dalliba were as 'free-for-all' as the Draper parties were exclusive. The enormous studio was the focal point for the neighbourhood's Sunday night bohemians, and good fare and impromptu music-making were always forthcoming. May Mukle, the 'cellist, and her gifted sisters, with Harriet Cohen, Marjorie Hayward, Muriel Besant, Shapiro, Rosing, and numerous other *habitués* formed a nucleus of the studio chamber music activities. If the Very Great were often conspicuously absent, the rest of us more than adequately managed to contrive admirable-sounding music, all the better because of its impromptu nature.

Such definitely was not the case at W. W. Cobbett's home just round the corner. This wealthy amateur violinist, who gave his name and money to the 'Phantasy' competitions from which sprang a whole sheaf of fine chamber music works by the younger Englishmen (conspicuous among them was Frank Bridge, the best string writer of his generation), carefully selected his colleagues for evenings of chamber music. Eminent quartet players were invited to participate in supper and music, and if at times the zeal of the keen amateur host prompted him to tackle—on a magnificent Stradivarius—works slightly outside his technical capacity, his associates never failed him in conscientious support. His *Encyclopedia of Chamber Music* remains still the best book of its kind available, despite its author's (at times) rather supercilious comments. Cobbett had a collection of fine violins; but his insistence on playing them for you—rather indifferently—instead of letting you try them for yourself often tended to obscure their finer qualities. On one occasion we read through the Arnold Bax *String Quartet*. Later that night at Bax's house, eating spaghetti cooked by Harriet Cohen, I regaled them with tales of our hazardous progress. . . .

Often en route to Hampstead I would stop at Cyril Scott's house in Bayswater. In an incense-laden, Gothic, Pre-Raphaelite atmosphere, this gifted, esoteric, intensely sincere man dispensed China tea and played me his latest work, with the setting sun filtering through a stained-glass window. At such times his finely chiseled, sensitive features took on the expression of a transfigured Chopin, strangely at variance with both his occult nature and the forlorn, melodic wailing with which he still accompanies his playing. How little appreciated and neglected are his works to-day; yet Debussy spoke of him as the most original of English composers. Known chiefly as a miniaturist, his larger, more important works still await the revelation which is their due.

Close by, in Campden Hill and Holland Park, lived more painters and musicians. Harold Speed, Glyn Philpot, Lamorna Birch, and Edmond Dulac had their studios there, while Frank Bridge, Arthur Bliss and I were near neighbours, in the days when I lived in George Davidson's home—with the Aeolian organ—in Holland Park. Dulac, whose erudite paintings and drawings for the Oriental classics entailed vast research of the most far-reaching kind, was an intelligent music-lover with a hobby for collecting flutes. One day I found him squatting crosslegged on his studio floor, producing diminutive but ethereal tones from an Indian nose-flute, to play which he had plugged one nostril in order to emit a steady column of air from the other —by no means a negligible feat. A profound store of Oriental lore made him a fascinating talker, and me an entranced listener. Once he offered me betel-nut, which I refused. . . .

CHAPTER LVI

On the fringes of Chelsea, to which eventually all good bohemians gravitate—or *did* gravitate in those days —and to which the 31 bus carries you from the heights of Campden Hill, lies Pimlico, where in George Moore's home in Ebury Street I once listened to A.E., the Irish poet, and Chesterton, discussing *The Ring* at dinner.[1] Neither knew very much about it, and when the author of *Esther Waters* joined in, confusion was more confounded as the trio indignantly—and wrongly—identified successively each of Wagner's *Leitmotifs*. By the arrival of coffee, and with the help of a convenient copy of Lavignac's *Voyage à Bayreuth*, I added my only words, by settling the argument, which proved again that eminent men of letters rarely hestitate to step in where ordinary mortals fear to tread. Arnold Bennett, a not too distant neighbour of Moore's in Cadogan Square, was the exception; except for Shaw, I doubt whether any writer of this period had read or acquired more knowledge about the subject of music than A.B. The following extracts from his letters and diaries reflect the absorption for detail which characterized his musical references:

75 Cadogan Square, S.W.1.
13 *February* 1923.

I really do think that that improvisation of Bax and Goossens* at the piano Sunday night was one of the most miraculous things I ever witnessed. I can't get over it. And I think they were pretty well impressed by it themselves!

* We improvised a duet.—Author.

3 *March* 1924

Goossens lunched with me. He wants me to compress *Judith* into a 50- or 60-minute one-act opera—in prose. It is a good scheme. I have promised to do it, in my own time.

---

[1] I was present at a similar conversation about that time between voluble Arthur Colefax and Hilaire Belloc on the genesis of opera, and this was equally abortive. It lasted, however, twice as long. The only two authors I ever knew who remained silent during discussions on music were Galsworthy and Walpole.

31 *May* 1925

I liked the three operas* much better than ever, and stand more impressed than ever by the bigness of Wagner. I used to be overawed by the mere achievement, apart from its creative force. Now I am not. After all, creatively, these operas are very simple, and the artist is tied by scarcely anything in them. He is in an ideal world. He hasn't got to think of half so many things as a novelist in a long realistic novel. The hardest mere 'work' is the scoring, and many composers could and do score with far more complexity than Wagner. Still, the power and the beauty of Wagner are staggering. There was great singing.   * *The Rosenkavalier, Tristan*, and *Valkyrie*.

25 *May* 1926

After dinner, Dorothy and I played for $1\frac{1}{4}$ hours, bits of *Petrouschka*.

27 *March* 1927

Dorothy and I played the first movement of a fine Haydn symphony. I've no recollection of ever having played it before, and the music was quite fresh to me.

16 *June* 1928

Eugene Goossens and Alick Shepeler came for dinner. Eugene began to play and sing our opera, *Judith*. He has evidently set out to do something not too incomprehensible. Better than I had expected. Dramatic. Effective. My libretto seemed quite good. He talked of a production at Covent Garden next year.

19 *October* 1928

We reached the Ravel Concert at the Aeolian Hall 20 minutes later, and Ravel himself came into the vestibule. We talked a bit. This concert was extremely satisfactory. It seemed to me to be all good music.

14 *November* 1928

Then I corrected over 60 pages of the pianoforte score of the new Goossens opera, *Judith*. Lots of errors in the text.

A five-minute walk from Bennett and Belgravia brought one straight to Chelsea and that other author, Compton Mackenzie, with his twin hobbies of clothes and music. I have never seen a larger or more variegated collection of well-tailored suits as hung in his wardrobes, or as many records as were stocked in his music-cabinet. A sensitive connoisseur, his knowledge of musical technique is by no means sketchy, as his writing shows. Once we discussed turning one of his books into an opera, but it came to nothing; I forget why.

Further up the King's Road, in their delightful Carlisle Square house, Osbert, Sacheverell, and Edith Sitwell, with William Walton as star boarder, held court. In those august but dangerously crowded rooms, in which one false move might unframe a Severini, consign to oblivion a tableful of Victorian knick-knacks, or shatter an ormolu clock, Osbert marshalled a never-ending procession of social and artistic lunch and dinner guests, on which occasions the air teemed with crackling and coruscation of epigram, witticism and criticism—often from the host's own fertile and perceptive brain. At one luncheon I recall the combined sparkle of Evelyn Waugh, Lord Berners, and Osbert made interpolations from the other open-mouthed guests trivial and superfluous.

Across the road, hospitable Sybil Colefax's beautiful 18th-century house was the scene of endless parties honouring, during the season, London's visiting and resident artist celebrities. More eloquent pens than mine must describe these much-sought-after gatherings of social Bohemia. Stravinsky and I were on one occasion joint recipients of the Colefax 'accolade'. Similar—but slightly less stately—functions took place a few doors away when the American, Hoytie Wiborg—and later Syrie Maugham—resided in the lovely house at the corner of Tite Street. George Gershwin, playing breathlessly intricate arrangements of his latest musical comedy hits, and accompanied by cigar, champagne glass and a bevy of starry-eyed ladies of society, is one of my outstanding memories of Hoytie's parties.

Over the street in Manresa Road were the studios of sculptors Epstein and Dobson. Both being 'moderns', their work and tastes followed the contemporary trends of music: Epstein, Stravinsky, and Dobson, Debussy. I was *persona grata* there, for, like the whole painting fraternity of that day, they welcomed the company of musicians. Augustus John, Fergusson, Laura Knight, Flora Lion, the Lovat Frasers, Margaret Morris, Stuart Hill, and a host of other Chelseaites lived in a world where music was an integral part of existence. For how many musicians, I wonder, can it be said that to them painting is a vital part and parcel of their lives?

But Chelsea was not the monopoly of the painters, and there were musical studio parties as well. The nearest approach to the Draper-Dalliba variety were the evenings at Herbert Hughes's studio-home. Hughes, composer of delightful Irish songs and Assistant Music Editor to Robin

Legge of the *Daily Telegraph*, kept open house on Sunday nights for his legion of friends, and there was always lavish music and good fare to transform those nights into Bohemian *soirées* of the first order. His untimely death left a gap in the musical community life of Chelsea which has never been filled.

At the art critic Wilenski's studio, further down the road, there were gatherings of painters and musicians where conversation usually included a full-dress debate on some more or less acrimonious aesthetic topic of the time. On these occasions the gathering would again take on the smoke-laden atmosphere of a French *genre* picture of the 'eighties. Round the corner, too, lived the witty and erudite author-critic, Francis Toye, whose chief delights were Verdi and French cooking of the Boulestin variety. On the first he has written a classic volume; of the second his small dinners at his home showed a telling influence. My friendship with his brother, the versatile Geoffrey, dated from college days. In turn conductor, composer, company director, and opera director, his early death confirmed that 'whom the gods love . . .'

Last but not least, there is Chelsea's own John Ireland, whose studio in Gunther Grove is the quiet haven of a few intimate friends, but for all others an unknown byway. A life-long friendship with him has been a rewarding experience. If the humility and artistic sincerity of a modest artist find their best expression in that artist's work, then John Ireland's contains the deepest known to me.

With a return to the same Thames-side from which I started, the circular tour of London's 'twenties comes to an end. After three decades, those nostalgic scenes and meetings have taken on in retrospect a grim aura, the causes of which are all too familiar, yet the growth of which I cannot—because of absence abroad in those years—pretend to discuss as eyewitness. But it is otherwise with the innocuous (by comparison) happenings of the world of music during the past twenty years. To these, and to the Goossens family's by no means unlively share in them, will be devoted a future instalment of these records.

APPENDIX A

SOME CASTS OF OPERAS PRODUCED BY EUGENE GOOSSENS I DURING HIS ASSOCIATION WITH THE CARL ROSA OPERA COMPANY

Royal Court Theatre, Liverpool, 8 *January* 1883

Donizetti's *La Favorita* (first performance in English)

Cast

Leonora (Favourite of the King)	Madame Marie Roze
Alfonso (King of Castile)	Mr. William Ludwig
Baldassare	Mr. Henry Pope
Don Gaspare	Mr. Wilfred Esmond
Ines	Miss Clara Perry
A Noble	Mr. Clarke
Fernando	Mr. Barton McGuckin

Conductor: Mr. Eugene Goossens

Royal Court Theatre, Liverpool, 17 *January* 1885

Massenet's *Manon* (first production in England. English version by Joseph Bennett)

Cast

Chevalier des Grieux	Mr. Barton McGuckin
Conte des Grieux	Mr W. H. Burgin
Lescaut (cousin of Manon) . . .	Mr. William Ludwig
Guillot Monfontaine	Mr. Maurice de Solla
De Bretigny	Mr. Hallam
An Innkeeper	Mr. Campbell
Attendant at the Seminary of St. Sulpice . .	Mr. H. Brooklyn
A Sergeant	Mr. S. Thomas
An Archer	Mr. Stewart
Pousette	Miss Clara Perry
Javotte	Miss K. Bensburgh
Rosette	Miss Marion Burton
Manon	Mme. Marie Roze

Conductor: Mr. Eugene Goossens

Royal Court Theatre, Liverpool, 18 *January* 1886

Maillart's Light Opera *Fadette* (first performance in English. English version specially written for the Rosa Company by W. Grist)

Cast

Fadette, a poor peasant girl	Mme. Marie Roze
Sylivia, Jerome's apprentice	Mr. Barton McGuckin

Jerome, a farmer . . . . . Mr. Wilfred Esmond
Belamy, Lieut. of Dragoons . . . . . Mr. James Sauvage
Pastor, leader of Fugitives . . . . . Mr. W. H. Burgon
Georgette, Jerome's wife . . . . . Mme. Julia Gaylord
Conductor: Mr. Eugene Goossens

Royal Court Theatre, Liverpool, 4 February 1886

Marchetti's Grand Opera *Ruy Blas* (first performance in English. English version especially written for the Rosa Company by W. Grist).

Cast

Dona Maria (Queen of Spain) . . . . Mme. Marie Roze
Don Sallust de Bazan (Prime Minister in love with
the Queen) . . . . Mr. Leslie Crotty
Don Pedro (Governor of Castille) . . . Mr. Campbell
Don Guritano . . . . . . Mr. W. H. Burgon
Dona Juana . . . . . Miss Jenny Dickenson
Don Mauel Arias . . . . . Mr. Hallen Mostyn
Casilda (lady-in-waiting to the Queen) . . Miss Marion Burton
Ruy Blas (valet to Don Sallust, afterwards under the
assumed name of Don Caesar de Bazan) . Mr. Valentine Smith
Conductor: Mr. Eugene Goossens

Royal Court Theatre, Liverpool, 26 January 1887

Nordisa (first production, 3-act opera, written and composed especially for
Rosa Company by F. Corder)

Cast

Count Oscard Lydal (a young nobleman) . . Mr. Edward Scovel
Lieutenant Fredk. Hansen (his friend) . . . Mr. James Sauvage
Andreas Brand (an old soldier) . . . . Mr. Max Eugene
Lavor (his brother-in-law, an innkeeper) Mr. Aynsley Cook (Mother's
father)
Pastor . . . . Mr. Henry Pope
Young Shepherd . . . . . . Miss Vadini
Baroness Nymark (Count Oscar's aunt) . . Miss Ella Collins
Minna (her daughter) . . . . . Mme. Georgina Burns
Nordisa (a peasant maiden) . . . . Mme. Julia Gaylord
Margit (Halvor's wife) . . . . . Miss Kate Drew
Conductor: Mr. Eugene Goossens

Note. This opera was a great box-office success in Liverpool, probably because of the introduction of an avalanche in the last act, one of Carl Rosa's most sensational stage achievements.

The *Liverpool Daily Post*, in its criticisms of the first performance, said: 'To Mr. Goossens, who has been mainly instrumental in creating the delightful exposition of the work which signalized the musical part of the performance, the thanks of all concerned are due. . . . Also to Mme. Goossens (better known as Mme. Sidonie) to whose artistic invention the charming and characteristic ballets are attributable.'

306

At the close of the opening performance, the audience called loudly for 'Goossens', but he could not be prevailed upon to come on to the stage.

Royal Court Theatre, Liverpool, 8 *February* 1888

Meyerbeer's *Robert the Devil* (first production in English)

Cast

Robert (Duke of Normandy) . . .	Mr. Francesco Runcio
Bertram (his friend)	Mr. Charles Manners
Raimbaut (a minstrel)	Mr. John Child
The Herald	Mr. P. Somers
Albert (Principal Knight)	Mr. Campbell
First Knight	Mr. Redmond
Second Knight	Mr. C. Stewart
Third Knight	Mr. Beale
Fourth Knight	Mr. Coleman
Alice (a peasant girl)	Miss Fanny Moody
Maid of Honour to Princess . .	Miss Annie Cook (my Mother)
Abbess of St. Rosalie	Miss Mayall
Isabella (Princess of Sicily)	Mme. Georgina Burns

Conductor: Mr. Eugene Goossens

The *Liverpool Daily Post* on the following day said: 'It was pleasant to see that after all the principal artistes and Mr. Rosa had been called at the close, loud cries were raised for "Goossens", who has done so much in this and other instances to perfect the musical elements of difficult productions, and *for the first time* he came on the stage with Mr. Rosa, and was the recipient of very warm acknowledgment.'

Royal Court Theatre, Liverpool, 1 *February* 1889

Meyerbeer's *Star of the North* (*L'Etoile du Nord*) (first performance by the Rosa Opera Company)

Cast

Peter, the Czar (a carpenter) . . .	Mr. Charles Manners
Danilowitz (a pastry-cook afterwards a Colonel) .	Mr. John Child
George Skavronski (teacher of music) . .	Mr. Wilfred Esmond
Gritzensko (Corporal of the Grenadiers)	Mr. Aynsley Cook (Mother's father)
Tcherendeff (a Russian General)	Mr. H. Brooklyn
Yermoloff (Russian Colonel)	Mr. Campbell
Ishmailoff (a Cossack officer).	Mr. Somers
Reinhold (a tavern-keeper)	Mr. Imrie
Prascovia (niece of Reinhold)	Miss Amanda Fabris
Natalie (*vivandière*)	Miss Kate Drew
Ekimone (ditto)	Miss Rita Presano
Catherine (sister of Skravonski) . . .	Mme. Georgina Burns

Conductor: Mr. Eugene Goossens

Gounod's *Romeo and Juliet* (first production in English)

Cast

Romeo	Mr. Barton McGuckin
Mercutio	Mr. F. H. Celli
Benvolio	Mr. Ellis
Tybalt	Mr. John Child
Friar Lawrence	Signor Abramoff
Capulet	Mr. Max Eugene
Duke of Verona	Mr. M. Albert
Paris	Mr. Somers
Stephano (a page)	Miss Kate Drew
Gertrude (the nurse)	Miss Annie Cook (my mother)
Juliet	Mlle. Zélie de Lussan

Conductor: Mr. Eugene Goossens

Here follows the programme for the Command Performance given at Balmoral Castle before Her Late Majesty Queen Victoria, 8 November 1892: Donizetti's Comic opera, *The Daughter of the Regiment*

Cast

Tonie (a young Tyrolean peasant) . . .	Mr. E. C. Hedmondt
Sergeant Sulpice (of the 20th) . .	Mr. Aynsley Cook (Mother's father)
Bruno (Steward of the Countess)	Mr. L. Pringle
Corporal Max (of the 20th)	Mr. Charles Campbell
Delve (a peasant)	Mr. P. Somers
Countess of Berkenfeldt	Miss Madge Stavart
Babette	Miss Kate Drew
Mlle. Beaupre	Miss Williams
Madame Duval	Miss Neuwirth
Marie (Daughter of the Regiment) . .	Mlle. Zélie de Lussan

Conductor: Mr. Eugene Goossens
Manager: Mr. T. H. Friend

In connection with this Command Performance, it may be interesting to quote a contemporary (Scottish) newspaper: 'The Carl Rosa Company at Balmoral: The visit of the Carl Rosa Opera Company to Balmoral on Tuesday evening was artistically and otherwise an entire success. The company left Dundee at ten in the morning, arriving at Ballater shortly before two. The management of the opera company was represented by Mr. H. Bruce, Managing Director, and Mr. E. C. Holle, Secretary, and Mr. Arthur of Her Majesty's Theatre, Dundee, accompanied the party. Luncheon was served in the Invercauld Arms, and the company then drove to Balmoral, where *The Daughter of the Regiment* was rehearsed, preparatory to its performance in the evening. A stage had been erected in the ballroom of the castle, and Mr. H. Brooklyn, Stage Manager of the Rosa Company, personally super-intended the whole stage arrangements, which, although room was limited, from beginning to end were carried out with the greatest success. A large assemblage was present when the Queen and Princess Beatrice entered—to the strains of the National Anthem sung by the company, and accompanied by the orchestra. The ladies and gentlemen of the Household-in-Waiting were in attendance, and the following, according to the *Court Circular*, had the honour of being invited: Lady Alfred Churchill and Miss Spencer Churchill, Sir Alan and Lady MacKenzie, Lady Kinnaird, the Rev. Archibald and Mrs. Campbell, Captain M. J. Hughes, 2nd Life Guards, Fleet-Surgeon H. C. Woods, R.N., Captain S. Paterson, Lieutenant S. E. Douglas and Lieutenant R. C. Gore, of the Argyll and Sutherland Highlanders, Dr. Profeit, Dr. Noble, and the Munshi Abdul Karim. The servants of the Balmoral, Birkhall, and Abergeldie estates were present. The opera was splendidly rendered [here the cast of characters is printed], and Her Majesty, who occupied an armchair in front of the centre of the stage, with a small table before her, watched it with evident enjoyment—catching up the points keenly and quickly, and applauding cordially. The performance concluded with the repetition of the National Anthem, Her Majesty rising with the rest of the assemblage while it was being sung. Shortly afterwards Mr. Bruce, Mr. Hoile, Mr. Arthur, Mlle. de Lussan, Mr. Goossens, and Mr. E. C. Hedmondt were conducted by the Hon. A. Yorke to the corridor leading to the Royal drawing-room, where they were received by Her Majesty. The Queen, before retiring, entered into conversation with the members of the company and spoke with animation of the pleasure which their visit had afforded.' Then follows a description of the supper where a number of Her Majesty's household sat down with the visitors, apparently a gay affair, concluding with toasts to the Royal Family, and especially to the Prince of Wales, whose birthday it was. A speech was made commending H.R.H.'s interest in music and drama. The party continued until three in the morning, when they returned directly to Dundee.

To continue with the list of operas and their casts, the next on the list is Meyerbeer's *The Prophet* (first performance by the Rosa Company 2 March 1892, Liverpool):

Cast

Jean of Leyden (the Prophet)	Mr. E. C. Hedmondt
Count d'Overthal	Mr. Max Eugene
Jonas ⎫	Mr. Alec Marsh
Mathisen ⎬ (leaders of the Westphalian revolt) .	Mr. L. Pringle
Zacharia ⎭	Mr. Rhys Thomas
Wilhelm (a peasant)	Mr. Somers
Bertha (betrothed to Jean)	Miss Alice Esty
Fides (mother of Jean)	Miss Josephine Yorke

Conductor: Mr. Eugene Goossens

Royal Court Theatre, Liverpool, 14 *January* 1892
Mascagni's *Cavalleria Rusticana* (first production in English)

Cast

Turiddu	Mr. E. C. Hedmondt
Alfio (a teamster)	Mr. Leslie Crotty
Lola (his wife)	Miss Alice Esty
Lucia (mother of Turiddu)	Miss Josephine Yorke
Santuzza (his betrothed)	Mme. Georgina Burns

Conductor: Mr. E. Goossens

Other first productions conducted by Eugene Goossens to be noted are:

A. C. Mackenzie's *Colomba*. Written and composed especially for the Rosa Company, and produced at Drury Lane Theatre, London, 9 April 1883.

Carl Millocker's new comic opera, *The Beggar Student* (*Der Bettel Student*). First performance in Liverpool at the Royal Court Theatre, 3 January 1885. This was the English version.

Arrigo Boito's *Mefistofele*. First performance in Liverpool, 8 January 1885.

C. Villiers Stanford's *The Canterbury Pilgrims* (written by Gilbert à Becket), specially written and composed for the Rosa Company. First performance in Liverpool, 29 January 1885. The first performance of this work was at Drury Lane, 28 April 1884.

Goring Thomas's *Nadeshda*. First performance in Liverpool, 11 January 1886. First production at Drury Lane by Rosa Company, 16 April 1885.

Victor Massee's *Galatea*. First performance in Liverpool, 12 January 1888.

Auber's *Masaniello*. First performance in Liverpool by the Rosa Company, 17 January 1888.

Verdi's *Othello*. First performance in Liverpool, 24 January 1893.

Auber's *Le Domino Noir*. First performance in Liverpool by the Rosa Company, 20 January 1892.

Halévy's *La Juive*. First performance in Liverpool, 10 January 1889.

Grandfather Goossens produced the following 33 operas during his tenure of the Carl Rosa:

Thorgrim (Cowen), 1 February 1889.
Esmeralda.
Nadeshda (P. Thomas), 11 January 1886.
Nordisa (Corder), 26 January 1887.
Troubadour.
Colomba (Mackenzie), 9 April 1883.
Canterbury Pilgrims (Stanford), 1887.
Mefistofele (Boito), 8 January 1885.
Othello (Verdi).
Tannhäuser (Wagner).
The Jewess (*La Juive*—Halévy), 1889.
The Huguenots (Meyerbeer), Rev. 1891.
Robert the Devil (Meyerbeer), 1888.
The Black Domino (Meyerbeer), 1892.
Midsummer Night's Dream.
Romeo and Juliet (Gounod), 1890.
Galatea (Massee), 1888.
Aïda (Verdi).
Cavalleria Rusticana (Mascagni), 1892.
Masaniello (Auber), 1888.
Favorita (Donizetti), 1883.
The Prophet (Meyerbeer), 1892.
Manon (Massenet), 1885.
Fadetta (Maillart), 1886.

Ruy Blas (Marcheti), 1886.
Star of the North (Meyerbeer), 1899.
Djamilah (Bizet), 1893.
L'Amico Fritz (Mascagni), 1893.
The Talisman (Balfe), 1891.
Adina (Donizetti), 1892.
Postillion of Longjumeau (Adam), 1893.
The Golden Web (G. Thomas), 1893.
Traviata (Verdi), 1891.
Mostly between 1883 and 1893—*ten years' work!* (E.G.)

Here follows a list of the names of the best-known members of the Carl Rosa Opera Company during Eugene Goossens' connection with it:

Sopranos
Marie Roze
Georgina Burns
Julia Gaylord
Fanny Moody
Zélie de Lussan
Ella Russell
Alice Esty

Tenors
Joseph Maas
Ben Davies
Barton McGuckin
J. W. Turner
E. C. Hedmondt
Valentine Smith
Philip Brozelle
John Child
Payne Clarke

Contraltos
Josephine Yorke
Marian Burton
Kirkby Lunn
Kate Drew
Miss Meisslinger

Basses
Aynsley Cook (Mother's father)
Charles Manners
G. H. Snezelle
Lempriere Pringle
Webster Norcross
F. H. Celli
Arthur Winckworth
Signor Abramoff

Baritones
William Ludwig
Leslie Crotty (husband of Georgina Burns)
Max Eugene
Alec Marsh (husband of Alice Esty)

After leaving the Rosa Company, Valentine Smith, mentioned as a tenor, started an opera company of his own. He made a point of advertising, 'Valentine Smith's Top C from the Chest', in allusion to his reputation for 'Mauries' aria, 'Strike Down that Dread Byre' in *Il Trovatore*.

[Much of the foregoing information came from Mr. Thomas Keates, Liverpool, through Mr. T. G. Gregson.]

Writing of the first concert, the critic of the *Liverpool Mercury* said: 'It is gratifying to note that, with the exception of about eight, all the instrumentalists are residents of Liverpool, and the quality of the performance under Mr. Goossens' direction was such as to afford hope that the dream of a permanent orchestra in this city would sooner or later resolve itself into an accomplished fact.' A pompously laudatory notice concludes with the following: 'Both at the beginning and the ending of the concert, Mr. Goossens was honoured with plaudits, in which was conveyed cordial appreciation of his efforts and talent. The Right Honourable the Lord Mayor and the Lady Mayoress occupied a box during the evening, and the gathering in the auditorium was representative.' The same paper opens its review of the second concert with the following: 'A musical function of unusual importance took place last evening at the Philharmonic Hall, when Mr. Goossens gave his second concert. The hall was not so full as it ought to have been. Indeed, the attendance was not commensurate with the occasion, but those who had the wisdom to attend must have experienced supreme enjoyment.'

APPENDIX B

EDITORIAL FROM LONDON *MUSICAL NEWS*
(*see p.* 226)

It may be a serious matter for music in England, for this reason. Most of us make the mistake of offering our wares to the wrong public at some time or another; but when we discover that we have made the same error of judgement as the legendary individual who offered pearls to swine, and are called upon to pay for our follies, we profit by the experience by seeking a more suitable market in future. Goossens is the most oustanding figure in the younger musical generation. He has been lionized in the Press, almost canonized by the musical public, and subsidized—by himself. Moreover, he has earned the interest of the Press and the praise of the public with his fearless enterprise in the cause of musical progress. Those who used to talk disparagingly of 'the wealthy friends who are behind him' must concede, now at least, that, in fact, *he backed his enthusiasm with his own financial credit.* All that is a matter of history and cannot be altered. What of the future? Even if it were possible, the victim of this splendid enterprise cannot be expected to repeat the process. I have no knowledge of his plans whatsoever, but if he has reached the conclusion that London is a bad proposition and is wondering mildly what New York might be able to offer to an energetic, versatile, and brilliant young composer and conductor, nobody could reasonably express either surprise or disapproval. Perhaps we shall wait until we pick up our newspapers to read that he has been offered and has accepted an appointment elsewhere before we trouble ourselves about the matter. Then we shall have letters to the editor by the hundred and deputations and sundry other British futilities. If, however, by way of a change from its usual lethargy, musical England displayed a latent sense of responsibility, we shall anticipate this disaster by a careful examination of the implication of the failure of the Goossens Concerts. It is not pretended that the departure from these shores of this musician would be an irreparable catastrophe. Ultimately, nobody is indispensable, of course. It is the fact that such an event would be a clear indication for all time to the Goossenses-to-be that England has no place for musical genius. Let it not be forgotten that the path trod by Eugene Goossens and anticipation for him is quite the British normal. Our complete lack of a sense of responsibility implies that if musical genius arises in our midst, we may be called upon to give support to-morrow which we owe to-day, and to pay our debt of lip service and of anything else that said genius may choose— except cash—and if the daring musician accepts the position, and if he packs up, well, after all, they do things differently in America, don't they? Nevertheless, let us avoid the imbecility of putting a blind eye to the telescope. That trick might make for heroics in naval matters—it is shirking in this case. If we care anything at all for the future of music in our native land, we shall realize that a policy of *leaving it to the individual to try* means that, in the end, we shall depend for our music-making upon humbugs with money and nincompoops with wealthy relations or friends. Men of the type of Sir Thomas Beecham will prove far too rare to save us from utter incompetence. This, indeed, is an odd position to contemplate after all the unctuous effusions of the years 1914 to 1918. Meantime, our leading orchestra,[1] the only one with any real claim to be regarded as national, is pottering about without a conductor. If its governing body really believed that no English musician is fit for the appointment, it would be more in keeping with the traditional spirit of the race if it forsook its policy of saying nothing, and told us of its conclusions on this important matter.

[1] The Royal Philharmonic Orchestra.

APPENDIX C

WORKS OF EUGENE GOOSSENS

1.* *Variations on a Chinese Theme*, for orchestra (1911).
2. *Miniature Phantasy*, for string orchestra. Curwen.
3.* Symphonic Prelude, *Ossian*.
4. Old Chinese Folk Song, for violin (or 'cello) and piano. Curwen.
5.* Symphonic Poem, *The Eternal Rhythm*.
6. *Suite for Flute, Violin and Harp* (or two violins and harp—or piano.) Chester.
7. *Five Impressions of a Holiday*, for flute (or violin), 'cello and piano. Chester.
8. *Deux Proses Lyriques* (Edwin Evans). Chester.
9. Two Songs (de Musset) 'Chanson de Barberine', 'Chanson de Fortunio'. Chester.
10. *Concert Study*, for piano. Chester.
11. *Persian Idylls* (Edwin Evans). Chester.
12. *Phantasy String Quartet*. Chester.
13. *Rhapsody for 'Cello and Piano*. Chester.
14. *String Quartet in C*. Chester.
15. Two Sketches for String Quartet, *By the Tarn, Jack o' Lantern* (*By the Tarn* arranged for string orchestra). Chester.
16. *Tam O'Shanter*, Scherzo for orchestra. Chester.
17. *Spanish Nocturne*, for 'cello and piano. Hawkes.
18. *Kaleidoscope*, 12 pieces for piano (also transcribed for orchestra). Chester.
19. Songs, 'Afternoon', 'Tea-Time' (G. Jean Aubry), 'Epigram' (Evans), 'The Curse' (Barbor). Chester.
20. *Four 'Conceits' for Piano* (also transcribed for orchestra). Chester.
21. *Sonata No. 1 for Violin and Piano*. Chester.
22. Prelude to *Philip II* (Verhaeren) for small orchestra. Chester.
23. *Quintet in one Movement for Piano and Strings*. Chester.
24. Ballet Suite, *Phoebus and Pan* (transcribed from the French Suites of Bach). Chester.
25. Three *Nature Poems* for Piano. Chester.
26. Three Songs with Piano or Quartet Accompaniment ('The Appeal', 'Melancholy', 'Philomel'). Chester.
27.* *Piano Studies*.
28. *Hommage à Debussy*, for piano. Chester.
29. *L'Ecole en Crinoline*, ballet. Chester.
30. *Rhythmic Dance*, for two pianos (also arr. for orchestra and military band). Curwen.

* Withdrawn.

31. *Silence* (de la Mare), A Fragment for Chorus and Orchestra. Chester.
32. Two Scotch folk-songs for voice. Chester.
33. Suite for Piano from Incidental Music to *East of Suez* (Somerset Maugham). Chester.
34. *Sinfonietta.* Chester.
35. *Lyric Poem for Violin and Orchestra* (piano transcription). Chester.
36. *Fantasy for Nine Wind Instruments.* Curwen.
37. *Sextet for Strings.* Chester.
38. *Two Ballades for Harp.* Curwen.
39. *Two Studies for Piano* (folk-song, scherzo). Chester.
40. Variations on *Cadet Roussel*, for small orchestra. Chester.
41. *Pastoral and Harlequinade*, for flute, oboe and piano. Curwen.
42. *Ships*, for piano. Curwen.
43. Song ('When Thou art Dead') and incidental music to *The Constant Nymph*. Curwen.
44. *Three Greek Dances*, for small orchestra. Curwen.
45. *Concerto for Oboe and Orchestra.* Curwen.
46. *Judith*, opera in one act (Arnold Bennett). Chester.
47. *Concertino for String Octet* (or Double String Orchestra). Chester.
48. Two Fanfares for Brass Instruments ('For a Ceremony', 'For the Regiment'). Chester.
49. Two Songs, 'A Memory' (Joyce), 'Searching for Lambs' (folk-song). Curwen and Chester.
50. *Sonata No.* 2, for violin and piano. Chester.
51. Six Songs from *Chamber Music* (James Joyce). Curwen.
52. *Nature Poems* (orchestral version). Chester.
53. *Four Songs* (Holmes). Chester.
54. *Don Juan de Mañara*, opera in four acts (Arnold Bennett). Chester.
55. *Three Pictures for Flute and Orchestra* (also with piano accompaniment). Chester.
56. *Two Piano Pieces* (Pikki's Lament, Bonzo's Dance). Carl Fischer. N.Y.
57. *Romance for Violin and Piano.* Chester.
58. *Symphony No.* 1 (1940). Carl Fischer. N.Y.
59. *String Quartet No.* 2 (dedicated to Mrs. Elizabeth Coolidge). Boosey and Hawkes.
60. *Phantasy Concerto for Piano and Orchestra.* Chester.
61. *'Cowboy' Fantasy.*
62. *Symphony No.* 2. Carl Fischer. N.Y.
63. *Phantasy Concerto*, for violin and orchestra.
64. *Apocalypse*, for chorus, soloists and orchestra.

APPENDIX D

STATEMENTS ON EUGENE GOOSSENS' DEPARTURE FROM CONDUCTORSHIP OF AMERICA'S ROCHESTER PHILHARMONIC ORCHESTRA

Mr. Miner's statement:

'For some time we recognized the fact that a conductor of his outstanding ability would continually be exposed to tempting offers from larger and more remunerative fields, yet we had hoped that the growing opportunities here, coupled with his past associations, would help to postpone it a few years. While the musical circles of Rochester cannot help but notice the passing of so eminent a figure, yet there is satisfaction in knowing that the programme of development of the musical life of the city which has been steadily growing throughout the years, and in which Mr. Goossens has helped so materially in recent years, will enable us to carry on in his absence without the temporary disorganization that would have followed the going of a less efficient master.'

Mr. Eastman's statement:

'I do not think that it could reasonably have been expected that Rochester would keep Mr. Goossens permanently. I feel that it is fortunate that we have had him here to accomplish so much that is important to the success of our project with orchestral music in this city. It would perhaps have been better for us orchestrally if we might have had Mr. Goossens for a time longer, but I believe his work has been so well done, that firm foundations are laid upon which it may stand in permanence.'

The *Rochester Democrat and Chronicle* said:

'In a way Mr. Goossens' departure means the end of a chapter in the musical development of the city. It will be impossible to think of the Rochester Philharmonic Orchestra without thinking of the one who took it when it was still in swaddling clothes and reared it to its present robust musical stature.'

The *Times-Union* said:

'When he came to Rochester from London, Mr. Goossens said: "It is my hope and aim to help establish an organization which will take a definite place among the leading orchestras in America." He has succeeded beyond his earlier ambitions, for the Rochester Philharmonic Orchestra is known around the world. In the brief span of eight years it has risen from comparative obscurity to a front rank position, into an orchestra, whose performances commend wide attention and admiration. . . .

'In his farewell statement Mr. Goossens says: "I shall leave sadly but proudly." It may be said that Rochester music-lovers, proud of Mr. Goossens' work in building up the Philharmonic Orchestra, will share the regret.'

317

APPENDIX E

EXTRACT FROM LONDON *MORNING POST*, 1922

(*see p.* 197)

Berlin, 18 *December.*

'It was by no means the first time since the war that English music had been performed in Berlin, but it was the first occasion on which it had been presented either on such a scale or under such auspices. The International Society for Contemporary Music, founded last year at Salzburg, was the titular concert-giver, and its German section claims to have enrolled nearly three-quarters of the German musical world. The orchestra was the Berlin Philharmonic. Hence, when Mr. Eugene Goossens appeared as conductor and composer, he had before him one of Germany's most important orchestral organizations and behind him an audience representative of the Berlin musical world. It is this that makes the concert a memorable event.

'Mr. Goossens quickly won the sympathy of the orchestra, whose cordiality increased as rehearsals progressed. There can be no doubt that he has made a deep impression as a conductor. The only notice that has appeared at the time of writing is couched in almost rhapsodical terms, and the conversation among experts gathered in the lobbies at the concert hall generally assumed the same character. Though the music performed aroused much interest, it was in very large measure a personal success, the significance of which lies in the fact that both orchestra and audience are accustomed to the very finest of conductors, and therefore usually inclined to be critical.

'The programme opened with Elgar's *Cockaigne* overture, which was, of course, not new in Berlin. It helped materially to create the right atmosphere. Lord Berners's piquant *Spanish Fantasy*, which followed, stimulated the prevailing curiosity, but left it somewhat intrigued, though not at the cost of appreciation. The event of the concert was Goossens' own, *The Eternal Rhythm*, which for a variety of reasons made the strongest appeal to his audience. Not even Holst's *The Planets*, which concluded the programme, could displace it from the first position in public favour, although that composition has also aroused much admiration. . . .

'Socially, also, Mr. Goossens' visit has been a success. The International has many friends in Berlin, and receptions were arranged to give them the opportunity of meeting the English conductor, who rapidly acquired popularity. After the concert an informal supper took place at the house of Hofrat Hartmann, among the guests being the chairmen of three sections of the International, the German, the British, and the American.

'The subject of the speeches, apart from those which were merely congratulatory, was the fostering of reciprocity among musical countries, tempered with the reservation that, whilst great art, creative or executive, should be assured of a welcome, this must not be construed as opening the door to a flow of mediocrities. So far as they are concerned, it is better that each country should maintain its own.

'These gatherings will have far-reaching effect. It was, in fact, remarked that musicians could accomplish more in a few hours than has been attained at many conferences.'

318

INDEX

ABERCONWAY, LADY, 187
Ackroyd, Vasco, 56
A. E., 301
Agate, Edward, 135
Akté, Aino, 82
Albanesi, Meggie, 192
Albert, King, 51
Alexander, Arthur, 238
Allen, Mr. and Mrs. R., 219
Allinson, Adrian, 111, 128
Amaya, Carmen, 230
Ancrum, Gladys, 143
Anderson and Sheppard, 118
Andreae, Dr. V., 223
Ansermet, 158, 223, 296
Antheil, George, 243, 244
Arbos, E. Fernandez, 60, 63, 64, 88, 98, 99, 100, 252, 253, 279
Arlen, Michael, 296
Asquith, H. H. (Lord Asquith), 126, 127
Asquith, Mrs. (Lady Asquith), 161
Atkins, Sir Ivor, 181
Auric, 147, 234, 235
Austin Fredk., 116, 120, 153, 154, 207
Aveling, Claude, 65, 69, 98
Ayres, Bindon, 116

BACON, ERNEST, 227
Bailby, Leon, 123
Bailly, 280
Baird, Jim, 94
Bakst, Leon, 179
Balanchine, G., 234
Baldwin, Mr., 267
Baldwin Piano Co., 212
Balfour, Lord, 126, 127, 176
Ballard, 270
Bampton, Rose, 285, 289
Bankhead, Tallulah, 187
Bantock, Sir Granville, 41, 75, 138, 282

Barbirolli, Sir John, 146
Baring, Maurice, 119, 187
Barrere, G., 232
Bartok, 223, 277
Battistini, 88
Bauer, Harold, 98, 100
Bax, Arnold, 75, 166, 167, 169, 170, 198, 200, 241, 282, 283, 284, 298, 299, 301
Baylis, Donald, 103
Beardsley, Mr. and Mrs., 219
Beaverbrook, Lord, 224
Beckworth, Arthur, 96, 97
Bedford, Herbert, 198, 199, 200
Beecham, Sir Thomas, 70, 79, 82, 85, 103, 116, 118, 120, 121, 125, 126, 127, 129, 143, 148, 149, 151, 181, 182, 187, 210, 249, 250, 265, 292, 293
Beigel, Victor, 94, 187
Bell, Clive, 297
Belloc, Hillaire, 301
Bennett, Arnold, 94, 97, 102, 161, 251, 268, 269, 270, 271, 281, 282, 301, 302
Bent, Arthur, 130, 134
Bernard, Anthony, 187
Berners, Lord, 158, 161, 234, 246, 247, 265, 266, 302
Besant, Muriel, 298
Best, Edna, 236
Beumer, 2
Bevan, Armine, 72
Binyon, Bertram, 95
Birch, Lamorna, 299
Blamphin, John, 57
Bliss, Arthur, 75, 156, 166, 169, 194, 200, 212, 241, 252, 282, 299
Bloch, Ernest, 208, 241, 263
Blois, Colonel, 255, 268, 269, 281, 282
Blondin, 42

Bodanzky, A., 253
Bolm, Adolphe, 86
Bonci, 88
Bonvalot, C., 200, 201
'Boonie' (Goossens), 146, 188, 189
Borodine, 106
Boughton, R., 208
Boulanger, Nadia, 7
Boult, Sir Adrian, 156, 283, 294
Boulton, Sir S., 95
Boulton, Miss, 96
Brain, Alfred, 91, 238
Breeskin, E., 254
Breitkopf and Haertel, 184
Brewer, Dr., 193, 194
Bridge, Frank, 212, 299
Bridge, Sir Frederick, 60, 64, 65
Brite, R., 276
Buckman, Rosina, 128, 152
Burgin, Quartet, 262
Burke, Edmund, 121, 144
Burns, Georgina, 26
Busscher, H. de, 91, 119, 238
Busoni, F., 205
Byrom, George, 61

CAMERON, BASIL, 283
Cammaerts, 114
Campanini, 77
Capell, Richard, 162, 168, 169, 273
Cardus, Neville, 241
Carpenter, 186
Carreno, Teresa, 102
Caruso, 69
Casals, Pablo, 98, 99, 100, 229, 231, 246
Case, Frank, 220
Casella, Alfredo, 146, 147, 223
Caston, Saul, 266
Catterall, A., 91
Caupolican, Chief, 285
Chaliapine, 100, 101, 102, 255, 256, 257, 258, 293
Chamberlain, Neville, 204
Chaplin, Charlie, 18, 239
Chaplin Sisters, 195
Chapman, Frank, 116
Charpentier, 77
Chatham, Pitt, 207

Chenal, Marthe, 125
Chester, J. and W., 191, 206, 224, 251
Chesterton, G. K., 301
Chotzinoff, 266
Chung Ling Soo, 18
Churchill, Winston, 107
Clark, Eric, 290
Clarke, Rebecca, 98, 212
Clarkson, Willie, 95, 204
Clemens, Clara, 262
Coates, Albert, 142, 148, 203, 219-26
Coates, Eric, 91
Cobbett, W. W., 110, 111, 298, 299
Coburn, A. Langdon, 136, 191
Cohen, Harriet, 298, 299
Colefax, Lady, 187, 303
Colefax, Sir A., 301
Connolly, Marc, 220
Cook, Alice A., 18
Cook, Annie (mother), 17, 23, 24, 39, 47, 103, 149, 163
Cook, Aynsley (grandfather), 8, 12, 17, 21-4, 43, 45
Cook, Elizabeth, 18
Cook, Fred, 17
Cook, Harriet, 21
Cook, Jim, 17
Cook, Katie, 17
Cook, Thomas (great-grandfather), 17
Cook, Tom, 17, 18
Cook, Willie, 17
Coolidge, Mrs. Elizabeth S., 194, 212
Cooper, Duff, 126, 187
Cooper, Emile, 255
Corder, Fred, 13
Corelli, Marie, 112
Cornelis, 6
Corriani, Mlle., 22
Cortot, 98, 100
Courvoisier, Carl, 56
Coward, Noel, 175, 176, 226, 236
Crooks, Richard, 285
Crotty, Leslie, 22, 26
Cunard, Nancy, 296

Cunard, Lady, 126, 127, 287
Cunliffe-Owen, 281
Cunningham, Frank, 219
Cunningham, Kathleen, 219

DALLIBA, MRS, 298, 303
Damrosch, Walter, 231, 253
Davenport, 13
Davidson (G.D.), 135, 136, 137,
  156, 191, 208 299
Davies, Ben, 10
Davies, Marion, 239
Davies, Walford, 282
Davin, William, 85
Deagan, 95
Dean, Basil, 189, 192, 209, 226,
  236
Debussy, Claude, 68, 69, 70, 75,
  77, 101, 167, 170, 181, 232, 267
Delius, 111, 112, 126, 127, 151,
  209, 232, 253, 291
Dengler, Dr., 258
Denyn, Jef, 51
Destinn, Emmy, 88
Diaghilev, Serge, 85, 86, 87, 101,
  103, 106, 145, 157, 161, 178,
  179, 180, 185, 229, 230, 233,
  234, 246, 247, 248, 258
Dieghem, C. van (grandmother), 3
Dolin, A., 247
Dobson, 303
Downes, Olin, 75, 241, 266
D'Oyley Carte, R., 6
Draper, Muriel, 98, 101, 252, 298,
  303
Draper, Paul, 98
Draper, Paul, Jnr., 99
Draper, Ruth, 99
Dukelsky, 234, 235
Dulac, Edmund, 299, 300
Duques, 232
Durey, 147
Dykes, J. St. O., 63, 64, 68, 69

EALES, PERCY, 141
Earp, Tommy, 296
Eastman, George, 202, 203, 204,
  214-17, 219, 220, 227, 231, 239,
  240, 286

Edward VII, King, 74
Edwards, Norman, 243
Egorova, 179
Eicheim, Henry, 238
Elgar, Lady, 298
Elgar, Sir Edward, 30-5, 114, 166,
  167, 168, 170, 193, 194, 196,
  208, 231, 298
Ellington, Duke, 244
Elman, Mischa, 280
Enesco, Georges, 267
Enna, August, 184, 185
Epstein, 303
Evans, Edwin, 111, 158, 163, 195,
  236, 241, 294

FAIRBAIRN, T., 224
Fairbanks, Douglas, Sen., 183, 184
Falla, de, 156, 157, 166, 167, 200,
  284, 293
Farren, Nellie, 18
Fenby, Eric, 210
Fergusson, John, 139, 208, 303
Fétis, 2
Fitelberg, G., 178, 183
Flagler, 231
Flecker, J. E., 209
Fleischer, 292
Fletcher, Percy, 192
Flonzaley, 280
Foch, Madame, 283
Foch, Marshal, 283
Fokine, 86
Forsyth, J. A., 122
Foster, 138, 148
Frankenstein, 241
Fransella, A., 91, 222
Fraser, Lovat. See Lovat.
French, H., 264
Fry, Roger, 297
Furber, Douglas, 296
Furtwängler, 284

GABRILOWITSCH, 262
Galsworthy, John, 94, 301
Garden, Mary, 115, 239, 246, 285
Gaul, Harvey, 254, 261
Gauntlett, A., 201

Genée, Adeline, 6
George V., King, 82
Gershwin, G., 303
Gertler, M., 297
Gevaert, 6
Giachetti, 88
Gieseking, 232, 267
Gilchrist, Connie, 18
Gilibert, 77
Gillet, 232
Glazounov, 79, 80
Gleason, Harold, 214, 215, 216
Godfrey, Dan, 207
Goldmark, Rubin, 7
Golschmann, V., 279
Gomez, Francis, 173
Gomez, Manuel, 172, 173
Gonitsch, Miss, 285
Goodwin and Tabb, 183
Goossens, Adolphe (great-uncle), 1,
    2, 3
Goossens, Adolphe (brother), 28,
    40, 55, 58, 89, 100, 103, 108,
    121
Goossens, Anne (daughter), 157
Goossens, Eugene I (grandfather), 1,
    2, 3, 4, 5, 6, 7, 11, 12, 13, 23,
    24, 26, 28, 29, 35, 36, 39, 58,
    59, 89, 128, 175, 240 (also
    Appendix A).
Goossens, Eugene II (father), 3, 4,
    5, 6, 7, 12, 13, 24, 26, 27, 37,
    38, 39, 42, 43, 53, 55, 59, 60,
    61, 67, 68, 78, 89, 103, 108,
    135, 149, 163, 164, 172, 195,
    240, 241
Goossens, Eugene III (author), 26
    onwards.
Goossens, Jane and Julia, twin
    daughters, 194
Goossens, Julia (great-aunt), 1
Goossens, J. B. M. (great-grand-
    father), 1
Goossens, Leon (brother), 36, 40,
    55, 57, 58, 89, 100, 103, 108,
    109, 121, 141, 158, 163, 164,
    222, 223, 232, 241, 252, 262,
    294
Goossens, Marie (sister), 28, 39,
    55, 89, 103, 141, 158, 163, 164,
    241
Goossens, Sidonie (sister), 6, 39, 55,
    89, 103, 141, 158, 163, 164, 223,
    241
Gordon, Cyrena, van, 289
Graham, Martha, 227, 290
Grainger, Ella, 95
Grainger, Percy, 94, 95, 218
Graves, Robert, 139
Gray, Cecil, 75, 111
Gregson, J., 5
Grignon, Lamite de, 246
Grigoriev, 180
Grisi, 22
Grossmith, Geo., Jnr., 6
Guidi, Scipione, 91
Guinness daughters, the, 187

Hahn, Reynaldo, 101
Hale, Philip, 233
Hall, Mrs., 255
Hall, Marie, 112
Hambourg, Mark, 296
Hammond, Aubrey, 296
Hanson, Howard, 214, 227
Hardings, the, 156
Harrison, Guy, F., 290
Harrison, Julius, 118, 167, 170
Harty, Hamilton, 166, 167, 199,
    298
Hatchard, Caroline, 116
Hayward, Marjorie, 298
Heath, John, 169
Heather, Alfred, 116
Hedley, Charles, 240
Heermann, Emil, 2
Heermann, Hugo, 2
Heifetz, Jascha, 293
Heming, Percy, 116
Hempel, Frieda, 232
Henderson, 266
Henry, Leigh, 167, 168
Henschel, Sir G., 93
Henschel, Helen, 93
Hertz, Alfred, 237, 275
Heseltine, Philip, 111, 112, 167
Hess, Myra, 110, 204, 212
Higgins, H., 255

Hill, Stuart, 303
Hilsberg, 266
Hindemith, 232
Hobday, Alfred, 72
Hobday, Claude, 72, 73
Hoffman, Josef, 148
Holbrooke, Josef, 137, 167, 181, 191
Holding, Frederick, 200, 201
Holst, Gustav, 166, 169, 181, 207, 229
Honegger, 147, 166, 229, 234, 291, 292
Hoogstraten, van, 237
Hopkins, Edward, 21
Horgan, Paul, 227, 290
Housman, 113
Huber, Frederick, 252
Hughes, Herbert, 303
Hungerford, Ed., 253
Hutchinson, St. John, 297
Huxley, Aldous, 297
Hyde, Walter, 73

Ibbs and Tillett, 158, 273
Ireland, John, 75, 158, 167, 171, 198, 200, 304
Irish, Mrs. L. A., 277
Ives, Chas., 233

Jackson, Barry, 208
Jacob, Maxim, 234
Jaenecke, 56
James, Cairns, 117
James, Henry, 99
Jean-Aubrey, G., 156
Jepson, Helen, 285, 289
Jeremy, Raymond, 96, 97, 200
Joachim, 62
John, Augustus, 296, 303
Johnson, Edward, 269
Johnstone, W. Dudley, 57
Jowitt, Leslie (Lady), 187
Judson, Arthur, 264

Kaminsky, 292
Karg-Elert, 215
Karsavina, 86, 101, 161, 234, 235
Kastner, A., 91, 238
Kaufman, G., 220

Kendal, Mr. and Mrs. W. H., 17, 18
Kennedy, Daisy, 99
Kennedy, Margaret, 236
Keynes, Maynard, 296
Kincaid, W., 266
King, George, 116, 152, 270
Klein, Herman, 8
Klemperer, Otto, 231
Kling, Otto, 75
Kneisel, Marianne, 252
Knight, Laura, 303
Kochanski, Paul, 98, 99, 100, 188
Kochanski, Zoischa, 188
Kochno, Boris, 230, 246, 248
Koechlin, Charles, 277
Kolar, Victor, 262
Komisarjevski, 144, 145
Koussevitzky, Serge, 75, 158, 186, 201, 232, 255, 279, 286
Kreisler, Fritz, 72, 109, 197
Kubelik, 41, 42

Labette, Dora, 201
Lachner, F., 21
La Fontaine, Rev. H. Cart de, 181
Lambert, Constant, 246
Langley, Beatrice, 94, 96
Langley, H., 116
Lara, Frederick de, 113
Lara, Isadore de, 113, 115
Largo, 24
Larner, 115
Lathom, Lord, 165, 166, 168
Laurence, Frederick, 183
Laurent, G., 232
Leacock, S., 274
Legge, Robin, 162, 181, 304
Lehmann, Liza, 198
Leno, Dan, 18
Leopold, King, 51
Leslie, Seymour and Shane, 187, 297
Letellier, 232
Licette, Miriam, 120
Liebling, L., 265
Lifar, S., 230, 234, 246, 247, 248
Liffschey, 266
Linley, Mr., 117
Lion, Flora, 303

Ljungberg, 268, 269, 270, 271
Lloyd George, David, 126
Lloyd, Marie, 18
Lockyer, James, 94, 96, 200, 201
Lopokova, 180
Lovat, Grace, 95, 188, 189, 309
Lovat, Fraser, 154, 188, 194, 303
Ludwig, 22
Luening, Otto, 227
Lunn, Kirkby, 10, 77
Lussan, Zelie de, 10, 23
Lutz, Meyer, 18
Lynch, Fanny, 62, 69, 74
Lynn, Olga, 187

McCarthy, Desmond, 297
Mackenzie, Compton, 302
McLaren, Mrs., 187
McPherson, 12
Maitland, Lena, 116
Malipiero, 156, 157, 167, 170, 297
Malsch, 56
Mamoulian, Reuben, 227, 290
Manet, 297
Mangeot, André, 146, 147, 263, 283
Manner, Charles, 38
Manners, Lady Diana, 126, 187
Mare, W. de la, 191
Marquis of Anglesea, 21
Marsh, Eddie, 127
Massenet, 13, 14, 15, 16
Massine, 106, 157, 161, 185
Mathias, Mrs., 178
Mathieu, 232
Matthews, James, 42
Maugham, Somerset, 189, 192, 211
Maugham, Syrie, 303
Maxwell, Elsa, 187
Mechelaere, 2
Meerts, 2
Melba, 142
Menges, I., 201
Mengelberg, 91, 259
Mestdagh, Carol, 49
Meyer, 21
Middleton, Mr., 222
Milhaud, Darius, 147, 166, 167, 170, 222, 236, 246, 247
Millar, Dorothy, 146

Mills, Florence, 233
Modarelli, A., 255
Moffat, Curtis, 296, 297
Moisewitsch, Benno, 99, 296
Molinari, 253, 254
Monaco, Princess of, 234
Mond, Sir Alfred, 161
Mond, Lady, 94, 186
Monteux, Pierre, 106, 275
Moody, Fanny, 38
Moore, Charles, 268, 269, 271
Moore, George, 301
Morales, Pedro, 98
Mordaunt, Miss, 139
Morley, Mrs., 187
Morris, Margaret, 138, 139, 140, 191, 208, 303
Morris, Mrs., 139
Mossel, Max, 296
Moussorgsky, 106
Mugnone, 253
Mukle, May, 94, 96, 100, 212, 298
Mullings, Frank, 116, 120, 128, 135, 152
Murdoch, William, 110, 152, 153, 293
Murray, Bill, 212
Murry, Middleton, 297

Nachez, Tivadar, 100
Nash, Paul, 297
Naylor, 175
Negri, Pola, 239
Nemtchinova, 231
Newman, Ernest, 163, 200, 241, 257, 271, 274, 275
Newman, Robert, 93
Nijinska, Bronislava, 179
Nijinsky, 86, 100, 101, 179
Nikisch, 54, 91, 195, 196, 197
Novarro, Ramon, 239

Oberhoffer, 237, 252
Odell, 296
O'Neill, Norman, 85
Ormandy, Eugene, 289
Ornstein, 137
Ossian, 115
Oubouhov, 147

PAERSCH, OTTO, 55
Pagani's, 75
Page, Philip, 161, 163
Palmgren, 214
Parepa, Madame, 7
Parker, H. T., 233, 279
Parratte, Sir Walter, 60
Parry, Sir Hubert, 60, 65, 79, 83, 90, 117
Parry, Mr., 137, 140
Parsons, Alan, 187, 296
Pavlova, 86
Payne, Harriet (grandmother), 17
Payne, Harry, 18
Payne, W. H., 17
Perris, Sarah, 39
Persinger, 98
Petipa, 178, 179
Philpot, Glyn, 94, 187, 299
Pickford, Mary, 239
Picasso, Pablo, 208
Pierne, G., 283, 291, 293
Pitsch, Georges, 140
Pitt, Percy, 118, 144, 255
Playfair, Nigel, 129, 154, 297
Poldowski, 296
Polignac, Princesse de, 181
Poltronieri Quartet, 263
Polunin, Vlad., 120
Pons, Lily, 292
Poulenc, F., 147, 167, 170, 234, 235
Pownall, Frank, 60
Pringle, Lemprière, 10, 28
Prokofiev, 166, 167, 246, 277, 293
Propert, W. A., 178

QUEEKERS, LEON, 49
Quilter, Roger, 94, 282

RADFORD, ROBERT, 73
Ranalow, Frederick, 116, 154
Rathbone, Basil, 192
Ravel, 68, 106, 147, 154, 156, 158, 167, 197, 206, 234, 263, 279, 289, 294, 302
Ravensdale, Irene, 187
Read, Dr. Ernest, 63
Reed, Willie, 194

Reillie, Bernard, 162
Reiner, Fritz, 255, 264, 286, 288
Réjane, Madame, 114
Respighi, 233, 273, 274, 279
Reynolds, Charles, 55
Reynolds, Walter, 108
Richter, Dr., 53, 54, 55, 73
Ricordi, 120
Rieti, 234, 235
Riley, W. J., 122
Rimsky-Korsakov, 106
Rivarde, Achille, 60, 63, 64, 66, 71, 72, 75, 88, 112, 130-4, 149
Robey, George, 18
Rogers, Helen, 219
Rohmer, Sax, 190
Ronald, Landon, 148, 283
Rosa, Carl, 7
Rose, Mrs. Connie, 112
Rosing, V., 95, 226, 227, 243, 289, 298
Ross, Alfred, 55
Ross, Charles, 55
Rouche, 258
Rousbey, Arthur, 27, 28
Roussel, 166, 167
Roze, Marie, 13
Rubinstein, Arthur, 99, 187
Rubio, 99, 100
Ruggles, C., 228, 233
Rumbold, Sir Horace, 118
Rumbold, Hugo, 118, 119, 129, 143
Russell, Sydney, 116
Rutland, Duchess of, 126

SAFONOFF, 91
St. Leger, Frank, 269
Saint-Saëns, 77, 79, 80
Salmond, Felix, 99, 110, 153
Salzedo, Carlos, 228, 233
Sammons, Albert, 96, 110, 152, 153, 293
Sanborn, Pitts, 266
Santley, Charles, 8, 22
Santley, Kate, 5
Sarasate, 63
Sargent, J. S., 94, 126, 127
Sargent, Sir Malcolm, 225
Saroya, Bianca, 278, 285

Sassoon, Sir Philip, 187
Satie, Erik, 147, 166, 167, 234, 236
Sauget, 147, 234, 247
Schmitt, Florent, 101, 147
Scholnik, 262
Schönberg, 87, 92, 167, 169, 201, 206, 277
Schuricht, 253
Scott, Cyril, 94, 136, 138, 140, 161, 170, 181, 200, 241
Scriabine, 102, 193, 194
See, Arthur, 290
Sergeev, 179
Shapiro, 298
Sharpe, Cedric, 96, 97, 200, 201
Shavitch, Vladimir, 214
Shaw, Bernard G., 161, 162, 163, 296
Shepler, Alec, 302
Sherman, Cecile, 243
Sherman, T., 280
Sibelius, 75, 76, 93, 109, 276
Sibley, Harper, 213, 214
Sickert, Walter, 297
Sidonie Goossens (sister). See Goossens.
Sidonie, Mme. (grandmother), 6
Siloti, A., 205
Sitwell, Edith, 187, 297, 302
Sitwell, Osbert, 187, 297, 302, 303
Sitwell, Sacheverell, 187, 297, 302
Sitwells, the, 187, 297
Smallens, Alex, 278
Smith, Valentine, 46
Smith, David, S., 252
Smyth, Ethel, 110, 115, 117, 118, 119, 282
Sobrino, 100
Sokolova, 231
Sons, Maurice, 64, 91
Sowden, Mr. and Mrs., J., 249
Speed, Harold, 94, 299
Spessivtseva, 179
Speyer, Edgar, 69
Stanford, Sir Charles, 7, 60, 80, 81, 82, 83, 88, 115, 117, 148
Steinberg, 91, 106
Stern, H., 219
Still, William, G., 233

Stock, Frederick, 286
Stokes, R., 266
Stokowski, L., 265
Strachey, Lyton, 297
Strangeways, Fox, 162
Strauss, Richard, 82, 87, 106, 108, 109, 167, 169, 186, 200, 271, 276
Stravinsky, 87, 106, 144, 158, 161, 163, 167, 168, 171, 185, 200, 222, 231, 235, 241, 260, 263, 273, 274, 283, 303
Stulik, Rudolph, 296, 297
Suggia, Madame, 99
Sullivan, Arthur, 6
Swanson, Gloria, 239
Swarthout, Gladys, 288
Szarvasy, 281, 282
Szell, G., 279
Szymanowski, 99

TABUTEAU, 266
Taft, Mr. and Mrs. C. P., 264
Tailleferre, G., 147, 233, 234
Tamagno, 120
Taylor, Coleridge, 224
Taylor, Colin, 112
Taylor, Mr. and Mrs., 219
Taylor, Peter, 195, 197
Tchaikowsky, 108
Tcherepnine, 101
Tchernicheva, 231
Temple, Richard, 6
Tertis, Lionel, 110, 153, 208
Thesiger, Ernest, 187
Thibaud, Jacques, 98, 99, 100
Thierry, Miss de, 188
Thomas, John Charles, 256, 285, 289
Thomas, J. H. (M.P.), 231
Thompson, Oscar, 265
Thomson, Virgil, 241
Thornton, Edna, 73
Thuman, J. Herman, 291
Thursfield, Anne, 198
Tibbett, Lawrence, 88
Tim, Chang, 191, 192
Timothy, Miriam, 89
Tinlot, G., 279

Toberman, 276
Todd, G., 202, 203, 215
Toscanini, A., 202, 233, 253, 264, 280, 284
Toye, Francis, 304
Toye, Geoffrey, 200, 304
Tree, Iris, 161
Tree, Viola, 187, 296
Trefilova, 179
Trend, J. B., 157
Turner, Father, 39

VARESE, EDGAR, 228
Vaughan, Kate, 18
Verbrugghen, H., 251, 289
Verhaeren, 143
Victoria, Queen, 6, 12, 17, 22, 23
Vladimiroff, 179

WALDEN, LADY, 187
Walden, Lord H. de, 159, 170
Walker, Edyth, 78
Walker, Sir Herbert, 229
Walpole, Hugh, 301
Walter, Bruno, 286
Walton, William, 234
Wanger, Walter, 182, 183, 184, 185, 186
Ward, Mr. and Mrs. H., 219
Warlock, Peter, 111
Warner, A. J., 219, 227, 290
Warner, Mrs., 219
Warner, Waldo, 96

Warwick Evans, C., 91, 96
Waugh, Evelyn, 302
Webern, A. von, 278
Weinberger, 91
Wellesz, 167, 170
Wells, H. G., 234
Weygand, General, 283
White, Felix, 166, 167, 200
Whitehouse, W. E., 60
Wiburg, Hoytie, 303
Widdop, W., 271
Wilenski, 304
Williams, Gerrard, 200
Williams, Vaughan, 112, 176, 200
Wolff, Frau, 197
Wolheim, Eric, 246
Wood, Dr. Charles, 63, 88
Wood, Sir Henry, 54, 69, 70, 72, 75, 90, 91, 92, 93, 102, 108, 109, 114, 148, 207, 237, 283, 298
Woolcott, Alex, 220
Wright, Frank Lloyd, 249
Wummers, J., 262
Wynn, Arthur, 116
Wynne, 29

YEATS, 94, 126
Yeiser, Frederick, 241
Ysaye, Eugene, 100

ZENATELLO, 88
ZUCCHI, 88

327

Printed in Great Britain by
The Camelot Press Ltd., London and Southampton